D1561492

Directing

FOR

Film

AND

Television

Christopher

REVISED EDITION

Lukas

ALLWORTH PRESS
NEW YORK

05   04   03   02   01   5   4   3   2   1

Published by Allworth Press
An imprint of Allworth Communications
10 East 23rd Street, New York, NY 10010

Cover design by Leah Lococo

Interior design by Jennifer Moore, Leah Lococo, Ltd

Page composition/typography by Celine A. Brandes

ISBN: 1-58115-201-9

Library of Congress Cataloging-in-Publication Data:
Lukas, Christopher.
   Directing for Film and Television/by Christopher Lukas.—Rev. ed.
      p.cm.
   ISBN:1-58115-201-9
1. motion Pictures—Production and direction. 2.
Television—production and direction. I. Title.
   PN1995.9.P7 L8 2001
   791.43'0233—dc21

                        2001003241

Printed in Canada

For Susan, who may not understand what I do for a
living, but knows all about me. And for Megan and
Gabriela, who are the best a father could have.

Contents

Preface to the Revised Edition

It has been a decade and a half since this book was first published. In the years that have passed, there have been many advances in technology—many clever inventions, new film stocks, new video cameras, and editing equipment.

But even though film technology has changed immeasurably, filmmaking—which began over 100 years ago—has remained remarkably stable. While aesthetics and experimentation always take us into new artistic realms, if we look at motion pictures from the vantage point of the craft—the requirements for creating a good story, the teamwork needed to translate those stories into film form, and the ability to conceptualize in advance—things are not very different from the way they were at the beginning. The practice of creating fiction films and videos—and documentaries in any medium—reflects the hard-earned lessons of the early masters:

- The ability to be a storyteller
- A good eye and a good ear
- Sensitivity to people's needs
- Some technical know-how

These are what make a good director.

For that reason, *Directing for Film and Television* remains a stable and, I believe, valuable guide to the craft. In it readers can descry the importance of learning how to:

- Write a good story
- Budget sensibly

- Think about look, style, and mood
- Make lighting suit that look, style, and mood
- Decide which cameras and lenses to use
- Accomplish competent casting
- Work with other members of the team

This book is about how to conceive and tell stories, how to employ the tools of filmmaking in whichever format one chooses. That having been said, today's filmmakers have one advantage over those of ten, twenty, and fifty years ago, an advantage that *does* require mention, and that led me to want to create a revised edition of *Directing for Film and Television*.

For most of the history of filmmaking there has been a huge gap between the professional and the amateur. In *still photography*, the introduction of Eastman's Kodak camera and Land's Polaroid closed the professional-amateur gap long ago. Only enhanced aesthetics and professional judgment keep the snapshot artist and the Magnum photographer apart.

Now, today, in *filmmaking*, the gap is also beginning to close. Equipment has gotten so small and so easy to use that amateurs and professionals are using cameras and edit systems that are remarkably similar. And while the craft of the professional filmmaker is still one that requires enormous amounts of expertise, judgment, and aesthetic ability, it is possible to make inexpensive films that can almost compete in quality with those made by Hollywood. Amateurs and professionals are closer together than ever before. It is this narrowing of the gap through technology that I address in a new chapter in this revised edition: chapter 9, "The Digital Realm."

One caution: The snapshot that Uncle Ted takes at a family picnic is still just a snapshot, no matter how easy it is to use the camera. The work of a talented, seasoned director is still superior to that of the man or woman who picks up a camcorder for the first time. In short, mastering the craft of directing requires talent, luck, a lot of experience, and the willingness to learn. Which is why I wrote this book in the first place: to give willing learners a place to begin.

How to Use This Book

"You can't *learn* directing, you have to *do* it; you certainly can't *read* about it in a book!" is the way it usually goes, followed by, "Besides, no one can be a director unless he's been an actor, editor, or writer first." The first of these statements is something of a paradox. The other is somewhat arrogant. And both, ironically, are partially true.

Directing is a complex craft, a sometimes art that assumes a certain amount of maturity and knowledge on the practitioner's part. It's the work of men and women who have been in the world and who bring to a film their vision. You can't teach "vision." You do have to "get out" and make a film, not just read about it; and, probably, you have to participate in some other area of filmmaking first before you direct. In other words, the naysayers are right: if you, or anyone else who reads this book, think that *simply* by reading it you can become a director, you're wrong. But that doesn't mean there aren't *some* things about directing that can be learned by reading. The special relationship between the theory of any art or craft and the practice of it demands that some things be learned about and some things simply be done. In my view, it would be foolhardy to assume that the only way to acquire knowledge about directing is to "get out and do it," especially since, in the world of film and television, getting out and directing is very expensive. (The exceptions-and there are always exceptions—are the "geniuses," those who seem "born to the art." Think of Hitchcock or George Lucas or Orson Welles. But look carefully: they usually surround themselves with skilled craftspeople with lots of experience. The Introduction looks at the "genius mystique.")

This book is designed for a wide range of readers, for those who are "out there doing it" and for those who have yet to try. For instance, some of you may have made a stab at some aspects of filmmaking and have decided they weren't for you. Perhaps you have been the producer of a film but didn't like simply controlling the purse strings. Maybe others of you have written a short story and wonder how to get your written words transformed into pictures and sound. There may be those of you whose first efforts at directing didn't work as well as you had hoped. Finally, there are some of you who have never approached the craft of filmmaking. In this book I hope all of you will find hints on how to make things move more smoothly, productively, and, perhaps, artistically.

Parts of this book explain how the professional, unionized world of directing works. For instance, chapter 2 and chapter 10 deal with large-scale productions in professional settings. On the other hand, some chapters, such as chapter 11, are deliberately keyed to independent, inexpensive productions. But most of the chapters approach directing from the point of view of craft, not of budget, from the assumption that there are certain things that have to be done by every director, regardless of the scale or cost of the production. Chapters 1, 3, and 8 fall into this category. If you read these chapters while you are actively studying film or making a film, I am confident that they can be of help to you. If, on the other hand, you wish to learn how things operate in Hollywood, the chapters on professional, large-scale operations will be of primary interest.

In other words, this book is intended to be used either as a manual, in which you can skip from one area to another, or, if you wish, as a book to be read from front to back. Afterward, you can experiment, enjoy yourself, make a film. Contrary to popular opinion, directing is not difficult. At this point I expect alarms to go off. "Not difficult! Does he think anyone can be a Fellini?" No, I don't think just anyone can be a Fellini, but why does everyone *have* to be a Fellini?) In fact, it's actually quite easy to direct, as long as you don't try to get in over your head and as long as you don't imagine that you can be a great director without a lot of work and talent. But . . . direct a film? Of course you can.

The most important thing a director needs to do is make choices. This is not too different from the most important thing a doctor or policeman has to do or a moral philosopher for that matter. But the choices that a director has to make require (1) a knowledge of certain physical and technical matters, and (2) the willingness and ability to make aesthetic decisions in a wide range of fields. It is this latter category that makes directing difficult at times (and easy at others), because the wide range of areas in which choices are necessary demands of the director a certain amount of education and knowledge, plus the ego strength to make decisions (choices) often and, occasionally, quickly or against the will of other people. (The word "director" itself implies leadership.) This book is intended to outline these required areas of knowledge, both technical and aesthetic, and to supply some basic information. What I cannot do is *endow* any human being with the ability to choose, much less choose well! That part is up to you.

A word about organization. The chapters that follow divide directing and its efforts into an almost sequential timeline, taking the director from his or her first glimpse of a film—the script or idea stage— through to the final print. Along the way, as the tension of getting the production under way mounts, I have tried to give hints on how to reduce the pressure. I also indicate shortcuts that are useful, and I show you how to know when you've gotten too far off the track.

Where I think it's especially important, I detail some of the knowledge that is worth having in the area of camera work or lighting or laboratory technology, but I deal mostly with those things that a *director* needs to know in order to carry out his or her tasks, leaving instruction in "how the camera works" to other people and other books (see the selected bibliography).

By the way, in this book I have used the term *television* to mean single-camera videotaping. For me, this kind of video work has a close affinity to film camera work. I do not intend to defend this statement, and I am aware that many practitioners of both film and video will quarrel with it, but my experience over the past thirty years has allowed me to travel back and forth between single-camera *video* work and single-camera *film* work precisely because I bring to both the same kind of approach and craft. As technology in the video industry has leaped into the twenty-first century, improving and almost eliminating the gaps between film and professional-format video, it becomes easier to talk about single-camera work, no matter what the medium (film or videotape) as if they were one and the same. For the purposes of this book, I intend to do so; where there are significant differences, I will attempt to point them out.

How should you use this book? In many ways. But if "use" makes it sound as if this is a textbook, I would feel very badly. I don't want readers to regard this effort as "instruction." I mean it to be an enjoyable book, one that gives you a *feel* for the world of the director as well as giving you some hardcore help in entering that world. Please—read on and enjoy!

Introduction: The "Mystique"

During the short history of the motion picture, the film director has acquired a fair share of mystique. Names come floating back to us from out of the past: D. W. Griffith, Abel Gance, Sergei Eisenstein, Carl Dreyer, Josef von Sternberg, Charlie Chaplin, Orson Welles, Howard Hawks, John Ford, Ingmar Bergman, Alfred Hitchcock, Akira Kurosawa. Out of more recent years, come a host of others: Stanley Kubrick, Francis Ford Coppola, Steven Spielberg, Spike Lee, Robert Altman, Steven Soderbergh, Quentin Tarantino, Martin Scorcese. If someone's favorites have been left out, it doesn't matter, the point has been made. These are giants whose work calls to mind a particular kind of screen image, of film genre. They were in command of the set, the script, the cast, the mood, and the temper of their films. They controlled. They directed!

In fact, at times they appear to have been in such control that, during the 1960s, the misuse of the French word "auteur"—conveying the concept of the director not only as the filmic leader but as "author" of everything—captured the imagination of the film critics. Writers, producers, editors—all were to be thought of simply as pawns in the director of photography's hands. The film was his, from start to finish. And what a giant he must be to so control!

What about this myth? Must we, for instance, in the manner of Kurosawa, be able to paint marvelous images of each frame during pre-production or, like Bergman, be a great symbolist? Like Coppola, do we have to pursue a single truth until it either bankrupts us or makes us ten million dollars? No, of course not, though these abilities (or passions) might make us more famous or more productive, if we could indeed acquire them. In any art or craft, a continuum exists. On one end are those artists whom nature, or perhaps hard work, has endowed with ability and insight so rare that they can create works of beauty and metaphor, apparently without effort. Beethoven certainly belongs on that special end of this artistic spectrum. But moving along the line toward the center, we soon come to artists whose achievements are more debatable, whose lives have been spent in fruitful but not necessarily stunning artistic endeavors. In music, Johann Pachelbel is a good example. Aside from his one rather sentimental and monotonous "Canon," few today have heard his music, and perhaps rightfully so. In painting, we all know artists whose works hang on our own walls or in a gallery, but who are not memorialized in museums or art books. And in filmmaking, the legion of directors whose names we don't know points to the obvious fact that one does not have to be a genius or a giant to direct film. But wait, the continuum has more room on it. At the far end, away from both geniuses and merely competent creators, are hundreds of others—musicians, painters, and directors whose art is so inept we not only don't know their names, we *never* see their work. Of course, the continuum is not rigid. People move along it, perhaps not from the genius end to the other end, but from the middle to one side or the other.

In all artistic endeavors there are incompetent, merely competent, and superbly competent artists. So it is in film. There are journeymen and -women (people whose work has been good enough to get them jobs, to earn them livings) and there are great artists. Of the four thousand directors in the Directors Guild of America (DGA), few would call themselves famous; fewer still, *auteurs*. If the public prefers to keep alive its fantasy image of the director-as-giant, with his hand resting upon the shoulder of a camera man gazing out over the Arizona desert—fine, but there's no reason for you to punish yourself with this fantasy. In fact, you would never have bought this book if you intended to buy such a myth.

Not that we can't *learn* from the work of the best and the brightest of the movie directors, or from the myth of the "artiste." All craftsmen, no matter what their potential, should want to know the work of artists better and wiser than they. But studying their work is not enough, not simply because they know things—perhaps instinctively-that we must acquire through our own hard labor, but also because the famous or extremely gifted person very often works in ways that we cannot emulate. I remember being in college and watching a young mathematician do a problem in calculus. He skipped several of what I thought were mandatory steps to arrive at the correct answer. For him, those steps were simply unnecessary; he saw past them, making leaps of the imagination. For me, they were essential, and I could not get *there* without them. Some of the best directors also make such leaps that others, perhaps less visionary, cannot make. And while we can learn much about the art of filmmaking from analyses of great films and from listening to the words of great filmmakers, we cannot create a great film simply by these methods. Other steps, other training, and another mindset is necessary. And that's what this book is about. It is a book addressed to the journeymen and -women *and* to the artists; to them and to those who aspire to be like them. It is a book about both the art and the craft of film, about the tasks and talents required to direct a reasonably articulate film or videotape.

Reality forces me to include a negative note at this point. There are over a hundred thousand students of film in colleges and universities every year. Most of those students want to direct. Obviously, few have a chance of becoming professional directors, since, for example, there are ten thousand members in the DGA worldwide (most are assistant directors, stage managers, etc., *not* directors), and of those, 25 percent work only sporadically. Going further, if you inquire how many women or minority members of the DGA there are, or how many women or minorities get to direct in unionized, professional situations, the picture looks worse and worse. In fact, when I recently inquired, the DGA had posted on its Web site the lamentable fact that the number of women and minorities entering the DGA is not what it should be.[1] But—to return to a positive note—there are thousands of working nonunion directors; there are thousands of films being made by students; there are lots of directors working in a host of strange and wonderful situations: cable television, industry, educational fields, hospitals, schools, and, of course, the commercial worlds of Hollywood and New York, Chicago

---

[1] "The percentage of minority members entering the DGA each year has remained stagnant at an average of 12.6 percent for the past 5 years, a figure less than half of the 28.6 percent minority share of the American population calculated by the U.S. Census Bureau. The Census Bureau figure for women as a percentage of the U.S. population is 51.1 percent, while in 1999 the percentage of women members entering the DGA was only 26.6 percent. This represents the lowest percentage of women members entering the DGA since 1995, and the second consecutive year of a decline."

and Houston, where both union and nonunion markets exist. In other words, there is a chance to work as a director, because there is always a chance for trained talent.

Ironically, much of that training comes from a background in literature and the arts and fields other than filmmaking. Some readers may think that I am merely stating the obvious, that everyone knows that directing is the kind of craft that requires a great amount of understanding in many fields, *along with* instruction in a few technical matters. Unfortunately, that is not the case. For every single person who believes in the myth of the "genius" director (with powers we cannot attain), there are dozens (many of whom are now directing) who have ingested *only* a technical competency and who think that that is all there is to directing.

Directing is neither the craft of those who are merely technically competent, nor the craft of those who know a lot about art and science but nothing about the technical sides of the filmic world. In short, aspiring directors must not think too big or too small. After all, look at what is required of you. Rhythm and pace must be judged, words must be weighed, actions watched, sounds listened to, human talents appraised, music considered, pictures cut according to symbolic or abstract judgments. Framing must be observed, judged, and set against values gained from the study of art or photography. Scripts have to be read and understood on a variety of levels. Actors and crew must be handled with care. So, the study of English and foreign literature, the creation of musical or visual art, the comprehension of philosophical and psychological concepts, all contribute powerfully to the ability to move the myriad participants, both human and inanimate, into configurations that produce a competent and perhaps artistic motion picture or television videotape. I therefore will assume that the reader of this volume has studied something other than frames and "glitches"; that he or she goes every now and then to museums or to the ballet; that reading and writing are pleasurable and often-indulged-in activities. In short, a director may not be a "genius," but he or she must be an educated person. (Once again, I hear the cries from offscreen, "What about all the hacks, the dullards? Who says they're educated?" My answer is that I am not talking about hacks. I am writing for those of you who want to do the best possible job of directing, and I am suggesting an avenue toward that goal.)

I began this introduction by saying that one doesn't have to be a genius in order to become a competent director, but I have also tried to say that there are *some* prerequisites for the work, more, perhaps, than many practitioners are willing to accept. One has to have a good intellectual background; one has to have luck and a predilection for hard work. *And* one has to possess a certain kind of talent. Assuming, however, that you have those things, and can pay careful attention to details, you should be able to do what thousands have done before you: direct a film .

Reading, Writing,
and Arithmetic

In the beginning is the written word. That's where a film starts. Of course, some people say that the beginning of a film is an image, or a concept. We could stay here and discuss the point all day, but rather than do so, let's take my idea that it's words that start the process and see how far that gets us. Basic words, at that, such as:

```
FADE IN:  EXTERIOR PHIL'S HOUSE IN THE BEKAA VALLEY, LEBANON
(NIGHT)

On the front of the house can be clearly seen the marks of the
latest shelling attack.  We HEAR rifle fire, but it is sporadic.

                                            DISSOLVE TO:

INTERIOR HOUSE - WIDE SHOT (NIGHT)

In the corner of a room that is dimly lit by moonlight, a family
is huddled.  The camera TRACKS slowly toward them.  They are
eating, but we can't tell that until we get close.  There is the
SOUND of the rifles and the SOUND of eating, but it could be
crying or sniffling.  As the camera MOVES very close, we find
four people:  Phil, the American husband of Mirra (a Lebanese
woman), and their two children.
```

These words, of course, are in the form of a "shooting script." They establish some very basic idea of where the film is to take place, who is in it, and the mood it establishes within a few seconds after "Fade In." Later, dialogue will come in, and we will have to read that and add it to our knowledge of what is happening. Other characters will appear, other scenes will take place. You will need to decide how to shoot such a script, but before you go that far, you must read it and understand it thoroughly.

In this chapter we will talk about how to know, by reading a script, whether (a) you want to make it into a film, and (b) you need to rewrite portions of it. We will discuss how to go about doing that rewriting. We will cover basic budgetary problems and how to know whether you will have enough money to make the film. We will also deal with some glaring problems that show up in dialogue, especially as we hear it on American television.

Take, for instance, a hypothetical line of dialogue ending a scene in a cafe, with a man saying to a woman, "I know we've just met, but wouldn't you like to come over to my house for a cup of coffee?" This is followed by a "dissolve" to an intimate corner of a house, with coffee on the table, the two strangers comfortably ensconced, and the woman asking, "What do you do for a living?" Now this isn't bad just because it's a terrible plot, or because the dialogue is so weak; it's bad because it leaves the viewer wondering what on earth the characters were saying to each other during the twenty minutes it took to get from the café to the house. In other words, this is an exchange of information that most likely would have taken place during the *unseen time* between scenes. The writer is so scatterbrained that he or she can't find a way of revealing information to us in the course of a conversation, but instead has to start at the beginning of the story in every scene. That's just not the way people behave. What could be done? Well, she might have said, after the dissolve, as they drank their coffee, "I've never been inside a military base, what's it like?" Or, "If you hate waiting on tables so much, why not a job in life insurance?" The same information is relayed to us, but we don't get the impression that these people have been sitting silently in a cab for twenty minutes, waiting to impart information to us!

Of course, you will develop your own objections to scripts and that, in a sense, is what this chapter is also about—developing your sensibilities.

READING

Whether you're a first-time director who has never made a film or a videotape, or a twenty-time award winner, every time you read a script in order to decide whether or not to film it is a crucial and wonderful moment. It is a time of choices. Or at least some choices, for you will fall between two extremes. On the one hand is that talented kind of director who writes his or her own scripts—many Hollywood directors, at least of feature films, do that these days—and on the other hand, there are those of you who will be hired by a production company to direct a script that's already written, cast, and ready to go, in which case you have very little leeway and very few choices to make. If neither of these is your lot, then, like most of us, you will be given a script by a friend or an acquaintance, and you will have to read it and decide whether to commit the next weeks or months or years to being tied up with that material. Are you, in other words, going to devote your life to this script?

Romance, suspense, terror, jeopardy, a decision point in someone's life. For thousands of years these have been the essence of drama, even of comedy. They are the meat of good stories. But how, your first time out, do you know if a script is going to "work," if it has enough of these ingredients? Well, that's a long process, but let's simplify matters by assuming you don't have a script, but merely a story-let's say a short story or a paragraph or two from a writer who says her idea would make a delicious movie. Start by reducing the script to a "one-liner" to see if it piques your interest, to see if you'd want to go further. If you've taken scriptwriting in college, that's very often where you've been told to begin, moving on from there to a paragraph, from there to a full-fledged "story"—that is, a few pages of summary—and then on to a "treatment"—the draft just before script—in which every scene and every character is described. If you've ever tried to sell a story or a script, you're familiar with this process: producers and executives ask to see a brief description, first. If they like it, they proceed to more elaborate efforts.

Okay, you have a one-liner, maybe something like the following.

A multiracial family in Lebanon tries to come to terms with the conflict surrounding it, but during a frightening month it comes apart at the seams.

Many one-liners will tell you that a story has no possibility, but do you really know enough to decide about this film? Probably not. Now, what?

Try the paragraph form.

> Phil and his wife Mirra live on the front in the Bekaa Valley in Lebanon. He is a wiry, tough-minded American journalist who has come to Lebanon to cover the war but instead falls for Mirra, whose husband has been killed in the civil war. He leaves his job and they marry, with a firm intention to remain neutral in the conflict. This proves impossible and, one year to the day after their wedding, Mirra and Phil take opposite sides in a battle that sunders their marriage just as violently as it tears the country apart.

This may or may not be your meat, but there's no doubt that you're better able to tell whether the script works as a story than you are in the one-line version, or, possibly, in a hefty, complex fifty-page version.

Okay, what is it we look for when we read such a paragraph; which things tell us this is an exciting possibility? (One thing we won't talk about is the film's commercial potential; that's something that depends on the place, the time, your position in the world of film, and a dozen other variables.) Does the story idea make you think it would be a good film? Why? The first thing I look for, whether in a student's paragraph, a professional script that I read, or a book that I want to make into a film, is if the story has a strong beginning, middle, and end. It's amazing how many stories don't. And it's amazing how many good writers claim that they know where something ends but don't know where it begins, or vice versa. (Middles, for some reason, are easier to come by.) Like so much in this business, this way of looking at a story may seem simpleminded, but the beginning–middle–end analysis is a wonderful place to start. After all, a film that fizzles out into a mediocre ending won't be satisfying to an audience; and a film that doesn't have a satisfactory beginning won't be satisfying either. What do I mean by a satisfactory beginning?

I want to make clear that this chapter is not a quickie course on screenwriting. We're looking at things from a directorial point of view, not a screenwriter's. So, what is it that you, as director, would put on the screen, and what just wouldn't go?

You want a beginning in which the conflict or goals of the main characters are evident or, if not evident, at least hinted at. A film that does not establish at some early point who the characters are and what they are trying to achieve (or escape from), leaves us feeling uneasy.

Which doesn't mean, I hasten to say, that we need to have that all spelled out in embarrassing simplicity; when I say "hinted at," I mean that a suggestion may well be enough and, indeed, is often very exciting and provocative. But we want to have an idea that the following questions can, soon, be answered: Who are they? Where are they going? Where do they want to go? What forces are preventing them from going? Do we know enough about them to (a) like them, (b) hate them, (c) fear them, or (d) find them intriguing and mysterious? This is a beginning.

We want an ending that "satisfies." Sorry, I can't define a good ending more than that. The likelihood is you'll know a vapid or non-existent ending when you read one.

And the middle? Although often overlooked, this is, after all, the substance of a story. Does your story leap from beginning to end without any interesting ups and downs in the center? Or is there a wonderful progression as it moves with its characters from one place to another, one problem to another? Do we feel we are coming to the end of the film only to have one more obstacle or one more achievement in our path? Along the way, do the characters grow or, if not, are we aware of the lack of growth which, by itself, becomes a dilemma to overcome?

It should be evident by now that all of this cannot be determined simply by a one-liner or, probably, even a paragraph. Hence the need, once a story intrigues you, to see it in an expanded form—the "story" of a one- or two-page length. Then, if you find that satisfying, move on to the "treatment," whether it's something you're writing yourself or being supplied with. Here, every scene is spelled out, dialogue is hinted at, and the entire story is there for you to see. Problems will leap out at you, as will images that make you excited.

Finally, of course, in order to determine whether the story is something you want to film, a script is needed, with dialogue intact. And here, when someone moves from a treatment or dynamite story line to a script, many of us find ourselves disappointed. What was a wonderful treatment seems vapid now that the dialogue is in place. Or overwritten. Or clumsy. How do you know if the dialogue is any good? The first and simplest test is to read it aloud yourself. (Many beginning writers don't do this—some claim they have a good "inner ear." Others just don't think of doing it—and many directors don't either.) After that, if you're ambivalent, get some friends who are actors to read through it. They'll appreciate your interest in their talents and ideas. If, after that, you love it, fine, go ahead with whatever business steps you need to take—call your agent, sign the papers, make the film. But what if you still don't know, or if you hate the dialogue? Is that the end of the project? To some extent, that depends on the reaction you've had to the rest of the film idea. Have you been wild about the story and a little discouraged with the dialogue? Or have you been so-so about the story and hated the dialogue? Or are you still puzzled about the dialogue, and think that with a little rewriting you can make it work? Or don't you know? It's with the last question that I want to deal. What makes good dialogue? What makes bad dialogue?

A line of dialogue needs to sound like it comes from the character who is saying it. That's simple enough. It should, in other words, not sound like it could come from just any character; nor should all the characters sound alike. Dialogue helps distinguish one character from another, and different people obviously talk differently; yet how many scripts have people in them who, on paper, all sound alike? Dialogue should meet a number of other requirements as well:

- Lines should not go on and on, stating every obvious fact that could be better shown with pictures. This is a well-known problem with American television, where the "radio with pictures" label is too often true.

- Pauses should be spelled out. By which I mean that what the characters are doing in between lines should be felt in the dialogue, not just stated in screen directions.

- We should feel in the dialogue that these are real people, not just narration lifted off the page. People should sound, sometimes, as if they have not listened with every part of their fiber to the other character but have actually had an interior life of their own going on. This is one of the most realistic things about Pinter's dialogue when he writes for film. Characters are obviously dealing with a rich inner life. In fact, they often don't respond to each other's lines, sounding more as if they were two independent characters, alone in the same room, but not aware of it. (This can be amusing, annoying, or, as in Pinter's writing, phenomenally realistic.)

- And, of course, it's more than nice if the writer shows a fine sense of wit, timing, intelligence, and character, all of which should leap out at you.

- Lines that cover a whole page and leave no room for action should be suspect; but if someone writes a lengthy monologue that makes you jump out of your chair with excitement, you'll probably find a way to make at least that speech work.

One of the most exciting kinds of scriptwriting is the kind that places us right in the midst of a scene. We see the lovers quarreling, but we don't know why—yet. The scene has reached a point of tension; we have to fight to keep up; they know so much more than we do, but it's exciting precisely because the scene has momentum. Conversely, a script in which dialogue *starts* as we dissolve to the scene, though we know that the characters have been with each other for two hours, limps along. A script in which every scene crackles with accepted facts that we perceive rather than receive, is a good script. A script that crackles, in general, that leads us from scene to scene, enticing us to want to see more, is a good script.

Given all these "rules," it is important to say something that I once read in a marvelous book on cinematography: "Rules were made to be learned so that you could know which ones to break." In other words, know what is supposed to be done, so you can then be free to use your own imagination and inventiveness to forge new territory. This goes not only for cinematography and lighting, editing and casting, but for scriptwriting as well. If something strikes you as "a good yarn," a story in which you can see something, even if no one else does, then perhaps you should go with it, even if it doesn't fit into anyone else's idea of what a good script is.

WRITING

Whether you've read a script that is very good or one that is only so-so but has a wonderful germ of truth in it, you will probably want to do some rewriting. If you're working with a producer by this time, he or she will tell you what your rights are vis-à-vis the writer (e.g.,

Writers Guild of America [WGA] requirements), but there's nothing to keep you from doing some of that writing on your own, before meeting with the writer-note-taking, as it were. Keep in mind that most writers are very wedded to their material, and if you want to have a good relationship with them, you'll need to use your powers of subtle persuasion and be tactful. I once made some changes in a script after detailed consultation with the writer, who said, "Hey, it's your film, go ahead, do what you want." After the film was shot, and the writer saw what I had done, he stopped talking to me. And that was an amicable arrangement!

First, look at scenes that are either missing or don't belong in the film at all or—to ring some changes, already—should be shifted from one place to another. That's a fairly easy problem to spot, though not so easy to solve, since, as a wise writer once observed, "scripts are like balloons: you squeeze them in one spot, they bulge in another." Next, you'll want to balance the length of one scene against another. Is this one too short? Does it follow too quickly on the heels of that one? And so on.

Are there characters who don't belong in the film? That's an interesting problem, and very frequently isn't seen until too late. But if a film is to work, the number of characters who demand our attention has to be just right. When you get to the editing phase, you will very often not only cut out a number of scenes because the film doesn't work without that excision, but you will cut out some characters as well. (Remember the actor's complaint, "I was left on the cutting room floor?") It's easier and cheaper to do those cuts at this stage. How do you know whom to cut? Look for characters who don't add very much, who are in there just to convey information. Can that information be delivered in some other fashion? By another person? By pictures? On the other hand, are there characters missing? Is the interaction of the two main characters so constant that we can't take our eyes off them but in the end feel somewhat bored by them? Try adding a scene with someone we haven't met before. It can be very refreshing.

Is there too much plot? This can be one of the problems with the middle that we talked about before. A script that carries us along from one important scene to the next may be very exciting, but it can also dissipate excitement by keeping us moving too much. Try inserting a

8

Sample Script
"Mirra, Mirra, On the Wall"

15. PHIL & MIRRA'S HOUSE - INTERIOR (DAY)

Bright sunlight fills the room, belying the sense of gloom that is
infecting the couple. Phil is mending some harness for the donkey.
Mirra is sweeping.

                            MIRRA
          Where are the boys? I worry when
          they go out like that?

[handwritten: Too explicit. Phil knows whom she means, LET HER VOICE tell us!]

                            PHIL (without looking up)
          They'll be fine. (beat)(he looks up)
          Do you want me to look for them?

Mirra hesitates, then shakes her head.

                            MIRRA
          No. I guess not. (she is not very sure)

[handwritten: obvious!]

                            PHIL
          If they're not back in an hour, I'll
          go. They're probably down by the river.
          You know how they love to paddle around.
          Don't worry, Mirra, there're no troops left.
          After last night's fierce battle, I doubt if
          there're any within twenty miles.

[handwritten: She knows, so leave it out.]

[handwritten: Too much.]

[handwritten: How often do couples call each other by name? Sounds stilted.]

Mirra goes on sweeping. Phil finishes the harness and stands up,
taking it to a hook on the wall. He stands looking out the window
for a moment.

CUT TO: PHIL'S P.O.V. (Point of View)

A distant curl of smoke rising up out of the valley. It could be
from a fire or from artillery.

CUT TO: C.U. PHIL

There is some concern on his face, but after a moment he relaxes,
dismissing the worry. He turns from the window.

MED. SHOT - INTERIOR ROOM

Mirra is looking intensely at Phil.

                            MIRRA
          What is it? What's out there?

                    PHIL
           I don't know.

                    MIRRA
           Damn you! What's out there?

                    "O.S." willdo

A sudden noise off-screen startles both of them. They whirl around,
and the two boys come running into the room. They are very excited.

CLOSE TWO SHOT - THE BOYS

                    SAMUEL
           Look! Look at what we found.

He is holding up a hand grenade, unexploded.

What? How old   SAMUEL (Cont.)
is he? Cut   It was down by the river bank. We
down or cut   were exploring for artifacts and couldn't
Out.   understand why the sand was torn up so much,
                        then we saw these soldiers, breaking camp.
                        We hid in the underbrush and waited until
                        they had gone. This was by a rock.

CU - MIRRA

                    MIRRA
           Phil!

CU - PHIL
                    PHIL   *I don't believe*
           Give me that, please, Samuel. — *this reaction.*

CU - SAMUEL

The boy holds back, suddenly putting the grenade behind his back.

                    SAMUEL
           It's mine.

MED - PHIL

Suddenly enraged, as if all his fears about the boys' welfare had
been transformed into anger at Samuel.

WIDER PHIL & SAMUEL
He grabs at the grenade, tearing it from Samuel's hand. The boy
bursts into tears.

CU - MIRRA

She is furious.

(handwritten: why so explicit?)

                    MIRRA
          Now, you get angry! When the Shi-ite
          soldiers came through here yesterday,   *(handwritten: Too long)*
          you did nothing. When the Christians
          came through the day before - nothing!
          But when my son is in danger, you get
          angry. Is there nothing better you can
          think to do?

(handwritten: OTHER: IF THE SECOND SON DOESN'T SPEAK, WHY IS HE IN SCRIPT?)

(handwritten: BE CONSISTENT WITH NUMBERS. ONE SHOT IS NUMBERED, THE OTHERS AREN'T.)

                    Revised Sample Script
                  "Mirra, Mirra, On the Wall"

15. PHIL & MIRRA'S HOUSE - INTERIOR (DAY)

Bright sunlight fills the room. Phil is mending some harness for the
donkey. Mirra is sweeping.

                    MIRRA
          Where are they?

                    PHIL (without looking up)
          They'll be fine. (beat)
          Do you want me to look for them?

Mirra hesitates, then shakes her head.

                    MIRRA
          No. I guess not.

                    PHIL
          If they're not back in an hour, I'll
          go. They're probably down by the river.
          Don't worry, there're no troops left.
          Not after last night.

11

Mirra goes on sweeping. Phil finishes the harness and stands up, taking it to a hook on the wall. He stands looking out the window for a moment.

16. PHIL'S P.O.V.

A distant curl of smoke rising up out of the valley. It could be from a fire or from artillery.

17. C.U. PHIL

There is some concern on his face, but after a moment he relaxes, dismissing the worry. He turns from the window.

18 .MEDIUM SHOT - THE ROOM

Mirra is looking intensely at Phil.

> MIRRA
> What is it? What's out there?

> PHIL
> I don't know.

> MIRRA
> Damn you! What's out there?

A sudden NOISE off-screen startles both of them. They whirl around, and the two boys come running into the room. They are very excited.

19. TWO SHOT - THE BOYS

> SAMUEL
> Look! Look at what we found.

He is holding up a hand grenade, unexploded.

20. CU - MIRRA
> MIRRA
> Phil!

21. CU - PHIL

He is stunned.
> PHIL (Angrily)
> Where'd you get that.

22. MED. SHOT - THE BOYS
Samuel is take aback, but John, not sensing Phil's fury, is still delighted by their find.

> JOHN
> Our river.

> SAMUEL
> Soldiers left it.

> JOHN (echoing)
> Soldiers lef' it.

```
MIRRA ENTERS the shot.

She is furious.
                          MIRRA
                    Now you get angry!

She takes a step forward, then remembers the grenade. Turning to
Samuel...

26. WIDER - THE BOYS AND MIRRA
                          MIRRA
               Sam -- give me the grenade. Please.
               It's dangerous. It's dangerous, Sam.

Slowly, the boy holds out the grenade. John watches silently,
dumbstruck by his brother giving over this prize.

Phil reaches into shot and takes the grenade, gingerly.

27. CU - PHIL

There is more fear on his face than anger.
```

scene that does nothing, a scene in which we learn a little about character or nuance, but which is basically there to let us relax, to take us away from the main action, or to let something happen offstage, to let time pass. It's not just that we need to move a little slower; it's that these kinds of scenes, in which "nothing" is happening, actually show us a little more about the personalities of our characters, and that makes us able to understand what is happening; it adds to our ability to believe plot.

In order to make all of the above a little more tangible, I've included a few pages of script, which I've marked up with suggestions for changes. Then, on succeeding pages, I show the revisions. This is not an all-inclusive example; there are no new scenes, no reams of new characters, but it should show one approach to the reading of a script.

RESEARCH

A great problem encountered by nearly all of us, whether we are writers, producers, actors, or directors, is the notion implied by the question, "Is it real?" When you read through my brief example, did you ask yourself whether I knew anything about the Bekaa Valley, about marriage in Lebanon, about the Shiites, about war? If you didn't, then I probably conveyed enough truth in that script for the pages of this book. But would it have been enough if you were going to be directing such a film? I doubt it. You would want to spend some time researching the subject matter discussed in the script. This is not a matter of trusting or not trusting the writer. It is far more serious than that. It has to do with the fact that you are going to take this script, if you like it, and spend a great deal of time—not to mention money—on it. It also has to do with the fact that you are going to be asked by the actors, producer, art director, and a host of other people how you wish to portray such and such a facet of the script, and that can't be done unless you know something—maybe a great deal—about the subject matter. That makes sense, doesn't it? So you're going to have to get out the encyclopedia, the history books, the catalogs; you're going to open up your favorite search engines on the Web; and you're going to have to go to places you want to make films about, or at least talk to people who have been there.

REALITY

When we asked before, "Is it real?" we were asking from a researcher's point of view. Now we are asking from the point of view of the audience. Does this script, as written, persuade you, the viewer, that the characters, the situation, the dialogue are real? Perhaps more than any other question, this one has to be answered. For how often have all of us, sitting in front of the television set, commented at the end of a particular film or videotape program, "I don't believe it"? How often do we look at the portrayal of a policeman, a lawyer, a lover, a "saint," a teacher, a child, in fact, practically any human being or human situation with which we have some acquaintance, and say, "No, it doesn't ring true"? It's your job as director to decide how much reality you want in your film and then to make sure you get it. (Some people don't care; comedies and fantasies are often specifically above reality—that is, surreal.) This is the time, when you're reading and rewriting your script, to make those decisions and make the necessary changes.

Now, this isn't simply a matter of saying, "Oh, it doesn't sound real." You have to know the characters with whom you're dealing, and you have to make a choice: Is the dialogue going to sound like the real characters, or sound like some abstraction of the real characters? What do I mean? Do you remember the first time you heard a method actor at work, with the mumbling, the tortured grimaces, the pauses. (I'm overdoing it; all good acting is, to some extent, based on method.) Did you at some point say, "Hey, that sounds the way real people sound"? Method actors often sound like real people because real people don't speak in whole sentences; they change direction, take pauses, mumble, and so forth. Some of that "real dialogue" feeling can come from actors' interpretation of any dialogue, but much of it must come from the writing itself. So when you're rewriting and deciding how "real" you want something, remember the method actor. How many clues do you want to give the actor about how you (or the writer and you) want the scene to go? Put in pauses; put in accents; put in your sense of reality.

After all is said and done, whether or not you want to make a script into a film depends less on the "rules and regulations" I have set down, or on your ability to rewrite dialogue, and more on your interest in the story and your willingness to stand by it through the long hard processes that follow.

Of course, sometimes you have little or no control over your script. And that deserves a little discussion.

TIME OUT

A word about the "business." There are all sorts of productions you may get involved with in the film and television industries. You might be directing a television series; you might be directing an "industrial" or an educational videotape. Other jobs may be directing for PBS in Washington or doing an in-house, closed-circuit informational film for a multinational corporation in Indiana. Most of what we directors do, alas, is not the kind of film we go to see at the local movie theater, and much of what we do is not originated by us. In point of fact, most of the working directors in this country are toilers in the field. They are hired for a specific project—for a specific term, often not more than a few weeks—to direct a film for one episode of an ongoing series, an educational documentary, a commercial, or a promotional short. (This happens both to staff directors and to independents, unattached to a studio, a television station, or a large institution.) Because of that you will often find yourself called upon to direct a script chosen by someone else, for which you will not conceive the idea or cast the characters or raise the money or hire the production team. You will be handed a script that is to be filmed within two or three weeks, for which the cast is already assembled or that is part of an ongoing television series. And that means less control than you would like to have.

What about such times? If you're at all like me, these are jobs you will probably decide to do, not so much because you're wild about the scripts, but because they pay well or lead to better work, or because you're a professional—it's what you do for a living. That doesn't mean, however, that you should take the script as a *fait accompli* without any possibility of change. You should read it just as you do any other script or story line and make suggestions you feel are appropriate to the story editor or producer or writer. What it may mean is that you may not have as much flexibility as when you're operating all by yourself or starting a new project. For instance, it's unlikely that you can get the producer to delete a character who is part of a running cast in a series. You may be able to get the story editor (see chapter 3) to insert more dialogue for such a character if you feel that he or she is not being used enough to justify his or her existence in the script, and you should certainly suggest changes in dialogue that sounds dull or wrong to you. How far you can go will depend on your relationship with the production company and your feelings about yourself as a writer. The worst thing you can do, in my view, is to accept bad scenes or bad dialogue without making some effort to change them. If you have problems, state them and see what happens. You may be surprised to find that producers and writers and editors are just waiting for someone to help them solve a problem that they had confronted but failed to fix.

Let's sum up the chapter so far. In a production, the script has to be paramount. No film can exist without one, and the best films are founded on the best scripts. Sometimes those scripts have been created by the writer, who sometimes works in conjunction with the director. Some directors spend months working with their writers, honing everything to perfection. Does this mean that on the set you may make no changes? There are two schools of thought. One says that the script, after thorough rewrites, is golden and cannot be changed on the set, when pressures may make you do things in haste. The other says that nothing is written in stone and that actors' tastes and characterizations, your own ear, and the producer's power all cause changes in the script, whether on the set, in the editing room, or at the lunch table. Whichever you choose, *both* schools accept the notion that the script itself is crucial as a starting point, even if you intend to improvise your way through the final filming.

TIME OUT

What about improvisation? Many of you will have read or heard about the actors and directors who like to make up dialogue around a concept. While the actor/director John Cassavetes was one of the best-known directors for this approach—using a corps of actors over and over again to create whole films around improvised dialogue—in recent years, improv has become a tool used by many in certain scenes. And while a filmmaker like Christopher Guest (*This is Spinal Tap, Best in Show*) can create enormously funny material through improvisation, most directors will use improvisation only to free actors or to get at a scene's underlying meaning or an actor's underlying emotions when all else fails. The use of improvisation, then, should probably be something that comes from a particular situation during a shoot, rather than as an approach to scriptwriting, unless you-and your actors-have demonstrated a real affinity for this technique.

ARITHMETIC

Normally, money and budget matters belong in a book or course about producing. I introduce the subject here because no matter how beautiful the script, no matter how enthusiastic the participants, films cannot be made without sufficient money. So, let's talk briefly about budgets.

"Sufficient." What does that mean and what does a director need to know about such things?

The answer to these questions depends, in part, on what your relationship is to the script and to the overall production, and how big the staff is. For starters, you should be able both to read and to create a budget. That's pretty upsetting to some people, especially those who can't balance a checkbook or do their own IRS forms, but I think I can lead you through the basics of budgets so that you will have a reading-and-writing capability in them. Directors need to know something about the financial side of filmmaking because (a) they have to know if there is money in the budget to *do what they want to do*, and (b) they may make a film all by themselves for which they serve as both producer and director. Ignorance of money matters in filmmaking is not bliss. There's a nice little paradox here: If you're working with a huge staff on a major project, you can simply tell the producer, "I need this. Find the dough." And leave the worrying to him or her. If you're operating in a tiny group, you and your producer will split chores because no one person can do everything. But in between—and that's where most of our projects fall—you'll have to know *something* about budgets.

There are a number of categories to deal with.

One Salaried positions. Who is going to be paid a weekly salary? How much do they get?

Two Craftspeople. Who is going to be hired for the duration of the shoot? For how many weeks or days? How much should they get?

Three Sets, costumes, makeup, film equipment, and so on. How much will these cost?

Four Cast. How many actors will there be for how many days at how much per day? How much should they get for overtime? How much are the agents' fees? How much for casting consultant?

Five Miscellaneous. Includes everything that doesn't fit into the above categories.

That's not difficult, is it? Look at the budget I've set up on the following pages. It's more complex than the five categories I've outlined, but if you look carefully, you'll see that everything in it fits into those basic categories. Where do you get the figures to plug in? That's a matter of experience or going to the proper rental catalogs, unions, or personnel to make the deals. Those numbers are available, and the production manager or producer deals with them on most films (see chapter 3), but you should have a beginning acquaintance with these figures.

N.B. The terms "above the line" and "below the line," which are traditionally used in budgets are omitted here. I find them unnecessarily confusing. If you encounter them somewhere in the industry, ask what they mean in that particular company. Also, what I've included here in "Category" and "Explanation" may not be entirely familiar. For the most part, these things are defined or explicated in the coming chapters or in the Glossary. For instance, personnel is discussed in chapter 3 and laboratory terms in chapter 9. However, the *basic notion* of a budget is laid out here.

BUDGET FOR A MODEST[3] 16MM FILM DRAMA[4]

Every budget should have, at the beginning, a note as to what it covers. Here's mine. *This budget is based on a four-week preproduction period; ten days of shoot; and ten weeks of postproduction. The film is to be shot all on location in Vermont.*

What I've provided here are the categories and the figures—the bottom line—for a forty-minute dramatic film with ten main actors. You should, hereafter, be able to read such a budget and, with some effort, write one.

What we now have to do is discuss whether this budget is sufficient to do what you want to do. First, look at the money included for you. Does that compensate you for the amount of time you must put

---

[3] I know that the word "modest" applied to a $325,000 budget must seem ridiculous for some, especially students, but keep in mind that a public television documentary these days costs between $200,000 and $750,000, and dramas go up from there.

[4] Here's a case where a difference exists between video and film. Depending on the kind of video you're shooting—BetaSP, Digibeta, Mini DV—the budget could go down from 10 percent to 15 percent because there would be no laboratory costs. Additionally, if you edited on video, the costs could be significantly lower. (See chapter 9 "The Digital Divide.")

in? If not, you may not be able to do anything about it because of your producer's financial condition; on the other hand, most DGA salaries are minimums—the contract clearly states you can bargain for more. Next, what about the time periods allotted for support personnel? Do you have enough time to consult with your director of photography, your prop person, and so forth? If you've never made a film before, some of this analysis may have to wait until you've read chapter 3, but suffice it to say for now that how much time you have with key personnel, and how much they're paid, is important.

What about settings and costumes? Is there enough money for these? Is this a period film to be shot in France, or a contemporary story to be made in the studio? The amount of money available for each costume multiplied by the number of costumes should add up to a sum that you can read off the budget. If it looks skimpy, put a question mark next to it. Similarly, for each piece of equipment or each actor, you should figure how many days or hours you feel you need and then compare them with the hours or days allocated in the budget. You may find that the budget doesn't spell out the number of days; it may be based on previous experience with similar films, or it may simply be a guess, an average, concocted at the beginning of a project, but not one that takes into account all the rewrites or added characters or changed settings you've decided on.

A lot of producers wouldn't dream of letting you see their budgets, but that doesn't mean you can't ask about certain categories that are important to you. Fireworks, for instance: Is there an allowance under special effects or props for that scene when the hero and heroine stand watching fireworks? If the producer says, "We'll buy some stock footage," and you know you want to shoot it "live," then you've got some bargaining to do. Some producers may simply say, "There's enough money, and if there isn't, we'll tell you when you're spending too much," or "You've got five days to shoot it, and we'll supply ample crew." A smart director won't stop there, even though that sounds like a monumental turndown. A smart director will say, "Okay, I understand, budgets are your business, but I do want to let you know some of the areas that are of special concern to me, where I've planned something a little more daring, a little out of the ordinary." And then you should go over the list. You don't want stock costumes, you want them made. You don't want a nine-foot ceiling, because you have in

ACCT. NO.	CATEGORY	EXPLANATION	TOTAL DOLLAR AMOUNT
901	SALARIES		
	A. Producer	flat fee	13,000
	B. Director	flat fee[5]	16,250
	C. Production Secretary	650 x 6 weeks	3,900
	D. Pension & welfare (10%)	DGA pension & welfare fund	1,625
	E. Payroll benefits (13%)	Social Security, insurance, etc.	4,310
Subtotal			39,085

ACCT. NO.	CATEGORY	EXPLANATION	TOTAL DOLLAR AMOUNT
902	CAST/BITS/EXTRAS		
	A. Principals (10) & bits (6)	AFTRA (American Federation minimum of Television & Radio Artists)	18,714
	B. Overtime for (A)		5,590
	C. Extras		5,200
	D. Casting Consultants	flat fee	1,300
	E. Pension & welfare	(9% x [A + B])	2,187
	F. Payroll Benefits	(12% x [A + B + C])	3,540
Subtotal			36,531

ACCT. NO.	CATEGORY	EXPLANATION	NO. DAYS	RATE	TOTAL DOLLAR AMOUNT
903	A. Production Manager	DGA			7,500
	B. First assistant director	DGA			5,500
	C. 2nd assistant director	DGA			3,250
	D. Director of photography	NABET[6]			7,500
	E. Assistant camera		12	$200	2,400
	F. Sound		11	350	3,850
	G. Boom		11	250	2,750
	H. Costume design	flat fee			5,000
	I. Wardrobe		14	200	2,800
	J. Makeup		11	200	2,200
	K. Hair		11	200	2,200
	L. Grips (2)		16/11	250	7,000

[5] A director's salary is based first on the DGA minimum, then on additional days, hours, weeks, and so forth. This was an estimate, but in all likelihood, the total length of time worked exceeded this rate.

[6] Production crews are paid a basic daily rate, then time and a half for each hour of overtime (OT). Some personnel, unions permitting, are paid a "flat rate" regardless of hours worked. NABET (National Association of Broadcast Engineers & Technicians,) is one of the craft unions, IATSE (International Alliance of Television & Stage Electricians) is the other. When you get to more than sixteen hours of straight work (sometimes twelve), you're paid "double time"; when you get to twenty hours, it's triple time—or "golden" time (which happens on sloppy shoots).

M. Props	18	300	5,400
N. Gaffer	16	350	5,600
O. Best boy	12	275	3,300
P. Art director	flat fee		5,000
Q. Script (continuity)	14	300	4,200
R. Production Assistants	(Unit manager, location, etc.)		4,100
S. Payroll benefits (13%)			7,476
T. Pension & welfare	(NABET 15.50/day)		1,843
	DGA (16%)		2,560
Subtotal			**91,429**

904	**EQUIPMENT/COSTUMES/PROPS/SUPPLIES**		
	A. Camera equipment	10 days	3,000
	B. Sound equipment	10 days	3,000
	C. Lighting/grip	10 days	12,000
	D. Costumes	estimate	10,250
	E. Props		4,500
	F. Electrical		1,150
	G. Shipping of equipment		1,150
	H. Hair/makeup/wigs		2,200
	I. Livestock rental		755
	J. Set dressing		4,000
	K. General film supplies		2,000
Subtotal			**44,005**

905	**TRANSPORTATION**		
	A. Car & wagon rental		2,700
	B. Truck rental		1,800
	C. Traffic control		750
	D. Gas, oil, mileage		1,900
	E. Local transportation	(NYC office)	1000
Subtotal			**5,480**

906	**LOCATION EXPENSES**		
	A. Train/air to location	24 persons x $200	4,800
	B. Hotel	550 nights @ $40[7]	22,000
	C. Per diem	550 days @ $60	33,000

[7]This is a pittance. Most per diems are $125 for food and hotel. In this case, however, the production manager and producer were able to find good food and good lodging for this kind of money.

	D. Catering	400 meals @ $10 (lunches)	4,000
	E. Location permissions		3,000
	F. Projector on location		1,100
	G. Preparation/ location scouting		2,200
	H. Location office/phone		3,500
Subtotal			**73,600**
907	**LABORATORY COSTS**		
	A. Raw stock/ process/print	fifty 400-foot rolls @ $150 (stock); @ $.60/foot (processing)	19,500
	B. Sound/transfer/print/ coding		4,500
	C. Opticals & titles		4,500
	D. Answer print		3,000
	E. Color Reversal Internegative (CRI)		4,400
	F. Sound effects		1500
Subtotal			**37,400**
908	**EDITING COSTS**		
	A. Editing package[8]	(room, editor, assistant)	24,000
	B. Negative cutter		3,500
	C. Dailies shipping		1,000
	D. Mix		4,000
	E. Effects editor		4,000
Subtotal			**36,500**
909	**OTHER COSTS**		
	A. Music rights		5,000
	B. Insurance		5,400
Subtotal			**10,400**

TOTAL PRODUCTION COST $374,430

---

[8] If possible, a producer will make a deal with an editor to supply a cutting room, equipment, an assistant, and him or herself in a "package" price, rather than get tied up with too much bookkeeping, overtime, and so on.

mind something grander. And so on. (Some of these details will be discussed again in chapters 5 and 6.)

If you are producing and directing your own film and you are uncomfortable with this kind of process, get a friend who isn't to work on it with you. That kind of partnership can be very comforting. What you may not do, however, is ignore the importance of the budgetary process and simply leave it to other people. That way disaster lies, not just because money is hard to come by, but because—unless you are incredibly lucky—sooner or later you will run into a scene or a shot or a costume or an actor for which you have plans beyond the scope of your dollars.

Throughout this chapter, I have made the assumption that you are working with a "narrative" script, that is, a script based upon a story. What if you are called upon to read, rewrite, or direct a documentary or educational film or tape? An industrial film? A commercial? Obviously, we cannot take up every film form in a book this size, but the documentary, encompassing so many important kinds of filmmaking, is a special case, one which is discussed in chapter 12. There, too, I will take up the question of how to read and write documentary scripts.

Reading, writing, and arithmetic. These are the basic three *R*s of grammar school. And they're very basic to filmmaking too: script and money. But, as you will soon see, there's a lot more coming.

The Team

The first day I appeared on a film set, when I was twenty-two, I was introduced to the cast, to my client (I was a dialogue coach on the *Lassie* television show), and to members of the crew. It was like a page out of Damon Runyon. "Here's Wally the Gaffer," one person said to me. "Meet Charlie the Best Boy." "This is Tommy the Mixer." The terms both amused and baffled me. "Wally the Gaffer," indeed! I now know that a "mixer" is the man or woman who handles the level of the sound as it comes from the microphone(s), as well as the person who monitors the sound in the rerecording studio (often called the dubbing studio) or on the music recording set. The gaffer, of course, is the chief lighting person, who takes orders from the cinematographer (also known as the director of photography, or, in England, the lighting cameraman) and bosses around a crew of juicers (electricians), the top dog of whom is the best boy.

The purpose of this chapter, however, is not to describe the peculiar names associated with the crew of a motion picture production, but to define the responsibilities of those crucial members of the crew with whom a director works and especially those with whom he or she will have the most important relationships. In order to do so, I propose to list the jobs that are associated with even a moderate, independent production in film and television, because such a list is astonishing to those who have studied film or video as a *low-budget* operation. The list of team members described below is only one kind of configuration. It is a Hollywood/New York, professional, unionized production crew. The list will be useful to the novice, however, precisely because it is so large, and because it lists the variety of crew positions to be found in many productions. Yours may vary. You may never have the luxury of some of the support to be found here. On the other hand, since the beginning days of the professional motion picture era in America, this has more or less been the traditional team.

FILM

First are those who are in the so-called management team: those who are responsible for running the show.

Executive Producer The man or woman in charge of the production from top to bottom. The title is usually reserved for someone who has helped raise the money or someone who is responsible for a number of productions, whether in feature films or in television.

Producer The person in charge of a specific production, who reports to the executive producers and is responsible for the day-to-day operation of the project.

Associate Producer In my view, this is someone who can take over the duties of the producer if that person drops dead or gets ill. In other words, a top assistant. Often the associate producer has very specific duties of his or her own that are quite different from a producer's. In other words, the associate producer is like a vice-president, either busy and contributing to the work or frustrated as hell.

Writer The man or woman who conceives and writes the story line, the "treatment," or the actual script that is used. Sometimes the writer and the executive producer are the same person. Often, as we saw in the last chapter, the director is also the writer.

Story Editor A position that seldom exists on a feature film. But in television, story editors are crucial members of the team. They are management personnel who work with the writer(s), making sure the writers understand the nature of the project. They often supply the writer with something called a "Bible" that outlines character traits and story lines permissible in the series, and they edit or rewrite scripts in order to ensure that they are supplied to the production team on time and in good shape. The story editor is often responsible for writing some scripts on his or her own and for making financial deals with the writers.

Production Manager (P.M.) Variously, a tough-minded, difficult human being who is responsible for making the business deals with the rest of the crew, getting the equipment that the director and others want, seeing to it that the location has precisely what's needed, *or* a tough-minded, difficult human being who is disliked by one and all because he brings the production in under budget by renting hotel rooms without private baths. In short, an indispensable team member who doesn't have a chance of being liked.

Unit Manager Person responsible to the production manager or to the company's business manager for the day-to-day financial operation. Sometimes the unit manager functions as a location scout; sometimes she or he simply helps the P.M.

Production Office Coordinator (P.O.C.) If the production manager is the most indispensable member of the management team, the P.O.C. certainly comes in as a close second. This team member was added to the cast of characters when production after production left the confines of the film studios in Hollywood and ventured out into the world to do "location" shooting. The P.O.C. is that lonely person who sits in the production office, which has been rented for the occasion, and holds down the fort. She or he is there throughout the day and often into the night, coordinating various members of the crew, overseeing technical operations, taking messages, finding the caterer, redirecting lost agents and lost property, and typing and retyping cast lists and location schedules. You can tell by the length of this list of duties just how important the P.O.C. is.

Onward now to the crew itself, those people who are hired when production is about to begin. As is the case with everything else in the industry, there are variations as to who is hired when. Sometimes, for instance, an art director is considered management, but I choose to think of management as those people who would be kept on even if there were a long delay in the scheduled start of shooting. So, people like art directors, who are not kept on in such circumstances, are listed here with the rest of the "crew."

Assistant Director (A.D.) Often hired *instead* of the production manager on a simple shoot, the A.D. is responsible for breaking down the script into segments that can be shot on a single day. The A.D. plots these segments on a board, into strips that contain, among other things, the scene number, the number of pages, the cast of characters needed for each scene, animals or special effects that are used, and a myriad of other details that make it possible to see at a glance how many such scenes can be shot on a single day, which ones can be shifted to another day, what to do if it rains or if a character in the cast gets sick, and so on. In short, the A.D. (or the P.M., if he takes on that responsibility) must plot the film in such a fashion that everyone knows in advance what will be shot when. And, of course, it all has to come in *on*, or *under* budget. The A.D. is also responsible, once the shoot actually gets under way, for running the set. The classic line, "Lights, camera, action" is never heard on a set. It's much more likely to come from the first A.D. in the following fashion: "Quiet on the set. I said, 'Quiet!'Come on, boys, let's get it quiet. All right . . . roll camera." The camera rolls, the sound rolls, a clapstick is made to close noisily in front of the camera, and only then does a quiet voice (take note of that adjective, please!) say, "Action." That voice, of course, belongs to you, the director.

Second Assistant Director This person is usually hired only a few days before the beginning of the shoot and has a terrible series of jobs. He or she must sign the actors in and out, make phone calls to the actors to change their "calls" (the times they're due on the set or location in the mornings of the shoots), take over the set only when the first A.D. is out changing the strip board, and do a great deal of dirty work, like rounding up stray extras or horses that have wandered off with their wranglers. The second A.D. also does a great deal of paperwork at the end of the day, filling in reports on how many scenes were shot, how many hours of overtime were used, and so on. Yes, there are sometimes third and fourth assistant directors. Using walkie-talkies, they will handle traffic, hold back crowds, and generally herd large numbers of extras around, especially when the shoot occupies a large outdoor area.

Cinematographer The fancy name for the director of photography, called D.P. for short (never "cameraman"), who is in charge of how the picture looks. I'll leave it at that for now, because I would need more than ten paragraphs to describe what this title really means. However, we'll come back many times to what the D.P. does and how he or she interacts with the director.

Camera Operator This position refers to filmmaking in 35mm or larger formats: the "big time." Because of unions and because of the many things a D.P. has to watch, it was decided long ago that he would not handle the camera during the actual shooting; that a camera operator would do this. On lower-budget productions, and with different union relationships or negotiations, the D.P. will in fact often handle his or her own camera.

Assistant Cameraman (A.C.) The person who assists both the D.P. and the camera operator, changing focus and lenses, measuring distances, and keeping everything neat and tidy. (Yes, there are second assistant cameramen, too.)

Mixer As I mentioned earlier, this is the person who takes care of all sound levels, whether in a studio, on location, or in a postproduction situation. In addition, the mixer is in charge of the rest of the sound crew on the set.

Boom Operator The person who handles the microphones.

Recordist On a big set, the recordist is the person who does the actual recording of sound. On most productions these days, due to simplification and miniaturization of equipment, this person and the mixer are the same.

Grips The key grip is the chief carpenter, stagehand, and dolly-pusher on the set. The other grips are carpenters, stagehands, and so on.

Continuity Person Formerly called "script girl" until everyone realized that (a) a lot of men did the job, and (b) it was a derogatory term. The continuity person is crucial. He or she keeps track of how many takes are made of each shot and of each scene, how long they ran, who was in them, what lines of dialogue were changed, where the characters lifted hats, chewed gum, drank whiskey, and so on. He or she will yell out when a line is mangled and no one else has heard it, take a Polaroid shot of the scene so that clothes and colors will match if and when it's reshot, and remember details about the scene that you would not think possible. The continuity person is also responsible for handing the film editor a detailed, notated script containing every possible kind of remark about what was shot, when, where it was, and who was in it. Truly, a monumental task.

Gaffer As mentioned earlier, the person in charge of the lighting crew. The gaffer takes orders from the D.P.

Best Boy The top electrician, who reports to the gaffer.

Juicers The rest of the electricians.

Makeup and Hairdresser(s) Depending on how many members are in the cast, there are one or more of these artists.

Costume Designer The person who actually designs the costumes.

Wardrobe. Not to be confused with the costume designer, wardrobe people handle the costumes on the set. There is usually one for men and one for women.

Art Director Sometimes called the production designer (depending on his or her importance in the production-or his or her contract), the art director is in charge of the overall setting, design, and construction for the production. In some ways the fact that I list this person here is indicative of the industry's mindset. In point of fact, the art director is much more important and belongs with the team that comes in before any shooting actually goes on. Whether or not the art director is brought in early depends on the way the producer, the director, and the entire production company treats the production. Is this a large feature film that requires much art design? Or is it a television show with a "standing set" that was pulled out of stock a long time ago?

Art Decorator The person who is in charge, on a large production, of actually filling in the details on a set. The art decorator works for the art director.

Props Oh, how easy it is to leave this one out and then regret it. The prop man or woman is a crucial member of the crew. He or she supplies not only the perfect prop, but many copies of it (for retakes), the director's favorite mints (from an unlimited supply), the right word of encouragement, and the perfect solution to a tricky but solvable special effects problem-when no one else thought of it. On big shoots, there are several categories of prop persons: special effects, "greensmen" (those who handle shrubs, grass, branches), and so on.

Postproduction There is a whole series of postproduction personnel, most of whom don't actually fit into the "team" or "crew" of a film or television set (mixers, dubbers, laboratory technicians, and so forth), but there is one person who absolutely must be considered a part of your primary team, especially since he or she will often begin work long before the production is "wrapped" (finished).

Film Editor The person who actually edits the film under the direction of the producer or director or other people. He or she has an assistant editor and sometimes, in Hollywood, an apprentice editor. (The rules for getting these jobs used to be arcane. In Hollywood, you might, for instance, have to be an apprentice for seven years before graduating to the job of assistant. In New York, being talented and adept is more important.) More about this crucial job in chapter 10.

What I've listed is the standard crew and production team for most motion picture shoots. There are even more, but they are not important for this book.

TIME IN

YOUR RELATIONSHIP WITH THE TEAM

You've noticed that this is a large team. To be sure, not all of the people I've described are actually on every shoot you're going to go on, but enough of them are-especially in the world of television, where many of you will end up-that you need to know how to deal with them.

First things first. You're not the king. Directors used to be, and on some movies they still are, but the days when the director was always the top man are gone now that series television is here. When I first went to work in Hollywood in 1957, my executive producer told me not to say a word on the sound stage; the director was in charge, and his orders were always to be obeyed. After a few days, I noticed that my boss was wandering on the set, pulling the director aside, and telling him what to do. I began to get the idea that the jodhpurs-and-megaphone days were gone, that there *might* be places somewhere in town where the director called all the shots, but where I was, he was just one of the boys. Twenty-five years later, that's truer than ever, and now that women are an integral part of the directing force, they will have to accept the fact that many times they, too, are just "one of the boys."

There are three rules to remember:

1. Know what the rights and responsibilities of a director are;
2. Know whom you have to deal with, what you have to know, and what you don't have to know; and
3. Say "thank you."

Rule 3 Before moving on to the first and second rules, a brief word about the third. Why do I bother to add it? For the same reason that I mentioned there are no more jodhpurs-and-megaphone days. If the director is no longer king, he or she is also no longer God, no longer able to push people around and get away with it. So, if I wasn't impelled to issue rule 3 just because it's nice to be a nice guy, I would be impelled to do so because it is a way of *getting things done*. In other words, it's to your advantage to be polite. Some people find that difficult when they're under pressure or when they're being "creative." I've seen this happen in film schools, and I've seen it under professional circumstances. But the fact is, the men and women a director works with, from the wardrobe mistress to the executive producer, *also* think they're being creative and, God knows, they're under pressure too. If they all behaved like boors and frustrated artists, the movie set would be chaotic. In actual fact, under the right circumstances, a film set is a remarkable place. People who may or may not have worked together before operate like a team. Props, sound crews, and grips put themselves out for each other and for the director, offering suggestions, help, and energy—*just for the sake of getting the thing done right*. But they won't do it forever, and if you don't get in the habit of saying "thank you," you may find that the energy, the help, and the suggestions get left behind, until what was a team becomes just a bunch of pressured people putting in their time. That's a sad thing to see and can be avoided by remembering rule 3.

Rule 1 Know what the rights and responsibilities of a director are. The DGA has a set of rules and regulations, called the "standard contract," which tells employers and directors alike what is expected of them. Some of the points covered in that contract include the hours a director may work before getting additional compensation, what rights he or she has in terms of casting, how and when he or she can supervise the first edit of the film, and so forth. In point of fact, while directors are indeed entitled to these things, much of the time someone else takes over those responsibilities. This happens because in television series the format, the cast, the script, and the money raising have all been arranged before most directors come on the scene.

Typically, an executive producer or a producer brings an idea to a studio or production company, after having gone through the origination of a pilot program with another director, or initiates the project without a director at all. Then, when and if money is raised, the original director may not be available, or he or she may be too expensive, or there may have been a quarrel (heaven forfend!) and so other directors are hired. Or, with an hour-long series, the production company may hire two directors to work on two episodes simultaneously (back-to-back) because of time restrictions. Obviously, *each* director cannot have casting approval over a cast that works in two different episodes. Additionally, a director may be hired to direct two or three episodes of the same television series, which naturally would prohibit him from having much, if anything, to do with the editing of the first episode.

All this information is simply intended to introduce the notion that the "directorial chores" as defined by the DGA, or as outlined in your head, may have to undergo some revisions. It is likely, for instance, that the *producer* will actually supervise the editing of the television production or that his associate producer may do it. (The physical editing, of course, is done by the editor and his or her assistant.) Similarly, casting, even for moderately important roles, may actually be done by the producer. You the director have the right and, if you enjoy such things, the pleasure of doing much yourself, but you need to be aware that if the producer has gotten used to doing these chores, you may be entering into a conflict, and that conflict may get in the way of your doing some things you are actually better at and from which you get more pleasure.

In other chapters I will be defending the importance of the director making the crucial decisions in the areas of casting and editing. How, then, can I say here that those chores can be passed on to others? It's simple: I'm of two minds. With one part of me, I believe wholeheartedly in a director doing every aspect of a director's job;

with the other part of me, I'm trying to retain a smidgeon of pragmatism. If other members of a team have, by dint of their position, taken over certain aspects of your job and you won't hurt your film or your reputation by letting them continue to do those tasks, then I suggest you do so. In other words, there are tradeoffs. Are there places to draw the line? You bet! One of these is how you direct actors. Another is what your shots look like. And there are many more. All I'm trying to say is that your relationship with the producer and the executive producer (and, often, the associate producer and even the assistant to the producer) requires giving a little so you can get a lot *more* in terms of creative freedom.

All of this may seem a little strange to those whose experience with film or television has been a three-person crew in a film school or in a low-budget operation. There was no producer, let alone an executive producer. There was no unit manager or story editor. You did it all yourselves. Well, as I mentioned earlier, this book is both for those who are going to do a lot of professional work and for those who wanted some information for more modest kinds of production. These suggestions are for those involved in a professional, unionized, formalized world.

Of course, *some* people who work in the professional world, who have had experience with, say, high-quality movies-of-the-week or feature films or single dramas on television, where the director is given a great deal of autonomy and input into all those areas of filmmaking that are so crucial to a quality production, will find my remarks equally strange. In those productions, for a variety of reasons, the director is treated with much more respect and assumed to be the master of the art form that, in many cases, he or she really is. There, the director is given control, or takes control, over 90 percent of the production aspects (the creative ones). So, when I say, "Know your responsibilities," it's a different matter for each situation into which you are thrown. This is true, too, for rule 2.

Rule 2 Know whom you have to deal with, what you have to know, and what you *don't* have to know. I listed many people that a potential director may have to deal with. With which of these should he or she establish a meaningful relationship, and whom may the director deal with in only a cursory manner? You can see by my discussion of rule 1 that the executive producer and the producer are crucial. You will have met them somewhere long before they hired you—you may even be college friends—and they will have discussed the project with you. Your relationship with them may stay good, or it may rapidly deteriorate if, once production is under way, you discover that their taste isn't nearly as interesting or good as you thought it was. (They may, incidentally, think the same about you.) And yet you will want to keep a cautious relationship with them, because the time will undoubtedly come when you want to demand something from them for the sake of the production. If you have alienated them, or vice versa, it's going to be hard to demand anything, your DGA contract notwithstanding. The following is a case in point.

Some years back, I was producing a program in the series *The American Short Story*. The director was a charming man who was making (I believe) only his second or third film. He had been a film editor, and a very respected and talented one at that, and he was now changing his career. In preparing the schedule, he said he thought he might need an extra day of shooting. The production manager and I thought the director could get by without it. We were going to be on location and it would cost us a large amount of money if we used that extra day. The director was a reasonable man; we got on very well, laughed at the same jokes, and shared some of the same tastes in food. I wanted it to be a very relaxed production, so I promised him that if he needed it, we'd squeeze in the extra day for some difficult scenes. As it turned out, the director finished early, didn't need the extra day, and that was that. We handled the whole matter in a casual, friendly fashion. The point is, had we ended up on location and the director really needed something, he could have demanded it from me—successfully, and without rancor—because our relationship had been established and was good. He was as much responsible for the comfortable relationship as was I. We both made an effort.

This relationship needs to be discussed a little more. The producer, believe it or not, may actually be a very creative person. We tend to place producers in a category with that of the executive producer—someone who is concerned with money, with coming in under budget and ahead of time. To be sure, all producers have responsibilities beyond the aesthetic perfection of the film. But so do you. You wouldn't dream of accepting a job as director, with all the responsibility that it entails, and then go off and make a film about something else, or purposely go over budget, or do any number of other irresponsible things. Well, neither would the producer. He or she has taken the job with a number of goals in mind. Some of those goals actually dovetail or overlap yours. The producer is very interested in making a good picture, in creative filmmaking. He or she just happened to fall into, or chose, a different way of coming into the business. So, don't make the mistake of thinking that the producer's interest runs counter to yours. Get to know your producer; find out what creative instincts he or she has that are similar to yours. Use those creative urges and talents to help you make your film even better.

This approach to producers doesn't mean that there aren't terrible human beings who produce films, or that you'll have a wonderful relationship with your producer every time. Being a director is actually a lot more *fun* than being a producer (I've been both), but both jobs weigh heavily, so you and your producer may, from time to time, not see eye to eye about how to make this film or videotape. You may even fight; you may stop speaking to each other. But it would be a shame if that happened, because there are probably a lot of things you two have in common, including the desire to make this film come out right. How to do that may be something on which you disagree, but a pleasant lunch or a good bottle of beer or a laugh may be the best (and most creative) way to iron out differences, not a fight that sours the entire relationship.

Who beyond the E.P. and the producer will you want to know well and have a special relationship with? Certainly, the director of photography. This craftsperson is an extension of yourself; it is the D.P.'s vision and experience that will allow you to carry out your vision. You should discuss any and all special ideas you have about the look of the film and the shots you want to have with the D.P. If the producer doesn't call him or her in early to go on location and to help make decisions with the art director, you will want to suggest in a very firm manner that it be done. But how do you communicate with a cinematographer? Don't try to use jargon if you're not comfortable with it. The D.P. isn't interested in your idea of what f-stop he should use, or in your technical knowledge of lenses. He or she really wants to know what you see, and that can best be communicated in your own words.

Sometimes the D.P. knows some arcane method for doing things that just can't be communicated to you because of a language barrier, or because you have never seen that particular effect—"pushing" film stocks, "post-flashing," using a star filter, or any number of other devices you may not know about. Get the cinematographer to run a test. For a few dollars you'll have your film to look at and be able to discuss it with the D.P., the producer, and the art director, and then you'll know for sure what will or will not work.

On location, the D.P. will have all sorts of suggestions. You and your art director (and the ever-present production manager) may have picked a place to shoot that presents problems for him or her. It may be on the second floor and lights can't be brought up there without a lot of trouble. It may be too dark, too light, the wrong color, too big, or too small. The cinematographer is obviously trained to see these things differently from you. Use that training.

During the shoot, despite all of the discussions beforehand, directors and D.P.s may come to a parting of artistic ways. They will usually give way to your taste and to your needs—that's part of their training—but don't be surprised if they sometimes put up a hell of a fight. The point is, a good cinematographer has his or her creative vision to satisfy, too. Of course, in the end, you're responsible for the picture, so your ideas must be heeded, but you might do well to listen twice (or even three times) before discarding the inner muse of your D.P.

A peculiar thing often happens in filmmaking. You begin to pay a tremendous amount of attention to the image and very little to the *sound*—that is, until something goes wrong. Such as when you're in "dailies" and all you hear is an airplane that you didn't even know existed. Or, God forbid, in the final mix, when you can't balance the two versions of the leading woman's dialogue, though your editor thought you could. How does that happen, when your producer paid for one of the best sound persons around, a mixer of unique talents? Very easily. A drawing of a typical studio set or a location shoot will give you a hint. There, in the forefront, is the action: the actors, the lights, the set. Next, facing the action is the camera, with the D.P. prominently displayed. Next to him is the director, whose face is also turned toward the action and, occasionally, looking through the camera to get a picture of what's going on (this is a good idea, which will be emphasized in later chapters). Where is the sound person? Well, there's the boom man, holding the "fishpole" with its microphone and keeping very quiet (on sneakers) so as not to make a sound. And there,

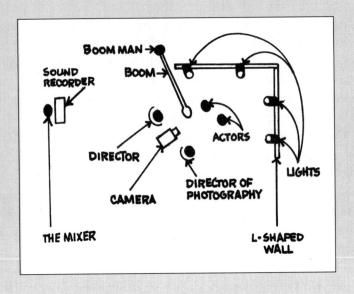

BOOM MAN →

SOUND RECORDER

BOOM →

DIRECTOR

ACTORS

CAMERA

DIRECTOR OF PHOTOGRAPHY

LIGHTS

THE MIXER

L-SHAPED WALL

at the very back, is the mixer.

Up there in front, with the *picture*, you assumed the sound was fine. (You'd never do that with the image, would you?) And, so, unless the mixer is not only talented, but somewhat aggressive, you sometimes end up with sound that is less than perfect. So, what should you do? Encourage the mixer to speak up. Spend some time with him or her. Tell the mixer what is happening, what kind of sound problems may occur. *Think* sound. That takes effort on your part, but it will pay off. Such encouragement can, of course, lead to problems. Someday your sound crew, usually so quiet, might actually speak up; a mixer might say, out loud, "Hold it! We've got trouble." And you'll find yourself saying, or muttering, "Why aren't they ever ready?" Which isn't reasonable, since they're *usually* ready, and since all sorts of other people are seldom ready as soon as you'd like them to be, but you say it, nevertheless, because *we're trained to think image, not sound.* So, now you're warned, and you'll behave differently on the set? Alas, I doubt it. You'll probably fall into the trap like most of us, and one day you'll hear some sound that's not as good as it should be and you'll say, "What was wrong with that mixer?" What was *wrong* was that you didn't establish the kind of relationship you should have with the mixer.

Some years back, I was doing a remote shoot at Orchestra Hall in Chicago. We had two thousand singers and an orchestra, and they were all doing Handel's *Messiah*. There was no rehearsal; this was truly a one-time-only chance. I had five cameras, ten microphones, and a crew of twenty. What did I pay attention to? The cameras. What did I neglect? The audio man. Why? Because (1) he had a sterling reputation as a live sound mixer, and (2) I always paid more attention to picture than to sound. The fact is, this particular man was better at mixing popular music than classical music. So, naturally, he mixed the audio for the concert with the orchestra being almost as loud as the voices. That was the wrong mix for the *Messiah*, but I hadn't discussed it with him beforehand. I'm not a careless director, but my bias toward picture had gotten in the way.

TIME IN

After you've established your relationship with the mixer, what is it you should listen for? What do you want this expert to do? We'll get to that in chapter 8.

It will probably be impossible for you to have a truly fine relationship with your production manager, who works for the producer and is responsible for keeping a tight rein on money. Therefore, it is unlikely that your blessings will be given very often to the kind of shortcuts that a good P.M. wants to make (and if you find yourself concurring too often, then maybe you should examine your own ideas). I suppose a word is in order to those people who think that production managers unfairly get a bad name. As I tried to indicate, the P.M. is an indispensable member of the team. There has to be someone controlling the purse strings and overtime at every moment. All I'm trying to indicate in this book is that the natural instincts of a director—to achieve perfection—almost always seem to run counter to some people's ideas of financial curtailment. On the other hand, it would be very foolhardy to set up an adversary relationship with the

P.M. You may be lucky and find a production where the word has gone out to slacken the financial reins a little in the interest of ending up with a better film. Or, if you've worked for this company before, they may know you as someone who keeps a reasonable control on your impulses and doesn't need a heavy hand. More important, for ten days or ten weeks you and the P.M. will work on the same film. A strange bedfellow the P.M. may be, but a bedfellow nonetheless.

Oddly enough, despite the title, the relationship between director and assistant directors is very slim. The A.D.s actually work for the producer (in much the same way that the P.M. does), and, aside from the invaluable work they do in running the set, you won't have a great deal to do with them. At the end of the day they may go over the strip board with you (after first giving it to the producer, of course) and ask if you mind them shifting around certain shots or scenes. They may say it looks like rain the next day and ask what shots you want to do indoors if the location shoot is canceled, but most likely this will simply be given to you as a *fait accompli*.

As I've indicated, the prop person is a special friend to, and helpmeet of, directors. Learn from the prop person. Got a problem? Grips and props are there to help.

Similarly, the continuity person is invaluable. It would be a mistake to turn away when that inestimable member of the crew cries out, "Wrong camera direction" (referring to which side of the camera a person was supposed to look toward), or "She dropped a line in that take." More likely, of course, the continuity person will not cry out, but will stand up out of his or her chair, carrying a heavy book, laden with twenty different color pencils and rulers (for marking the script), and whisper in your ear the necessary suggestions. The continuity person is often a writer and often a highly intelligent person, someone worth having lunch with during the shoot and worth chatting with about arcane matters.

I don't know what to say about the writer in this part of this chapter. I suppose I ought to admit that I've been one myself and felt very upset when a director changed my lines. I ought to admit, too, that I've been on the set as a producer and been very angry when a writer came on and said we'd changed lines and shouldn't have. (It's in their contract; they can come on the set.) On the one hand, you may be a writer and feel that it's your project, your idea; you've got to see it through from start to finish. On the other hand, you may not be the writer, and you'll be damned if you want someone telling you how to do your film. That scene doesn't belong there; and that one over there doesn't belong in the film at all. In part, it comes down to how you've gotten involved in the project. If you've started the film yourself, your relationship with the writer will be self-evident: a friend, a hired gun, a co-worker. If you've been hired to an existing script and cast of characters, you may not even see the writer. If you do, you would do best to be very polite, listen carefully to his or her suggestions, and then do about them what you think best. (Writers are strange people. Sometimes they actually have very good ideas about filmmaking.)

Your relationship with the film editor may not even exist. If, as I've suggested, you've been hired on a television series, you may not get to work with the editor at all. If it's a feature film or a movie-of-the-week, then you may. In that case, let's reserve comment until chapter 9.

The rest of the film crew and management team really will not have much contact with you, the director, in any deep sense. The "key" (that is, chief) grip may banter with you from time to time or make very good suggestions, but that's more in the nature of good humor than an attempt to establish a friendship. The crew knows that a director is concentrating on getting the best pictures and the best acting possible, and that very often means being left alone.

How much you want to get involved with specific craftspeople (such as the costume designer, art director, and so on) really has to do with your own particular feelings about that craft or about its importance in your film. The people I've discussed thus far warrant your special attention. The others, I leave up to you. There is something called the "chain of command" in film as well as in the Army. People work through other people. You will go through the A.D. for certain things (getting the wardrobe person on the set, calling actors, moving props). You will go through the producer for others (hiring an art director or a production manager). If, however, you have a particular desire to work closely with someone, then do it, whatever the chain of command. Just let your compatriots know you're going to do so. I like talking to costume designers. I like going to the costume fittings. Many people don't. I just let my producer and the production manager know that any conversation about costumes will be handled by me. Similarly, some people think that art directors should be handled with kid gloves; that a production manager is likely to rub them the wrong way—giving instructions, for instance, not to spend too much, before the art director has even read the script. If you want a stunning set, you'd better intervene early on. Don't leave sensitive matters to other people if you are comfortable handling them. On the other hand, if you can't bring yourself to talk about money, then don't start making deals or discussing contracts until your producer or your production manager has done so. In fact, don't discuss them at all.

There's the team. Not many with whom you will need to have a close relationship, but the point of making films is not to form friendships.[9] Of course, these are only guidelines. It's perfectly possible that a particular associate producer may turn out to be your closest friend, or that the assistant cameraman is an old buddy. It would obviously not do, either for your own sake or for his, to ignore him just because I said a relationship with your A.C. isn't important. You probably won't see the P.O.C. much after the initial days in the production office, but if that voice on the phone is important to your sanity during the shoot, obviously you're going to call and keep in contact.

JOB FUNCTIONS OF THE DIRECTOR AND THE TEAM

We come now to a tricky discussion. The question here is which of the many job functions do you, as director, need to understand, and which jobs, conversely, can you simply assume to be someone else's work, and leave it at that? If you've attended classes in film, or practiced the crafts in the real world, you may have been led to believe that the director's job encompasses everything in the world of film, and therefore he or she must know *all* the crafts. That may work well, indeed may be a necessity, in film school where four students go out to make a film and act as D.P., director, producer, gaffer, best boy, and grips all rolled into one. It may also be sound in a setting that takes as a given that the students will decide *later* what to do with their talents and, therefore, need training in *everything* simultaneously. Lighting, sound recording, filming with an Arriflex and a CP, writing, carpentry, all may fall under the cur-

---

[9] There are many worse reasons for making films than the relationships you establish and keep. But it's just unlikely that anyone will hire you if you say, "I want this job for the friends I make." Nor is it likely that you actually went into the film business just because of the friendships you knew you'd make.

riculum for a filmmaker in a film school. In the practical world, however, as you have obviously gathered by now, there are many more crafts
and specialties than one person would want (or could manage) to learn
and to master. In the highly unionized industry, many of those craft
functions cannot be undertaken without a union card. So, as long as
we're talking about the organized film world, we need to make distinctions between those crafts that a director needs to master and those that
he or she simply needs to acknowledge exist.

Which are which? I've suggested in chapter 1 that writing is an art
in which a director *must* have some skill. Now, I'd like to add to writing the fields of lighting and cinematography, but with strong caveats
on the *amount* of proficiency one needs to acquire in those areas. In
camera work, a director should be familiar with lenses and their effect
upon the film image; he or she should know the difference between
various film stocks and *their* effect upon film image; he or she should
know whether a particular camera can be equipped with a wild motor,
whether "super 16" refers to a style of dress or a particular kind of film
format, how fast a camera can rotate on a tripod, and similar points.
But directors do *not* need to have a working acquaintanceship with f-
stops or with the actual mechanism of a camera. In fact, a director
should retain a healthy respect, but also a healthy distance, from the
myriad mechanical facts about cameras and how they handle film.
Nothing impresses a crew more than a director who can rattle off a
series of facts and figures about depth-of-field and Wratten filters, but
simply impressing the crew is not what directing is about. What's needed is to
be able to articulate what kind of a look and what kind of a shot is
desired, and to request that look or that shot from the D.P. If it cannot
be achieved, he or she will suggest an alternative; if it's artistically right,
he or she will go along with it or suggest a shading. A modicum of
knowledge is desired so that the director will be able to have a *range* of
possibilities, but not in order to instruct the camera crew in how to
achieve the look or an effect.

As always, there are exceptions. In the world of commercials, for
example, many directors are actually D.P.s who have taken on the dual
role of cameraman-director. Obviously, they know, and need to know,
everything about camera. And there are directors, some of them
famous or extremely capable, who believe in knowing everything. But
in the broader world of film and TV, the world that you will inhabit, a

director needs to know some basic language, the effects produced by the parameters of light and film, lens and filter, and let it go at that.

Lighting is a similar craft. It is obviously essential that a director know the difference between "key" light and "fill," between a "2K" and an "inkie." A director should know what kind of light will make the shot work, understand that sunlight is bluish and tungsten light is reddish, and that filters or other tricks will be needed to make them compatible. But a director need not know how to balance lights, how many amperes are needed, or how to protect a house circuit from becoming overloaded. The technical names for various cables ("pigtail" being my favorite) are quite irrelevant for a director. The gaffer is a trained technician whose associates should know everything about getting the lights up and focused. Even the D.P. will leave a request hanging in midair without appending the really technical language to it. "Bring that baby over there and flood it" may be as far as he or she goes. For you, the director, study light and study the moods it creates.[10] Stay away from the wonderful, but relatively irrelevant, world of lamps and amps.

For the rest, you don't need to know how a dolly is put on its track, but you must know whether or not track is needed and that it takes time to get the dolly set—otherwise, you will be constantly baffled why certain shots take so long to get. You *don't* need to know how a continuity person makes his or her notes, but you need to know that such notes are kept and how they can be useful to you. You need to know that props can take a long time to acquire and that discussions about special effects must take place long before the shoot is to begin, but you certainly *don't* have to know how the prop person makes a dead seagull look like a live duck. In fact, it's a lot more fun to be ignorant of such processes, so you, too, can take pleasure in the transformations, in the magic of it all.

In videotape, you certainly must know that a video camera has to be "white balanced" (the magic way in which a video camera is electronically tempered to the actual color of light falling on the subject). You *need* to know that video requires more even lighting than film

---

[10] This, of course, is not a simple matter. It can take a lifetime. We'll discuss the part of it that can be discussed on paper in chapter 4.

does (because of something called "contrast ratio"), but it is certainly not important that you can read a vectorscope, or that you know how to repair a broken image enhancer.

In fact, there is a certain balance that must be achieved between knowledge that helps you and knowledge that gets in the way, knowledge of other people's crafts that makes it possible for you to say, "I see your problem; I'll do it some other way." This makes you very popular with the crew, but also makes it possible for them to very gently steer you away from the stringent artistic course you have set yourself. Helpful knowledge, on the other hand, is precisely that knowledge that allows you to say, "I think I can see a way you can accomplish my goals, without breaking your spirit or your equipment." Helpful knowledge is that knowledge that advances your artistic goals. Sometimes it's simply a matter of a director knowing something well enough so that he or she can devise a shot or a scene ahead of time that is easy to shoot. Sometimes it's a matter of knowing enough technically so that you can help the craftspeople get around a problem that you created. That, too, can make you very popular, but it more importantly *helps* you accomplish your aims. How much of any one craft you must acquire in order to be knowledgeable enough, but not too knowledgeable, is essentially a matter of balance—and experience.

The self-taught approach has severe limitations. Sometimes one cuts out a kind of shot or a kind of scene precisely because one thinks, "I know that it's too expensive or too difficult." How much better it would be, with an extremely difficult shot, to go to a D.P. or a prop person and say, "Here's what I have in mind. Can you do it?" Sometimes the answer might be, "Oh, sure, we just bought a new lens that does that kind of thing," or, "Have you heard of the Cricket Dolly? It's built for just that problem." If you tried to keep up with every technical development, you'd probably fail at both the technical and the artistic sides of your career.

A FINAL NOTE ON YOUR ROLE AS DIRECTOR

I have given a picture of film and television crews that may lead one to believe that the director has, in many cases, been reduced to an adjunct. The director doesn't write the script, doesn't hire the actors, doesn't supervise editing. On the set, the director calls the shots, but only in conjunction with a large number of people. This is a different image from the one given by books and newspapers, certainly a far cry from the notion we have of the film director from the early days of the industry. All this is true, but not universally so.

There are, for instance, those feature films where the director is not only king, he's Superking: the legendary Orson Welles, of course; Francis Ford Coppola; George Lucas; Robert Altman; Ingmar Bergman; Martin Scorsese. These are (or were) directors fully in charge, hands-on in script, design, everything.

Sometimes, such directors will feel the need to take on the title of Producer as well, to keep total control. Such was the case for John Sturges (*The Great Escape, Gunfight at the O.K. Corral*). But other directors prefer to keep the roles separate, as does Woody Allen, for instance, who leaves logistics, money, and other important jobs to his longtime producers.

Directors who take on the producer role are called "hyphenates," as in *producer-director*. (There are also writer-producers, director-cameramen, etc.) Of course, on any feature film, even if the director isn't the originating force and doesn't take the producer credit, he or she will have the absolute right to do casting, rewrites, and so on.

What I am trying to do in this chapter, however, is prepare you for the majority of directing positions, those in film television series, or in commercials, or similar occupations, where the producers have taken more and more control of certain functions.

This does not mean that you have had your artistic authority usurped. It does mean that you will have to alter your image of the director's role somewhat. Relax. Enjoy it. In fact, it's nice not to have to worry about many of the details. When the knock on your door comes at 6:30 in the morning, and the A.D. says, "We'll be ready in five minutes for your first shot," you may indeed find it a pleasure not to have to worry about all the details that you concerned yourself with as a film school senior. On the other hand, if you're one of those wonderful individuals who find every detail important and like to do it all yourself, you may simply have to work somewhere else than the "real world" I've been describing. If you don't, you may find yourself constantly at odds with a system that has decided, for good or for evil, that the producer, the executive producer, and other team members are going to perform some of the functions you thought were yours.

3
Casting

Conventional wisdom is that the script and casting are the two most important elements in making a film. I believe conventional wisdom is right. We've discussed the role of the script in chapter 1, so now it's time for the next step.

Shortly after World War II, when the "neorealist" films from Italy were stunning American audiences with their powerful stories and their powerful looks, inquiries were made by critics into how the directors (men like Vittorio De Sica and Roberto Rossellini) were able to achieve such brilliant acting from an infant movie industry emerging from a war-torn society. Imagine the critics' surprise when they discovered that many of the actors used by these brilliant directors were amateurs, "real" people who had been chosen for their character and look, not for their professional experience. While much of the Italian movie-making world has taken a different track since then— using brilliant actors, schooled in acting techniques, such as the pre-eminent Italian actor of the last three decades, the late Marcello Mastroianni (who can be seen in many Fellini films)—there are many, both in Italy and in other countries, who still employ nonactors in order to acquire a sense of utter reality in their films. More importantly, the concept of using people for their "look" is a crucial part of the skill of European casting. Fellini, as is well known, would use an actor or actress whose voice was very unpleasant or untrained, but "dub" a voice in later by someone more skilled or whose sound was more mellifluous. The result, as all who have seen a Fellini film can attest, is marvelous faces, marvelous films.

In Hollywood, "look" is also important, but it is a different kind of appearance that counts. We prize beauty in our faces, but not angular planes; we prefer style and grace to awkward, often more realistic action. Which is not to say that Americans cannot get good performances from their actors. It is to say, however, that our star system leads us to hiring some of the same beautiful or handsome-faced actors time and again in order to get "box office," whereas Italian or German filmmakers hire those special faces and special voices that make that particular film come to life. How often have you said, coming out of a movie, "What a real world that director created," as opposed to, "What a great performance Brando gave"? The difference may very well be laid to these two entirely different styles of casting. Recently, American film critics (led, I hope, by American audiences) have begun to recognize that films with unknowns (by which is meant actors whose faces have not appeared too often on the screen, not actors who haven't worked before) can zero in on our emotions and our intellects in a way that films filled with familiar faces may not. Let me call your attention, for instance to the casting genius of Peter Weir in *The Year of Living Dangerously,* or Woody Allen's *Zelig. Zelig* is filled with fine, still relatively unknown character actors. Some of those actors, by the way, were in fact nonactors; they were real people reading lines and being directed by a man who knew his job. What all the "unknowns," actors and nonactors, gave to the film is a sense of reality, the same thing that that fine war film, *The Boys from Company C,* got by using sterling actors whose faces simply hadn't been seen to death, though many have become regulars on the Hollywood scene. (These include Michael Lembeck, who starred as as Abbie Hoffman in the 1987 TV-movie special *Conspiracy: The Trial of the Chicago 7,* who has also directed TV series including *Mad About You, Everybody Loves Raymond,* and the Emmy-Award-winning *Friends;* and another "Company C" actor named Noble Willingham, who played the role of Clay Stone in both of Billy Crystal's *City Slickers* comedies, who has a familiar face, even if his name doesn't resonate with everyone.)

All right, let's assume that you, too, want to cast the best actors for your film, that commercial success (that is, box office) is not your primary concern. In other words, you want to come up with the best actor for the job. Let's say that you have never cast a film before. How do you go about it?

STEP ONE: VISUALIZING THE CHARACTER

Let your script, your dialogue, and your ideas dictate to you who your character is, what he or she *looks* like, *sounds* like, and how he or she moves. Don't start by rifling through pictures of actors and saying, "Is he right for the part?" *Don't even ask your friends what well-known actor would be right.* Just close your eyes and picture the person.

Right away, I hear a voice saying, "Dreamer! You'll never get someone who looks and sounds like that. You're ruining your chance of ever being happy with the actors you *do* get." Well, yes—and no. Yes, it's unlikely that I'll find the specific character I'm dreaming of. But, no, I won't be foolish enough to refuse all others. And—this is the important part—I'm identifying to myself which characteristics are important to me in the character I've read on the page. A stubby nose, a growl in the throat, tall and elegant, short and ugly. Whichever you choose, these characteristics may tell you more about what you want to do with the part than all your script study beforehand.

STEP TWO: FINDING YOUR ACTORS

There are a number of ways to find actors. Let's assume you aren't going to use amateurs because you don't feel confident enough, but you do want to try to find the physical (and psychological) types you've been dreaming about. You might start by wanting to cast someone you've seen in a recent film, but that may immediately turn into a monetary nightmare. Or someone from a play. Or you might turn to The Book.

The Book

This is the route tried by so many before you: buy the two big sets of books (*The Academy Directory* and *The Players' Guide*), which are divided into categories ("Ingenue," "Leading Man," "Character Actor," "Children," and "Specialties") and which are put out for both the New York stage and the film world. In them, actors and their agents have put not only small pictures of the actors and actresses, but short descriptions as well. Here you can find what telephone number to call to get the actor's agent; here you can sometimes see a second picture, perhaps with the actor wearing a toupee or a pair of glasses. For you, rummaging through these books can provide a quick tour of the available actors in the category you're seeking. Did I say "quick"? Well, not quite. In fact, the Book can be a very discouraging way to find the person for your role. Among other things, he or she may simply not be in there (not all actors can afford the fees), or the actor may have had pictures taken to make himself look like—well, like everyone else. There are thousands of listings and, pretty soon, everyone begins to look "wrong" or, worse, everyone looks "right." Finally, and perhaps most importantly, you have no way of knowing how these people can act and, after all, isn't that the point?

Acting Schools

If you've ever cast a film for work in film school, you may very well have gone to the theater department and asked for a chance to cast students who are studying acting. Many of our best actors *do* come out of acting classes, or continue to take them after going professional, so this is actually a good idea. Broaden your search to include professional acting classes. The teachers and students will welcome the opportunity to try film, even though they may get nothing for it monetarily.

Casting Calls

You could have casting calls. These are very simply arranged. Your producer will handle it for you by calling up the *Hollywood Reporter* or *Backstage* (if you're in New York) and inserting a brief announcement that such and such a film is having an "open" casting call. Or, because open calls usually bring in thousands of actors, you might call a limited number of agents, tell them what you have in mind, and seek a limited casting call. Your producer, if he or she has made a film before, will have relationships with actors' agents and may even begin suggesting actors. And that, after all is said and done, is how most new directors start casting: with the aid of others. This has its positive side—the producer, your associate producer, the P.M., your friends, all may have favorite actors for your roles. You may be directed to go to this or that small theater, or to see this or that film, to catch this or that actress who is perfect for the part. (You should be doing that on your own, anyhow. I keep Playbills from every play I go to, as references for future films; and I make notes about movies I've seen.) There is a negative side to this, too—you may begin to lose control over the casting process because others are flooding you with ideas. So, let's look for another process.

The Casting Consultant

The casting consultant is sometimes called a casting agent or casting director, and there are two basic kinds: those who operate out of a movie studio or production company, and those who have their own agencies. Some of the latter (you can find them listed in the Business Yellow Pages or, better yet, in the special directories put out by various film organizations such as the Television Academy or the DGA) have done a land-office business casting for commercials, so you may be tempted to doubt their ability to cast your important film. Don't. Some of the best casting in recent years has come out of these kinds of organizations. Their job is to know every actor and actress around, to do videotapes on new actors or actresses, and to scour the countryside for fresh faces, special looks, great voices. They'll read your script, listen carefully to your ideas, suggest faces and voices, show you pictures, call the agents, arrange the readings, and make the financial deals. What more could you want? Oh, yes, there's a price for this, ranging from $500 a day to more than three times that amount. But in my view, if you're new to the casting game, it's a price well worth paying. (Try that argument out on your producer.) If you can get an independent casting director to come on salary for a smaller fee, and he or she has proven ability in this area, do so. You'll have to supply office space and your producer will have to deal with agents, but that's what he or she's paid for, isn't it?

What if you think you can't afford a casting consultant? There are two things to be said about that. One: Don't be sure you can't. Some of the best casting agencies get tired of doing commercials and would welcome doing a drama or a comedy or an educational film. They may give you their second- or third-string consultant, but she or he may be better than you at ferreting out fine actors; or they may not give you their full attention, but it will be good work and a good opportunity for you. They may also realize that you're an up-and-coming young director who will be doing feature films for MGM someday, and they may want to start a relationship with you now. Two: They may give you a big break on the price, down to $250 a day, but you call the agents and make the deals, and that's certainly worth doing, especially if it's a small film and you can do the casting in one day

Casting by Yourself

What if you don't have even $250, or what if you want to do the casting yourself, how do you go about it? Put that ad in *Backstage* or the *Hollywood Reporter* or *Variety*. Have actors call you before you see them, or have them send in their pictures. They'll be delighted to do so. If it's a really inexpensive film, tell them you can't pay—will they still do the film? Or tell them it's non-SAG—can they do a nonunion film? Then, set up appointments, thirty minutes apart. Read the actors, with at least two other people there (to bounce off). Use the tools for listening that I will discuss in a page or two; keep an open mind—and keep your dreams. If you get tired, take a break. If you have to "let them know," call them later. There will be a lot of paperwork and phone calling involved. That's what your producer is for! Your job is to look and listen for the *balance*, the *character*, the *look*, and the *sound* that will make your film work. Take your time.

STEP THREE: THE READING

Whether you cast by the Book, by casting consultants, or by hook and crook, you will eventually come to the Reading. (There are exceptions. Occasionally, you will land big stars. They aren't going to read for you. They may sit still for an interview. They *may* talk over the phone. They will certainly read your script and decide whether they want the roles. But they won't read for you.) You will sit and listen to actors reading parts; you will take notes; you will do this with some of the production team, probably the producer and the associate producer; you will discuss; you will choose. But how?

An Important Note on Your Knowledge of Acting

What do you know about acting? Anything? A lot? Nothing? Have you ever acted in a production? Was it in high school, college, professionally, summer stock, film, theater? These are not idle questions. There is nothing that says you have to be a fine actor in order to direct actors, but there is no doubt that acting experience helps greatly in understanding what problems and what needs actors have. So, if you've had absolutely no experience as an actor, go take a class or two. I'm not going to suggest what kind of a class you take; in fact, I'm going to suggest it doesn't matter whether you study with a method teacher, a classical teacher, a Chekhovian, or an Alexandrian. What's important is that you get a chance to experience the kinds of things that actors go through in order to prepare for a role and, more important- ly, the kind of language that helps actors grow in a role and deliver in a role.

You'll find, among other things, that asking an actor to read lines "louder" or "faster" is not only counterproductive, but makes you sound like a dumb director. Why do you want the lines louder or faster? Is it to help out a microphone that's too far away, or is it because the character is in a hurry and has to get out of there right away? Motivation, in other words, is clearly a crucial matter. End results are generally not help- ful; the reason why generally is. That doesn't mean that you will end up being a psychologist. It does mean that you may learn a few things about what actors need in order to make a role work for them.

Acting classes have another very beneficial result for directors. They enable us to see a variety of actors at a vari- ety of levels of talent and ability. Because we are participat- ing in a class, we hear things progress at a slower pace than during filmmaking; and we can analyze what works and what doesn't work, not only from the viewpoint of ourselves as actors, but as potential directors. The teacher, on the other hand, is suggesting ways in which to achieve depth in our roles, and this too can be very helpful to a budding director. Finally, in an acting class, you may learn what doesn't work, and this is just as useful as what does.

I hope after your first experience with the study of acting that you will enjoy it and enjoy actors; that you will stay with the acting, learn some parts, even play them. It doesn't matter whether you're any good. What matters is that you're learning the profession from the inside. Among other things, you'll find that actors have to work hard. They have to know how to move, so they take movement classes; to speak, so they often take speech or diction classes; to think about roles, so they study texts; to feel, so they work on their emotions—learning not only how to bring them to a particular line or a particular speech, but how to *repeat* those emotions. There is nothing so devastating to a film as an actor who can *feel* an emotion on the wide shot but, by the time the close-ups have come along, is dry, or vice versa. Or an actor who cannot be consistent in reading the same lines time after time.

You may hear some jargon, but don't be upset by it. Theater has a long history. Pay no mind to terms you don't need; retain those (like "beat"—a particular moment in time) that help you work with actors. Some actors need to talk about "goals"; others work with "as if"; everyone needs to know what "conflict" is involved in any script, whether it's Shakespeare or the latest TV sitcom. Questions I think you will find valuable to bring to your work as a director are: "Where am I going?" "Where are you going?" "What needs do you have?" "How do my goals get in the way of your goals?" "What experience in my past life can I bring to play in this role at this particular moment in time?"

The Actual Reading

What happens at a reading? You will meet an actor or actress and you will ask if there are any questions, but you won't give any direction at this point. There are two reasons for this: (1) you want to see what the actor brings to the role, and (2) you want to see what possibilities there are in the role that you haven't already seen. Sometimes you'll hate an actor but love something he or she brought to the line or the role. And you will use that later, shamelessly.

At the reading the candidate will read the part. Someone in the casting agency, or the associate producer, will read the other roles. They will read through the scenes you've chosen (called "sides") at least once. At the end of that, you will have some idea whether you want the scene read again. You will listen very carefully to intonation, to understanding, to emotion, to the characteristics that you had dreamed about when you first thought about the role. You may be confused. Some of what you heard you liked, some you didn't. The voice is right, but the face isn't. He's too young; she's too old. Don't hurry. Have the actor read again, but this time ask for something that was missing. Don't be too specific; don't say, "I'd like the line read like this." Mimicry can work very well in a casting session, but not necessarily on the sound stage. It's shallow. If, after the second or third reading, things are getting better, and you begin to see the character, fine. If not, don't worry, there are others waiting to read.

What if you love what you hear the first time around? Is that cause for euphoria? Maybe, maybe not. There is a curious pronouncement that I've heard that often turns out to be true: "A terrific reading means a bad scene." Why? Because there are some people who are very good readers but who can't get any deeper than that. And conversely, some actors are lousy readers but have depth and can bring that out when they are worked with. I did a film in which I chose the handsome man who auditioned and who read the first time around with absolute brilliance. I asked him to repeat the scene and it was quite different. I asked for a particular change and it didn't come. I was dumb; I hired him anyway. Each time he played the scene, in wide shot, close-up, and medium shot, it was different, and never any deeper than that first reading. If an actor is fine, ask for nuances; ask for changes; make the actor read with a different actor; probe. Similarly, if an actor is less than satisfactory, give him another chance and listen again.

STEP FOUR: THE DECISION

As soon as an actor or actress leaves the room, talk with the casting people. Is he experienced in film? What has she done? Is he always as casual, as quiet? You like the intensity, but is she neurotic? The casting people may or may not know all the answers to these questions, but they will be able to find out a lot from other people. Next, start asking about whom they have in mind to "pair" with this actor. One of the big problems in a cast is getting a balance—a variety of actors and actresses. It isn't enough to have fine actors in the film; you must have actors who work well with each other, who don't all look alike or have the same characteristics. Or, conversely, if it's a production of Shakespeare, you need to make sure that accents and style can be matched the way you need them to be. All this must go on at casting time; all this can be discussed with the consultants—and, of course, with your producer—during the casting sessions.

Don't be surprised if you get tired and restless very easily during casting. It's not easy listening to people reading the same lines (and many of them doing badly) while you're looking for your ideal character. Which brings us back to "the dream" you had when you first read the part. If you keep that dream uppermost in your mind and don't detach yourself from it, you're probably going to be disappointed. Casting, like shooting, requires an unbelievable amount of compromise. With one part of you, you're holding on to an ideal; with the other, you're looking for that spark of imagination or excitement that *someone else* can bring to the project. With actors, that means listening and looking for something that is new; something that you didn't expect; some reading of a line or some character in the face or body that tells you that that person can bring a wonderful quality to the role—a quality that you hadn't thought of or, perhaps, even known was there. That may mean giving up your dream—but getting much, much more. On the other hand, the opposite may happen. You may hear a lot of banal reading, and nothing you can say to the actors helps. After several days of this, your producer gets very upset and says you're being too picky. He knows that the actress you heard yesterday has done beautiful things and you're being pigheaded about the whole thing. Indeed, you may be pigheaded, and you should be. Your vision of the film is what counts, and your need to have the right actor or actress is terribly important. Which doesn't, of course, mean that you will find one, but it should be your decision to compromise, not someone else's. (Of course, they are paying the bills and you may have to sleep on that decision a little.)

What happens in the end is that you, the producer, and the casting consultant will come up with a tentative list of those you want for your film. Some of them will have sounded fantastic, others will be *ifs* that you think will work. Take time to think about the list before giving your approval. If you have doubts, talk them over with someone (if you're still talking to anyone). When you've decided, the producer will try to make deals with the agents and then, if you're lucky, you'll have your cast. If you're unlucky or someone is too greedy, you may have to go back and cast one or more parts anew.

All of us want to know if the actors we've chosen can truly deliver. If you've come up with a cast list of well-known actors whose work you've seen, then that won't be much of a problem. If, on the other hand, you've taken someone else's word for the acting ability of one or more of them, you may have a few tremors in the stomach during the next few days. And if, as sometimes happens, you've gone for a completely unknown cast, who made you feel very excited while you were casting, but very nervous when you were away from the reading, you will have to find some way of coming to terms with that uneasiness. Rudolph Serkin, perhaps the world's greatest interpreter of Brahms piano concertos, was asked on his seventy-fifth birthday whether he ever still got stage fright when he went out to play. His answer was that he always got stage fright and he wouldn't trust a performer who didn't! I feel somewhat the same about all stages of film directing.

Certainty at all times is probably suspicious. At the same time, constant doubt and anxiety aren't very productive either. Talk over your doubts with people, like the producer and the casting director. Go back over your notes (you did take notes, didn't you?) and see what it was that made you so excited about this or that actor at the time. If it's a nonunion production, go talk to your actor on some pretense or other—such as a discussion of character or dialect—to reassure yourself that you've done the right thing. (You can also do that if it's a union production, but money may get involved; "rehearsal" isn't free.) I can't give you any suggestions how to handle things if you want to get out of a signed deal, but if you haven't signed and you have grave second thoughts, tell the actor or actress that you're rebalancing the cast and want to replace him or her. It's not nice; it's not even ethical, but it is necessary if your film is to be the way you want it. On the other hand, if you find yourself doing this sort of thing often, then you ought to examine (a) your judgment, or (b) your behavior.

Casting is crucial. I said that at the beginning. It's crucial because your actors and actresses are the vehicles for getting your picture across to the audience. It's crucial because it is in the casting that we create a sense of reality or unreality. It's crucial because casting can give the twist that we need. It's crucial because the right actors will often do three-quarters of the work that needs to be done. They will see things in the lines that you and I will never have seen, or they will make our dreams come true because of their extraordinary ability. Anyone who has even once chosen a less-than-perfect actor for a part will know what I am talking about. Which is not to say that directing is all casting; there is more to it than that, but it's a huge part of it.

When you see a film in which casting has been imaginatively done, you come out believing in the mood, the style, the realness of it: a short, ugly man plays a leading character; a woman with blazing red hair plays the ingenue; a Brooklyn accent shows up in the middle of a Midwestern scene; unknown faces and unknown voices show up in a crime movie, making it seem like a documentary; actors move rhythmically, because they've been chosen for their ability to move; a man and woman are identical heights, making it easy to believe in their "twinness"; a midget plays a role written for a full-size person, bringing a quality of originality to the film that could never have been achieved with other casting. We have all seen films that worked because of that casting skill.

And, on the other hand, we've seen films ruined by casting: Hollywood in the 1930s and 1940s, intent on proving its patriotism or its ability to rouse us from our doldrums, plugged into each film its "stable" of "contract players," giving us one pretty face or one rugged, handsome physique after another, but not the originality that European films of the 1950s and American films of the 1970s began to achieve.

4
GETTING READY (I):
LOOK, STYLE, AND MOOD

This could have been called the "look, style, mood, feel, emotion, and content" chapter. In some ways it's the most important part of this book. It's about how you're going to shoot the film—the actual shots you're going to use, the way you're going to translate the script into image. It's difficult to talk about these matters in a general way, so let's try to be specific: *where* you will shoot the film to give it the right look; *how* you will plan shots so they will accomplish your goals of mood and style; *what* you will do to achieve the effect you've decided upon; *when* you will bring in other members of the team for consultation; *what* you should do when you're stumped; and, finally, *how* and *when* you should improvise. These are thorny but crucial matters.

In one sense, this process starts the day you decide to do your film at all, even while you read the script. It continues through the precasting period, and on into every successive day. Bruce Beresford, director of *Breaker Morant* and *Tender Mercies*, was once quoted as saying that too many directors simply photograph a film rather than *direct* it. What he meant by this is that they simply place the actors in front of the camera, rather than planning each shot so that it is superbly right for the film and the moment. He talks about doing a drawing of every shot in the entire movie, and researching carefully. "I have to find my locations first. I can't go somewhere and start shooting. It doesn't work. I find the locations, work with the production designers, and get plans of all the rooms so I know where all the windows and doors are. Then I work out every camera angle for the entire film." What a director says in print when he's publicizing a film may or may not be an accurate reflection of his true beliefs and his true behavior, but this statement rings true to me and, with one exception, I find it an incisive description of a very important process that all directors need to go through. The exception is that Beresford, for me, places too much emphasis on the groupings, the lenses, and the framing of the shots and not enough on script, actors, and directorial efforts *apart* from the camera work. A few examples will help explain what I mean, though they will push me out onto that strange limb called "taste."

Fanny and Alexander, Ingmar Bergman's 1983 film, utilizes the director's great cinematographer, Sven Nyquist, and Bergman's own impeccable sense of taste to create great framing. In the film there are scenes with absolutely unbelievable opulence (a Christmas dinner and a christening scene) and others with the utmost simplicity and purity. I found it difficult to keep my mind always on the story because the visual side of the film was so perfect. At the same time, the power of the story and the shimmer of the acting brought me back to the film, as it told its kind of grown-up fairy tale. I do not think I would have felt that way if it had been a film that was *only* well shot.

A perfect example of the latter, I think, was James and Stacy Keach's *The Long Riders*, a film brilliantly photographed, directed by Walter Hill. This retelling of the Jesse James myth had some of the most marvelous cinematography, some of the most brilliant shots I've seen. Framing and lighting were magnificent, but the story itself was banal, the acting oppressive, the film, in the end, a boring failure. And yet let's take another Bergman film, *Scenes from a Marriage*. This low-budget miniseries, shot for Swedish television, is basically without exceptional framing or lighting. The images are good but by no means great. Yet the story and the acting, brought out by Bergman, make this an unforgettable film. So, too, Steven's Soderbergh's first film, *Sex, Lies, and Videotapes*, was shot with the most minimal use of camerawork, yet his fine sense of story, dialogue, suspense, and acting, created a wonderful film. So—for me—story before picture. Always!

Yet I can agree with Beresford that how a director sees his film and how he translates that vision to individual frames of celluloid is of great importance. I said "individual" frames of film and I mean that. As you probably know, there are 24 such frames in every second of film, and 1440 frames in every minute. In a very real sense, then, there are 24

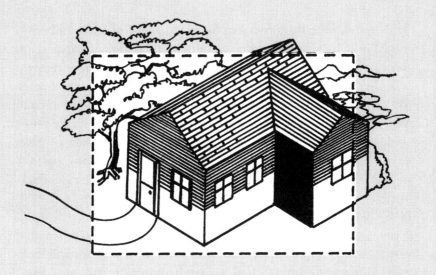

The real-life house has a whole tree, a long path, and mountains in the background. On screen, the "frame" reduces path, tree, and mountains to "partials." Putting a frame around reality changes that reality for the viewer, forever.

still photographs to be framed and shot every second, and 1440 every minute. To consider only how a whole shot or scene looks ignores all the nuances of the frames in between.

This is especially important when one considers how a film is *edited*. You may think a shot should be cut at a certain point and another shot spliced on. Your editor, on the other hand, may think that the timing or rhythm of the scene requires that a cut be made a fraction of a minute earlier or later. What does the *frame* look like at that point? And, here, it is in fact the frame we are talking about, because the film editor has stopped the film from running at the rate of 24 frames per second, and is looking at it *frame by frame*. Are they all composed equally well? Not if you haven't given consideration to each of those thousands of frames when you were shooting. Since every shot involves movement of actors or movement of camera (pans or tilts, truckings forward or sideward), you may have to give consideration to dozens of separately composed frames within each shot in order to come out with shots or with a scene that is properly framed. It's like considering the composition of a whole series of still photos, not of one continuous, moving shot.

Now to some this may seem like a great deal of farfetched nonsense, but it has actually proven to be a very exciting and important concept. It means that as an actor moves toward or away from camera, or as the trees pass the camera on a tracking shot, if you think frames you won't be sandbagged by the misframing of any individual instant. And when you and the editor are struggling over a cut in the post-production period, you will at least have given him or her a whole series of wonderfully composed frames from which to make any single edit. That, to some extent, was what Beresford was talking about.

THE LOOK

If you're a director, the first thing that will happen to you when you start to read a script is to have fantasies about how the film will look when you start making it. If this doesn't happen to you, prod your subconscious a bit by closing your eyes and formulating a setting. The lines and the stage directions will take on a new meaning; you should begin to actually see the shots and the characters in them. How *do* they look? A lot of wide shots, showing countryside and large rooms? Or close shots, very dark, with lots of "eyelight"? This "look" will vary from film to film, sometimes subtly, sometimes grossly. (It doesn't matter whether your "film" is a drama, a comedy, an educational short, or an industrial; everything has a look, and that look should be planned.) If this isn't something you've ever done before, you may very well wonder how to actually *see* scenes and shots in a *frame*, as opposed to the way we normally view: through two eyes. Akira Kurosawa, the late great Japanese director, painted every shot of his films ahead of time and had actually exhibited those paintings, but you may not have an artist's eye or an artist's hand. If not, try a still camera.

Beginning students in filmmaking have often been required to study still photography, which makes a lot of sense. To me, the beauty of using a still camera is that it makes you look at a single frame, not simply as one piece of a moving shot, but as an artistic entity to be considered all by itself. Besides, it's a great deal of fun. To cut down the cost, and to concentrate on the essential elements of framing, minus the bogus influence of color, do black-and-white photography only.

Take your time; no one is looking over your shoulder. Use a

The tree branch and leaves help make this an interesting frame.

Some might think this branch interferes with the shot. I think it helps make a very interesting and unusual shot.

Three people, when spaced like this, help balance the frame.

The tree and the person overlap and unbalance the frame. With the wrong lens, the tree would actually look like it's growing out of the person's body.

sophisticated camera or a Polaroid, it makes no difference which. You will suddenly notice, as you take stills, that a tree branch coming into the top of the frame (see the drawings on the previous page) can be a contributive force to the frame, or it can be a distracting one. You will notice the interplay between light and dark, between negative space and positive space. And all of it will be frozen on paper to study and to change as you see fit. You can take stills to suit your mental image or create a mental image with stills, then remind yourself of those images later. All the while you will use the stills to help you continue your preparation for your film.

But, of course, your frames aren't all static like a still photograph. Actors move, and so do movie cameras, which brings us to an important element in this area of discussion. To Move or Not To Move. There are those who say that moving without purpose is a travesty of the whole film process, that it distracts the audience from the story and from the essence of film: the characters' interaction with each other. But since many filmmakers (especially in the Italian school of filmmaking—Antonioni, Bertolucci, Visconti) made movement an integral part of the look of their films—so much so that one cannot imagine a film by them without movement—a great deal more has to be said about *movement*. I am assuming that the concepts of montage and mise-en-scène are meaningful to you. In case they are not, a word or two is in order.

Montage and Mise-En-Scène

Montage? That's the basic technique of cutting between
· shots of various actors and objects. Classically, a director
would shoot his scene first in a wide shot, taking in the
whole set, or a large piece of it, and most of the characters.
This is followed by a medium shot, then a three-shot or two-
shot of some of the actors, then singles (close-ups), then
(sometimes) extreme close-ups (ECUs). Usually you match
close-up for close-up, or vary the shooting with over-the-
shoulder shots (part of the back of one actor and the full
face of another) that are also usually matched (that is, you
shoot two over-the-shoulder shots, not just one.) In current

filmmaking, especially television, practices concerning size and variety of shots have changed. Very often the wide shot (sometimes called the "master") is not used and is traded for closer shots early on, or for some kind of moving shot: a pan, a dolly, a tracking shot from one part of the set to another. There will be much more about the technical side of shots in chapter 8, but, basically, the concept of montage implies that you will shoot a *variety* of nonmoving shots, and the *pacing* and *timing* of a scene will be altered, its *impact* will be changed, by editing from one shot to another.

Mise-en-scène, on the other hand, is both a conceptual way of looking at film and a way of shooting it. Without knowing it, you will have seen this technique on many television shows and in many movies. Once the *steadicam* came into use—a device that allows very steady handheld shots—programs like *ER* and *West Wing* incorporated long, complex, winding shots into their work, following people who move around and around a room from a variety of seemingly endless angles. So mise-en-scène is the use of the camera so as to constantly place the actors and the setting in a flexible relationship to each other by *moving the camera and the actors*, not by cutting from one actor or group of actors to another. The effect of this use of the camera is often called "fluid," precisely because of the small number of cuts and the continuous camera movement.

For example, a camera tracks from one room to another, "carrying" (that is, staying with) one actor, who leaves the frame as another actor, coming from the opposite direction, passes the first; the camera then reverses direction and follows the second actor into another room where, in a mirror, we confront the second actor and his character's wife, who have an argument. The camera pushes in on the wife in the mirror, and we now dissolve to a shot of the same actress fully dressed at a dinner table. The camera moves from actor to actor along the dinner table, with each actor talking to the one next to him or her, thus "passing" the camera along from actor to actor. Obviously, this use of the camera requires a vision that goes along with it. It also requires a great deal of rehearsal time, because the pace, the timing, the impact of the scene *must be built into the movement.* In other words, since mise-en-scène is built along the notion that a scene will be carried in one long,

Wide shot

Medium-three shot

Two-shot

Close-up

Extreme close-up

Over-the-shoulder shot

fluid shot, there is no way for the editor to make pacing and timing changes later on.

Perhaps the most famous film mise-en-scène shot is the opening of Orson Welle's *Touch of Evil*, in which at least seven minutes is spent in one continuously moving shot, so well choreographed that camera and people come in touch with each other in close shots, then disappear into wide shots, only to return close again. In the director Robert Altman's *The Player* a similar opening seems to mimic Welles and creates a unique feel.

I doubt if you will ever sit down and say, "Shall I do this film mise-en-scène or montage, with a lot of movement or not?" The look that has come to you in your head with this particular script, the kind of filmmaking training you've had, the basic nature of your personality, and your artistic vision will dictate whether or not you are—almost by birth— a mise-en-scène kind of director. This statement sounds almost mystical, I realize, but it's based on a good deal of experience with a variety of filmmakers and directors. How and when you move the camera will have a lot to do with your inner vision as well as some basic rules that seem to work well for most of us, whether endowed with a passion for mise-en-scène, or rooted firmly in montage.

I said before that moving without "purpose" is considered anathema by many. But what is a good reason for moving the camera? That depends on many things. If you are a mise-en-scène director you will probably answer that differently than if you believe strictly in montage. (By the way, just wanting to move the camera doesn't make you a mise-en-scène director; most of us, due to practical circumstances, use a mixture of mise-en-scène and montage. A director who philosophically believes in mise-en-scène will shoot his film in such a way that a preponderance of the shots are created to avoid any intercutting.) As a mise-en-scène director, you might say that camera movement is justified in order to keep the screen "fluid." Others, who are less mise-en-scène oriented, might issue a set of rules that looks something like this:

Rules of Movement

Rule 1 If you have a character who is moving, moving a camera to keep up with this character is legitimate, whereas moving arbitrarily is probably not.

Rule 2 Try to keep your move at the same pace as the person or people who are moving.

Rule 3 Don't pan away from one set of actors to another set of actors if neither is moving. It looks bizarre.

Rule 4 If actors aren't moving, use a cut to get from one place to another, unless the move (pan, tilt, track) is an intrinsic part of your filmic approach and style.

The sum of these rules is: don't move without motivation—a motivation that comes *from* the scene, not one that is imposed *upon* it.

These rules may seem self-evident, but it's amazing how many beginning directors break them time and again, ending up with a film that gives a new meaning to the term, "motion pictures." Such movement need not be large to be distracting. Even a slight pan can disturb a beautiful shot. Try thinking back to the still photographs you started with; sometimes, a series of still frames, cut one to one, can be the most impressive kind of filmmaking. Imagine an exquisitely framed shot of a riverbank, close in on an exposed tree root, as a single drop of water is poised to fall from it into the river. It falls—the only movement in the frame. Now, imagine a slow panning shot along the same riverbank where any such detail of movement would be lost. Which do you prefer? Of course, I'm now verging too close to matters of taste, which I shall leave to your discretion. Every rule in filmmaking was made to be broken by someone; every choice by one director is anathema to another. The question of movement, however, is one that you must decide early on, whether by careful examination or by instinct; and you must write your decisions into your script, along with your other notes.

A Couple of Practical Notes on Movement

Hint 1 *You* need not be a mise-en-scène director to want to get from one shot to another without making cuts. You may simply want the scene to flow a little more. The easiest way to do this is to move your actors. But having said that, you have to realize that an arbitrary move may be more harmful than an arbitrary cut. Use *dialogue* and the content of your scene to make your moves make sense.

Look at the accompanying drawings. In the first (Drawing 1), a man and a woman are arguing. She is restless; *he* plants his feet and won't move. You could shoot the scene with a series of static shots of each actor, planning to cut back and forth between them in the editing room. But if the woman moves around the man, and the camera pans and tracks with her (Drawing 2), it is possible to get a "tie-up" shot involving both of them (Drawing 3), and for the camera always to be "featuring" the actor who is talking (Drawing 4), or, conversely, from whom you want a "reaction shot." This is more complicated than simply setting your camera down and getting static shots of each from which to make an edited scene, but it is also more interesting; it is powerful to keep two participants in an argument in full view, without giving up the necessary close-ups. (The over-the-shoulder shots involved in such a camera-actor move give you both people; they give you movement, realism, and close-ups all in one.) In order to observe this kind of move, pay attention the next time you go to a feature film or watch a high-budget movie-of-the-week. There are always shots like this in such films. They are quite elegant. Of course, they have to be well rehearsed so that the pace and timing of the scene is all there, and they often require a large number of takes to get right. You will sometimes find, by the way, that such a tie-up shot requires a couple of extra close-ups to "punch up" the action, but this doesn't ruin the basic effect of the "combination" shot itself (so called because it combines a series of close-ups or two-shots with moving shots).

Hint 2 When a character leaves a scene, make a decision early on whether you are going to follow the character (that is, pan with him) or *let him go*. If you follow, then you will have to be a lot more careful when you "pick up" the same character in your next shot. He or she will have to "match" movement and pace in the next shot, whereas if you let a character go out of a shot, you can pick up that character in a new shot with a different background or time frame and no one will be the wiser. In other words, it is easier to let people exit the frame so that you are free to pick them up in your next shot wherever you wish.

Hint 3 It's generally more pleasing to cut from a *moving* shot to another *moving* shot, and to cut from a *static* shot to another *static* shot, though people break this rule all the time. Take a look next time you're editing, and see which you prefer.

1

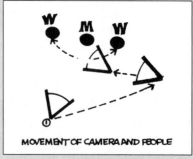

MOVEMENT OF CAMERA AND PEOPLE

2 As woman moves to position 2, camera moves to its second position, keeping both people in a well-framed shot

3

4

A FINAL NOTE ON MOVEMENT: HANDHELD OR TRIPOD?

I suppose there is almost no director who hasn't experimented with handheld camera movement, even before the invention of the Steadicam and other gyroscopic devices. The conventional wisdom is "Don't cut from tripod or dolly movement to handheld and don't go handheld unless you're absolutely forced to." This has led a lot of us down a difficult road. Even in high-budget dramas, there are times when the laying of dolly track is too difficult or too time-consuming, or where the space we're using is too confined and we are forced into static shots, using a tripod because we're afraid of the handheld cam-era. But as cameras become lighter and more flexible, as more and more camera operators are trained in handheld work, and as lenses become wider and less distorting, the use of handheld movement becomes more and more useful. A tracking shot on dolly, which might take a half hour to set up and another half hour to rehearse to perfection, might produce a shot only half as exciting as a good handheld shot on a wide-angle lens. Again, this is one of those areas where consultation with your D.P. will produce a quick answer that you might agonize over for hours alone.

Handheld Rules

Rule 1 Try not to plan a handheld shot where there's a great deal of movement of *camera* and no movement of *people*. You can walk alongside a jogging horse with a handheld camera and never notice the camera movement; the same shot of a static figure seated on a bench will produce a picture in which the camera seems to be jogging, which is likely not to be the effect you wanted.

Rule 2 Try not to use a long lens on a handheld shot, even if the camera isn't moving. Jiggles do show up on camera. Your D.P. (especially in documentary work) may think that he or she can easily hold steady with a long lens, handheld, but experience shows that when you come to edit such a shot into a sequence of shots, some of which are handheld and some of which are on tripod, the shakiness of the long-lens, handheld shots, renders them useless.

PLANNING THE LOOK

Plotting Shots

Once you have a look in mind, you will want to know how to translate that look into film. Start by plotting your shots directly onto your script. Some people do this by drawing actual pictures of the shots as they will appear on the screen, others do it by making diagrams of the camera angles with the way the characters will appear (see script page). Still others will actually paste the still photographs they've shot into the script. (Even if there are no actors in those stills, they convey a great deal.) Whichever you do will have to do with your artistic ability or your energy.

One or the other approach is almost mandatory. If, for instance, you've planned a whole series of wide shots to begin your film, conveying the sense of open space, you'll want to show that in your script with something other than "series of wide shots." What better way than to specifically draw the shots and label them clearly? Similarly, with a series of close shots, each shot—let's say, of a tree trunk—could be filmed in a dozen ways. Remind yourself of your particular vision by diagramming or sketching it carefully. (When you get to the shoot itself, it's remarkable how many details of your vision go completely out of your head. Then, you're left with improvising, a sure way for your look to change without your knowing it.)

Using Storyboards to Plan Shots

Another way to jog your memory is to use a "storyboard." As the name suggests, a storyboard is a large sheet of paper, broken down into frames, onto which you can draw as many shots as you need to tell your story. Some directors, especially in commercials, plot every shot. For animation, the storyboard is even more complex, illustrating moves *within* a shot. For longer films or tapes, you may choose simply to put down the major changes in the picture, or the beginning of every shot, or the shots that involve complex camera moves, or, you name it. If you can draw fairly well, a storyboard is a lovely way to show your shots to D.P.s or producers. If, like me, you can't keep a straight line from turning wavy, you may not feel comfortable doing them. I use line drawing in my scripts, as suggested above, but as seen from overhead (see next page), not from the camera's point of view, unless a very complicated visual effect is desired. But I happen to have a very good visual imagery mechanism working for me, so that how a shot looks is very clear to me without any drawing; the note in my script is merely a reminder of the shot that I can clearly see in my mind. For those who don't have such imagery, *some* form of drawing, from a camera's point of view, is a marvelous aid. It's not only useful for you, but also for your team. Imagine if you could show a version on paper of all shots, as you planned them, to your D.P. and producer. Those who can do this tell me it gives them a rich environment in which to "swim" while they're planning a film. There's no doubt that some of the best directors in the world use storyboards of every major shot as a way of mulling over the shots and of showing art directors, prop persons, D.P.s, P.M.s, and costumers just what they have in mind.

My doubts about storyboards center on two things: (1) a fear that

Revised Sample Script
"Mirra, Mirra, On the Wall"

15. PHIL 7 MIRRA'S HOUSE - INTERIOR (DAY)

Bright sunlight fills the room. Phil is mending some harness for the
donkey. Mirra is sweeping.

> MIRRA
> Where are they?

> PHIL (without looking up)
> They'll be fine. (beat)
> Do you want me to look for them?

Mirra hesitates, then shakes her head.

> MIRRA
> No. I guess not.

MEDIUM 2-SHOT

> PHIL
> If they're not back in an hour, I'll
> go. they're probably down by the river.
> Don't worry, there're no troops left.
> Not after last night.

Mirra goes no sweeping. Phil finishes the harness and stands up, taking
it to a hook on the wall. He stands looking out the window
for a moment.

16. PHIL'S P.O.V.

A distant curl of smoke rising up out of the valley. It could be from
fire or from artillery.

17. C.U. PHIL
There is some concern on his face, but after a moment he relaxes,
dismissing the worry. he turns from the window.

18. MEDIUM SHOT - THE ROOM
Mirra is looking intensely at Phil.

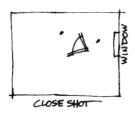

CLOSE SHOT

> MIRRA
> What is it? what's out there?

> PHIL
> I don't know.

> MIRRA.
> Damn you! What's out there?

those who cannot draw will believe they can't *visualize* just because they can't put the images on paper, and (2) my belief that what *lenses* can do just can't be shown properly in a drawing or watercolor. Still, storyboards have a venerable and useful role in film and television, and you might as well give them a try.

Choosing Lenses

Among the things you will want to indicate to yourself in your notes is the kind of lens you wish to use. I don't mean a 2" versus a 3" or a 28mm versus a 75mm. I mean whether the distortion that your shot demands is the kind that makes the background out of focus (a long lens) or one that stretches focus out into infinity (a wide lens).

"Distortion," I said, and distortion I mean, for the idea of a "normal" lens is really a fiction. Sure, books on lens use will tell you that the 50mm lens in 35mm format or the 25mm lens in 16mm format is a "normal" lens, and they'll give you a lot of technical reasons why this is so. But consider the following: the camera shoots with one eye, while humans have two; humans see in three dimensions, cameras in two; the human eye has almost complete depth of field, but camera lenses must be "racked" or stopped-down to achieve anything similar. In point of fact, *any* lens on a camera is a distortion of "normal" human vision. How much further you wish to distort, then, is a choice of the director, but distort you must, in order to focus the attention of the audience on the precise part of the scene that interests you. Here is a brief example.

Merce Cunningham, the American choreographer and dancer, made many videotapes and films about his dances. He used to use a man named Charlie Atlas to do the films. When they used the Steadicam, they usually used a wide-angle lens. This allowed a large number of dancers to be on-screen at the same time; it also allowed the camera to move in a small room and to be very close to the dancers and *still* hold focus with a low amount of light (wide-angle lenses have greater depth of field at lower f-stops). All this probably does create a certain "distortion" in the look of the dancers compared to, say, a 50mm lens. So what? Messrs. Cunningham and Atlas were achieving what *they* wanted, and so can you—by fitting your lens to your imagination.

Lighting

With your basic shots written down so you can visualize and revisualize them, move on to the second part of the look: how the scene will be lit. Overall, you will have seen a kind of lighting as you previsualized the film. (This is not the same as what I call "mood," which has to do with atmosphere, or "style," the manner in which actors will play the film.) You are not interested here in how your D.P. will light the scene, or how the gaffer will place the lights, but in what the light looks like. Is every scene overcast? Does the sun shine through brightly? Are there very noticeable shadows (à la Bertolucci)? Is the light without any sense of direction, as if the sun were bounced off soft fabric? You may even think of the color you want to dominate, using lights or fabrics or costumes or set pieces. (Think of how Antonioni must first have visualized *The Red Desert*.) A young filmmaker envisioned a film shot entirely around sunset, because she loved the idea of that golden glow that you get. Everything was to be "burning up." This required not only a wonderful vision, but all sorts of technical preparations: "gels" on windows to cut out most of the blue light; lots of backlight, with careful attention to direction of light at all times (a sunset is very directional, while noon sun seems to emanate from many directions at the same time). Attention was paid as well , too, to costumes and makeup so that everyone wouldn't appear to have a fever with all the red light being cast around.

Lighting is exciting. Think about it. Dream about it. Observe the world around you. In preparation for his seminal black-and-white film *The Seventh Seal* (1957), the Swedish director Ingmar Bergman and his director of photography, Sven Nyquist, went to the North Sea and stood there for hours looking at the light at all times of day. This is very good preparation for the shoot. Look at the light coming into your bedroom when you awaken, at midday, and at sunset. Does it create an effect? Can you re-create that effect on the set? On location?

What kind of lighting do you want? Beginners—in still photography as well as in film and video—think of the "key" (that is, main) light as coming in from the front, the "fill" (supplementary light to smooth out shadows) as coming in from the side, and the "backlight" (light that hits the top of the head and the shoulders) from above or behind. But take a look at the real world and, the next time you're watching a boring film where the story doesn't interest you, look at the lighting used by most professionals. In fact, in the real world, light almost never comes straight in at the front of people. The strongest light in a room is often from the windows or from an overhead light. Depending on which way people turn, they may get that light from behind, the side, or, sometimes, the front. What does that do? What effect does it have?

Do you remember the first time you saw someone use a flashgun for still photography outdoors? That's called "fill-in" flash, and it's used to soften the shadows on a person's face when the sunlight is providing a strong backlight. That's done by D.P.s and directors, too. And it can create marvelous effects. In fact, as in still photography, direct flat light from the front isn't very attractive (though it's used throughout much of television and in comedies on the big screen). But sidelight, backlight, filtered light, alternating shadows and light, can *all* have the effect of making a two-dimensional screen seem *three-dimensional*. The human eye, having as it does a partner, creates depth by the use of stereoscopic vision. It is aided by distance cues, such as color, falling off of light, and so on. The camera has fewer cues and can't use stereoscopic vision at all. But we do have light, and the real world—that is, the world in which we move daily—has an extraordinary variety of forms of light. The color changes, the saturation changes, there are shadows in corners, there are backlights and highlights, filtered light on walls (as when the sun comes in through venetian blinds or trees)— the list is endless. By using the same techniques in filmmaking, the real world can be created, or at least, re-created.

Let's take another tack. When you go to a museum and see paintings by Vermeer, Rembrandt, and other members of the Dutch school, are you struck by the extraordinary directionality of light and by its almost magical quality? Some filmmakers, especially from France and Italy, have taken advantage of that quality for their films, but many American directors and D.P.s have not. I wonder why. It seems to me that the way in which light can come at us from a wide variety of directions, how it looks in fog or mist, what happens when it's bright outside and dim inside, and a multitude of other variations are opportunities to alter the look of your film in a way that can add to the quality of the script, the acting, the entire production. (See a few examples of the way light varies on the next three pages.) I have never forgotten the first time I saw Bergman's *Wild Strawberries* (in the 1960s) nor Bertolucci's marvelous *The Conformist* (reissued in 2000 in an expanded version). In both cases, it was *light* that I remembered. One film was shot in black-and-white, the other in color, so it was not the color that impressed itself on me, it was the light. Use it wisely and the benefits can be exceptional.

Make notes to yourself that you can discuss with the D.P. when you get around to it. If you've experimented with lighting—by your-

Light can vary in quality, direction, and intensity. Here are three possible varia-tions. Here, the intensity of the light is low and, because it's sundown, the qual-ity of the light is very even and diffused.

self, in film school, or in other films—you already realize how intricate and detailed such work can be. You also know that most modern D.P.s will not use natural sunlight but prefer something called the Halogen Mercury Incandescent (HMI), a wonderful invention that puts out the hot (blue) light of sunlight at a fraction of the heat of earlier "arc" lights. Why don't D.P.s like sunlight? Because of clouds, and because the sun moves. If you are shooting all day long outdoors, and the scene has to be lit from a certain position, then errant clouds may cover your key light, or the movement of the sun will mean that what was "backlight" is now front light, ruining the lighting *continuity* of your close-ups, wide shots, and mid-shots. Of course, if you can shoot the entire scene in a half hour, then you won't need to lug cable and two or three HMIs out with you, but that's pretty quick shooting.

I go into all of this not to scare you away from your ideas on lighting, but to get you to formulate them carefully enough so that you and your D.P. can *plan* for them in advance and get the right lighting equipment ordered. For instance, if you are shooting indoors and you want strong, bright sunlight to come pouring through the windows, let your D.P. know. If, on the other hand, everything can be lit from unobtrusive "practicals" (the real lamps in a room), that changes the entire look of your film and the way it has to be lit. Like everything else in directing, the more you decide in advance, the more flexible you can be. That sounds like a contradiction in terms, but in fact, giving warning to your team about what you want to do means that when you do change your mind on the set, you will not be looked at as if you had ruined everyone's lunch ("He's changed his mind again!").

TWO FINAL NOTES ABOUT LOOK

One You will want to establish a "point of view." To some extent, this has been predetermined by the script. It's seen from so-and-so's point of view. But what does this mean filmically? Will you, for instance, go so far as to do what was done in the classic *Lady of the Lake*, directed by Robert Montgomery, where the camera *was* the protagonist, or at least took the view of Marlowe, the detective protagonist, taking blows from a criminal's fist, tilting down to see its own feet, and so on? Or will you take an "objective point of view," with the camera standing back and viewing everyone the same way? Going beyond that, will your shots take into account objects and settings, or will they stay

Here, a sharp unidirectional source creates quite a different feeling.

Deep in the woods, on a hot day, a small pond provides cool relief. The sunlight filtering down into the woods clearly states heat, and the shadows and bright spots create a sense of mystery.

strictly with humans? Can the camera show the outside of a building if the narrator of the film, or even the central character, is not present? When a couple is wed, from whose point of view will you show the two hands and the ring: from that of the groom? The bride? Or the priest? These things will make a very important difference.

Two How large will your shots be? Is a close-up, to you, full face, or face and neck? Is an ECU the two eyes, eyes and nose, or what? Is a medium shot down to the waist, or is it chest height?

The impact of your film or videotape will be determined by all these variables. Taken together, they define the look of your film; how and when you envision them and carry them out will be crucial to the aesthetic effect of the story you are telling.

If you are on a producer's staff or the other members of your team have already been hired, you will want to start conveying some of your ideas for the look to the D.P. and the art director as soon as possible. You will certainly have formulated an idea about whether you want to shoot this film on location or on the studio set or a combination of both (see chapter 6), because your visions of the look will have dictated what kind of place fits the film. Talk over these ideas with the D.P. Can he or she accomplish what you have in mind inside the studio, or does it demand the location in southern France that you visited last year?

A film student of mine wanted to do a short video project. He picked the basement tunnel underneath the administration building of our college. There, in a dirty, noisy space, with pipes and cable running here and there, he figured his World War II scene would have a sense of realism. The problem was, he wanted to use a dolly for the scene, and the floor of this tunnel was much too bumpy for that. In addition, he hadn't taken into account the problems he would have with sound. On the other hand, all other locations were too banal, too clean, too square for the war-torn scene he had in mind. In the end, he decided to shoot in the tunnel, compromising by using a smoother portion, farther from the steam valves, with ample headroom for the lights. It was a compromise that didn't hurt his film; by discussing it in advance with me (the titular producer for the piece), his D.P., and his sound person, he saved himself all sorts of problems during the shoot and the edit.

STYLE AND MOOD

Molière or Odets? Shakespeare or Beckett? Realistic or Impressionistic? This is a matter of style, and it is a decision quickly made, but often erroneously. Comedy is perhaps the most difficult kind of film to direct, because every actor and every set designer has his or her own idea of what it is. Doubly difficult is contemporary comedy, where the settings and the environment give audiences reason to believe that this is a realistic movie. The lines, however, and the plot, may lead us to another conclusion. How should the actors play it? With a belief in the outcome, but in the grand manner (high comedy)? Or with no belief whatsoever in the result (farce)? You must decide this early on, for it will be important that set and costume designers know which you have in mind, and the actors, of course, must all play in the same style.

As I suggested earlier, the mood of a film is established not by lights or by settings alone, but by the plot and the way you direct the actors. Does a female character step in and say, without any fuss, "Sir, Mr. Marlow is here," or does she say it with a whisper, slyly? Or does she say it with her face in the shadows? Or does she, finally, say it with a shriek? How do you want your audience to take the film: as a realistic, contemporary story? As a mystery? As an allegory? As a comedy?

All this has to do with the mood of the film (others may give it a different name—no matter), and all this requires a great deal of thought as to what you want and how to achieve it. When the film opens with a panoramic sweep of the countryside, birds twittering, sun shining, and comes to rest on the corpse of a man, his body strangely mutilated, we are establishing one kind of mood. If the same pan found a couple on a bed, making love, with the bed in the middle of a stream, we have obviously established another, less serious, mood. The same shot, ending with a wide shot of a house, quietly sitting in the middle of a clearing, smoke curling out of its chimney, but not a thing stirring, may well establish yet a third mood, not one of chilling surrealism, not one of comedy, but one of neutral expectation, for a still house, with nothing stirring in the middle of the day, should give us a little sense of suspense.

Your perception of the film's message, of the script's dialogue, and of the import of the film, all will play a role in making you think about how the audience is to receive it and, therefore, how the actors are to play it. This is the time to think about that, and to think about all the settings and trappings that will help you convey it. Naturally, your choice of style will be one of the ways you do this, as will your use of lenses, light, color, and so forth. Most important, however, will be the way you instruct your actors to behave, the way they talk, the pace at which they move and speak, the lines of dialogue you keep and those you throw away. Here is an example.

The time is 1905. The setting is a little town in—well, the script doesn't make it clear—it could be New England, it might be the Midwest. Two men are sitting on a porch, rocking (or at least that's what it says in the original script). One turns to the other and says,

SAM

They're coming today.

PHIL

Who says?

SAM

Frank saw them in town.

PHIL

What does he know?

The script is about a couple of women coming back to a small town and giving the men a shock by their big-city ways. Is it a serious commentary on feminism? Is it a light comedy? Is it a quasi-serious tract on how far we haven't come? Or is it a gentle story of how a woman in the early part of this century can be both a loving helpmeet and a liberated woman? Once you've decided that (based on the writer's intentions), you will have to decide a number of things about those first four lines of dialogue. For instance, will they be spoken with a dialect? What dialect will it be? How strong will it be? A Southern accent will tell us one thing, a Vermont twang another, and a Midwestern drawl yet another. Will they really rock, giving us a comedic twist to the beginning? Will they, as in many television sit-coms, snarl their lines or, as in Pinter, merely say them? Look two or three times at the lines and try reading them in a variety of ways, to convey the different parts of the country or the different moods you want to establish *right at the beginning of your* film.

Once the acting approach and the pace have been established, you will have to match them with the lighting, lenses, shots, and other visual choices you have made. Is this the house we panned to in my earlier paragraph? Or do we open on voices coming from a part of the set that we can't see, while our camera lovingly tracks past photographs and other memorabilia of the woman who is about to return from the big city? You can see that there are a million choices, and that any two of them make your audience react differently from any other two. Try thinking of how some of the famous directors you know about might do such an opening. Fellini, Coppola, Mike Figgis, Jim Jarmusch, Ridley Scott, Spike Lee. If you've seen films by those directors, you will see right away that there is something in the personal style of those directors that would probably dictate how they would open any film, yet there is something so creative about the same men that that mood would be different from the mood of any other film. Your choices will make the difference, not only at the beginning of the film, but all the way through it.

EMOTION AND CONTENT

Up to now, in preparation for your film, we have been concentrating on translating a particular look and feel about a script onto the screen. This has involved some technical matters and some purely aesthetic ones. What we are now going to discuss involves something a good deal more intricate: the decisions you will make about how to translate a particular line of dialogue or a particular emotion onto the screen. Much of this is a matter of trial and error, but some general hints can be given—or at least some general areas of *choice* you must make.

One. Is your story to be told in a straightforward manner or do you wish to use symbols? This depends, of course, to a large part on your script, but since the director has an opportunity to change script, you can add or subtract such things. Once again, we can call upon Ingmar Bergman for our discussion. In *The Seventh Seal*, light is used to symbolize the struggle between Death and the Knight who has just returned from the Crusades. Anyone seeing the film is immediately struck by the dark shadows that surround Death, and the halo of light that surrounds the juggler and his wife, symbols of virtue. In Bergman's hands the symbolic use of light (and of the chess game between Death and the Knight) is powerful. In another director's hands, such symbolism might be clumsy.

A less well-known film provides another example of the use of symbolism. *Ways of the Night* opens with a deer being killed. It is 1944. The German soldiers who have killed it discuss whether killing is a good or a bad thing per se, or whether the *way* in which one kills is important. Such a discussion could have been carried on without the deer, which I found a little heavy-handed. The director must have felt it was a necessary precursor to the killing that would go on later in the film *and* that it set the scene for the whole movie: a pastoral setting into which brutality would come. This, then, is more than mood. It is a symbol that plays upon our intellectual and emotional beings.

Two Where should a scene take place? A writer may choose an open field or a barn, a bedroom or a dining room table. Where the scene takes place is very closely tied in with the emotion and content of that scene. Would you be better off taking the discussion on brutality in the aforementioned film out into the fields or into a cold, white room in a requisitioned chateau? Do you wish to "telegraph" your message or let it develop? Is a love scene played out on the tennis court (with lovers batting balls toward each other) a good love scene? Or should it be, more conventionally, played in the bedroom? Do you recall *Tom Jones*, where the lovers wooed each other across a table laden with food? I have no idea whether that was the writer's original idea for a place to set the scene, or the director's, but it was a marvelous choice. Do you want to establish a stressful situation? Place the characters in a factory or a work yard where the noise of the mechanical goings-on is pitched to their feelings about each other. Do you want to make the audience think that everything is peaceful? Place your characters against a herd of lowing sheep (but watch out for the sound problems!). A writer placed a scene about a character who is ruining people's lives in the boardroom of a corporation. The director placed it, instead, in a hallway, with half a dozen doors opening to either side of the characters. At any moment, the image seemed to say, someone may come out of those doors. The danger of the scene was perfectly matched by the *locality* of the scene. These are but three possibilities for matching scene and locality among thousands of such choices. The message is: don't let the locality of your scene be a haphazard or frivolous choice.

Three What is the color and light quality in a scene? Here, think "Ingmar Bergman," for the color and quality of light in films such as *Cries and Whispers* and *Fanny and Alexander* so perfectly match the emotion and content of the scripts that they fairly cry out their message without dialogue. But you don't have to be a Bergman to use light and color to establish (a) the emotion and (b) the content of your scripts. You can do this as subtly or as openly as you wish. What is happening in a scene? Should this take place at night, with a little light filtering into the room through the open door or window? Should it take place in full daylight, with shadows on the walls from the hot sun, or, perhaps, in a room devoid of shadows? Is there an argument? Does this call for "angry" colors in the decor or lighting? Or is this too obvious? Are the characters depressed? What do you want in the room that calls attention to this? Or, conversely, do you want to play the dialogue outdoors in the fog to match emotions with the weather? Or, as a final possibility, to call attention to the fact that your character is at odds with nature, play it in a wooded glade with the birds singing and gentle light falling from a sun hidden by trees? Are there plants and flowers in the room in which a scene is played? Is the character in bed really sick or just pretending? The color of the flowers and the light that plays on them can give us a hint. (One doesn't have to have the plant die as in Spielberg's *E. T. The Extra-Terrestrial* [1982] to do this effectively; there are subtler means.)

Your art director and your costume designer will play major roles in this kind of determination. What kinds of clothes and what color of clothes are the actors wearing? Is the light coming at them from behind, or in front? Does their dialogue tell us how complex the situation is, or do you need shadows from moving fans overhead to cross their faces, giving the impression that they are somehow caught up in a great big web that entangles their every move? Too obvious? Perhaps not. It's your choice, of course.

Four What is the *sound* you choose for a scene? For some directors, this is something they choose not to think about until the scene is "in the can" and they are editing, but others want the scene to be shot with the appropriate sound built in. (In the days of silent films, string players serenaded actors during sentimental scenes so they would feel the right emotion.) Play a scene in a whisper and it's quite different from one spoken at normal pitch. An argument spoken under hushed circumstances may convey a sense of anger much better than one that is shouted.

What about "ambient" sound, or the surrounding noises? Birds, crickets, automobiles, rock music, radio news—all give a different feeling to a scene. And only you can make the determination, from the script, as to which is proper. Some of that ambient sound should be laid in afterward (editing is difficult when too much sound is actually on the primary dialogue track; it has to be matched with little pieces of "room tone" as you cut and paste various tracks). But a scene that takes place in a totally "dead" location or where you have *made no choice* as to what sound will eventually occupy the room, is a scene strangely empty. For example: have you ever seen a film in which the director or editor later decided to put in the sound of a noisy machine, but in which the two characters in the scene are speaking at a *normal* voice level? To compensate, the machine is "held down" on the sound track and the reality of the scene is ruined. To do this right requires actors who feel comfortable shouting at each other in a quiet room or a quiet field, but since it is necessary to the successful outcome of the scene, you must think about it *ahead of time*.

While we're talking about sound, think about the way you want your actors to talk. With an accent, dialect, or special characteristic? Or "normally." What does normal mean to you? What does it mean to them?

Five You must give a great deal of consideration to the reading of each line of dialogue. You cannot wait for rehearsals to determine how a line is to be read. You must know what every word means and how it is to sound. This doesn't mean you won't change your mind—especially when you hear how your actors read the lines (see chapter 8), but it does mean you must have a conception and a preconception about everything associated with the script. This must be done over and over again as you approach the shoot. If it is, you will discover an amazing thing: you will begin to translate how you feel about, and how you understand, the dialogue into *changes* in all the other matters we've discussed before. Shots, moves, lighting, color, costumes, make-up, cutting plan—*all* will shift as your knowledge and conception of the characters and dialogue gets honed.

Which brings us, in these final paragraphs, to the crucial question, "What is the point?" I don't mean of filmmaking but of the film itself. What is the story about? What is its moral or pragmatic point? Where is it going? You thought about all that when you were reading or rewriting; thought about it when the producer made a pitch to you—or you to the producer—in order to sell the project. But, as you go along with all these details, have you kept *that* point *uppermost* in your mind? Have you continued to think of your *goal*, which is the message of the film itself? Even if the film is a light comedy, it has *some* point. In the middle of all the costumes and makeup and camera angles, you can easily lose your path. There is no miraculous way to keep that "point" firmly fixed in your mind. Writing it on slips of paper, and sticking them in various places may help ("God is good"; "Anna wins"; "George loses"; "War is bad"; and so forth). Having it all thought out and continuing to think it all out, every day, is perhaps the best way. Each scene must lead somewhere, and every detail you work on must contribute to that goal. And they all must add up to one or two final points, or else everything you're doing is a waste.

The processes we've been discussing in this chapter start the day you hear about or read the first piece of the story that will become a shooting script. They continue during fundraising and casting, rewrites and hiatuses. They should also continue during the entire shoot. You should not be afraid to *think about* changing shot lists and localities of scenes even after you've started, if the change is crucial to the changed perception of your script; though you should consider *carefully* how often you want to do so, since nothing is more threatening to a producer or production manager than the director who always changes his mind at the last moment! In the next three chapters, we will discuss preparation for the shoot in three different ways: how to get ready on a technical level, how to prepare your shots, and what to do when things go wrong. Nothing should interfere, however, with the continued analysis of the matters discussed in this chapter. They are the essence of your aesthetic approach to the film.

5

Getting Ready (II): Technical and Artistic Preparations

This chapter gets down to the very important business of making arrangements with other team members—such as finding the proper location, designing the set, having a say in who will do costumes and makeup, planning rehearsals (if you're lucky enough to have them), and other technical or logistical matters.

As already stated in chapter 3, your producer will undoubtedly do much of the preproduction work on a television series, less on a feature film, and more or less on an independent production, depending on who the director is and what his or her relationship with the producer is. Since there is nothing for you to do if a producer has already made most of the artistic or logistical choices, we will proceed on the assumption that they're all yours to make, that your contract (or your personal or professional relationship) stipulates that you will be in on everything, right from the beginning. What do you have to think about?

> Designing the set
> Picking locations
> Designing costumes
> Designing and planning makeup
> Arranging for rehearsals
> Special effects and props

You have read the script, plotted your scenes, and discussed them with appropriate people—the artistic and technical staff who help you find the right artistic expression for your film. First of all, that means the producer. The producer need not know everything you want to do with your film—the specific shots, the pacing, and so forth—but he or she will certainly ask pertinent questions about how you intend to visualize the film, where you want to shoot certain things, and how much money you need. Though some directors like to keep certain aspects of their production plans quiet, discussing them only with the D.P. or a friend, open discussion is generally the best policy. Then, if there's a fight to be had, it can be had early on, before shooting begins. (You may be surprised. The producer may think everything you're doing is wonderful.)

The production manager is certainly someone with whom you will want to discuss all your needs. You may get real help from him or her in terms of suggestions. You may also get interference, but once again, know that in advance.

As we saw in the last chapter, you will discuss *everything* with your director of photography.

You and the art director will talk. In chapter 3 we merely mentioned the work of the art director, but now that we're looking at several areas of the production that call for his or her expertise, we should know more. An art director may have worked up from jobs such as prop person or set decorator. He or she will have studied art history in college, or be a painter or an architect manqué. Very often, too, a film art director will have done the same kind of work on the stage. The ability to draw, to design, to research, and to conceive overall visual appearances will be a specialty. It is the art director's responsibility to discuss all possible sets and all possible locations with the director; to accompany the director on location searches, then make suggestions whether such places are appropriate for the scene(s); to design original settings and alterations for locations; and to present estimated costs to the P.M. or the producer and to supervise the construction of the finished sets. That's a lot of work.

A director will want to spend a good deal of time with an art director, giving his or her gut feelings about the script and discussing how much detail is to be portrayed, and whether the film is realistic or expressionistic, humorous or serious, and so forth. Do not take it for granted that anyone who has read the script—no matter how gifted—*automatically* knows what the proper tone of the film is. Only you can share *your* vision. Other people may find no humor or too much humor; too much pathos or not enough; colors that are too bright or too dull—in something you think is just right. Express yourself completely about the look to your art director.

THE SET

Gooid art directors know how to use a little and make it look like a lot. They are also trained to know that it is the little details that make a set look "right." They will tell you, for example, that when pots and pans in the windows of stores are painted, rather than being three-dimensional, the artificiality of a Western can be given away. This is true even if the shot is to be a wide shot. Fakes look fake. On the other hand, an art director often is so intent on creating the perfect set, he does not see the essence of a shot. It is not possible, for instance, to get rid of power lines across a landscape, without extremely expensive digital manipulation, the cost of which is seldom in the budget of most productions. So if you and your cinematographer have decided that they won't mar your scene, you may have to override the art director's judgment.

Your discussions with the art director will involve the look you have decided upon, but they will go much further. You will want to give him the "feel" of the place; you will want the art director to supply you with information that you can use in your shoot. For instance, you want some valid activity for one or two of your characters. If the writer hasn't suggested what your characters should fuss with, your art director may know what kind of equipment or furniture makes sense in that period, in that room.

The art director will do drawings and/or paintings of anything that has to be constructed, but you must *check* on small details, too. In Hollywood, one day, our show was doing an episode in which a little boy bought a dog. The signs on all the stores (which were located on the "back lot" at MGM) had to be painted for this particular day's shoot. They had a sign shop at the studio that did such things in a standard simplified style that could be read very easily on television. What the art director did not realize, in this case, was that the director was going to take a close shot of the sign and that he wanted it to look old and worn. The sign shop printed a nice, clean, simple sign that *looked* nice, clean, and simple in close-up, ruining the effect the director had in his head. "In his head" is the key here. You must know what you want; communicate it to your staff (in this case, the art director); *and* check on it before it's time to shoot.

There are other things you will have to do. Convey to the art director how much space you need for your scenes, so that sets can be built accordingly. You will need to decide ahead of time whether you need "wild walls"—walls that give way to allow the camera and lights to be placed there, so that you can shoot from the "other side" of the room. You will have to learn how to read drawings and blueprints, so that you don't end up being shocked at how small a room is after you saw the original drawing and thought, "plenty big." Don't be afraid to ask questions if you're puzzled. Heights of walls are especially important. You will have to decide how low your camera will be and how it will be angled. You may need extra protection in wall height. On the other hand, don't have walls higher than you really need them, because that means that your lights will be placed higher than you want them. Higher walls also mean more expensive sets, and you may want to trade that expense for a special piece of equipment later on.

BUILDING SETS VERSUS SHOOTING ON LOCATION

Because sets do cost so much money, more and more producers have decided to film on location. (We'll look at locations themselves in a moment.) What are the pros and cons of building sets as opposed to making films on location?

The Pros

One You have the possibility of getting things exactly the way you want them. This can range from wanting a set that represents a nineteenth-century butcher shop to the need to shoot everything from very high up—looking down into the room. The latter isn't easy on location, and the former means either a long search or a great deal of restoration. Sets can be built for the specific look you have in mind.

Two Sound is generally easier to record in a studio setting. You have no fourteen-wheelers roaring past the microphone. I remember being on location and having to wait for the airplanes to pass on their flight run to La Guardia Airport in New York. We hadn't heard them (or the flight patterns were different) when we looked at the place, but we certainly heard them (and waited for them, endlessly) when we went to shoot.

Three Lighting is easier in a studio. You have all the electric power you want, and special effects can be achieved effortlessly. If you want night, you make it night; day, and you can make it day. For television cameras, the "hot" (that is, bright) sky can be dimmed with a twist of a knob in a studio or on a sound stage.

Four More time can be spent actually shooting, less, running from one place to the other.

The Cons

One Despite the "perfection" that may be achieved by building a set the way you want it, a location that has the *actual* look because it is the *actual* place, can be far more successful than a set. This may be because the texture of the place is right (remember our art director saying that it's *details* that make the difference), or because the hills behind the characters are real hills and not a painted backdrop. (Did you see *Brigadoon*? The heath always looked to me like a studio at MGM—which it was.)

Two The indoor sound for an outdoor setting may be just what you *don't* want. In other words, indoors you may get a silent background, but you may also get an unrealistic echo. (See, or rather hear, the same *Brigadoon*.)

Three Cost is a consideration. In point of fact, a lot of the money that goes into a movie set doesn't show on the screen, and a lot of the expense of shooting in someone else's movie studio might buy you two or three different locations.

Four It can be a lot of fun to be on location, creating a spirit for a picture. That's hardly something the P.M. or the producer will characterize as a valid reason for choosing location over studio, but it's something for you to think about. (Of course, it can also be a nightmare. Imagine shooting *The African Queen* or *Apocalypse Now* in the jungles, which is exactly what was done!)

Five Believe it or not, although lighting may be more readily achieved for some shots in a studio, there is nothing like real outdoor light. As I said in the last chapter, arguments vary on this; some D.P.s will not use sunlight even when they're outdoors, and others swear by natural light.

The upshot of all this is that, very often, a film will be shot partly in the studio and partly on location.

LOCATION

Let's say that the script has approximately thirty scenes, ten of which take place outdoors. You and the art director will want to sit down and discuss where that "outdoors" is. But first, if you have a specific feel for a scene, one that tells you, for instance, that it's in the backyard of the house you grew up in, you may want to go there, just to check out whether that space still speaks to you in the same way. You may get there and discover that a freeway has been built next to it. Or you may find it's perfect, just the way you remembered it. Keep in mind, however, that you'll need to have plenty of extra room for your equipment and crew, that a busy street will have to be blocked off, and that if the scene to be shot there is short, you'll want to have a place nearby where other scenes can be shot. (Your production manager will keep these things in mind, too, but it's smart to be ahead of the game.) If the film is not contemporary, keep an eye out for anachronistic things like TV antennae, new automobiles, or new buildings that come within the sight lines of your shots.

Being out alone in potential locations is wonderful, and if they're not far from production headquarters, go there first by yourself. You'll want to sit down and look through your script, to see the exact lines of dialogue and the exact angles you want to use. Then, after you've visited a number of the places, go back again with your art director, with the production manager, and with your director of photography. Now, the places will look different.

First of all, the art director will point out the very obnoxious yellow of the building in the center of your picture. "But that's a background," you will protest. Indeed, it may be background, but it may be a distracting background. Or it may be a yellow that wasn't around in 1857. "We can repaint it," says the art director. "Not on your life," answers the P.M., and suddenly a discussion about the right look has turned into a question of money. The P.M. may also object to the location because the nearest motel that can accommodate the crew is the most expensive, and the cheapest is too far away to ferry the crew every morning and evening. Then there's the fact that the location is close enough to a big city so that members of the Teamsters Union will be required for the vehicles, but not close enough so that the cast and crew can sleep in the city and make it comfortably to the shoot every day. Finally, to complicate things further, the D.P. points out that the horizon is so low there that you will see too much sky and not enough people.

How could you have missed all that? Maybe you didn't; maybe you missed only some of it. Or, maybe you have answers, such as, the yellow doesn't bother you, you'll get by with it. The angle of shoot is such that, in fact, you'll see more characters and less sky than the D.P. thought. And, by angling the shot a little, that barn over there (a lovely rust color) will provide a contrast to the sky. As for motels, you intend to use this location for only half a day's shoot, and your next location is going to be near a chain of motels that's noted for low prices and catering to movie crews.

Of course, you may not have all these answers. The D.P.'s thoughts on the location may disconcert you, and you'll be depressed for a few days. But then you'll think of an alternative spot (or maybe you had it in mind anyway) and everyone will be happy with that. Another course of action may be that you put your foot down and tell the P.M. that this is a perfect location, that the trees up there are fine for the bandits to come swinging down, that the barns are authentic, and that you discussed repainting the yellow barn with the owner, who would be delighted to split the cost.

It may seem to you that some of the work that you are doing in your location search and in your discussions of sets comes perilously close to a *producer's* decisions. I promise you, they are very much a director's decisions. On a big feature film that uses lots of locations— for instance, *Ragtime*—a director (in that case, Milos Forman) would not hesitate to suggest a location that needed a great deal of "dressing" and repainting. He would find a house and pay the owner a great deal to get it right. Woody Allen is famous for that kind of search. You want your film to look right, and you will have to find the right location and defend it, if money or blindness to its beauties gets in the way. On the other hand, as we discussed in chapter 3, you may have to give a little here, to get a lot more there. Money is never easy to come by and getting the right set (in the studio or on location) may require more ingenuity than money, or more money than is available. Compromise where necessary, bargain where possible.

Some directors hate this work and there is a person called a "location scout" whom a P.M. will often use to do it. But when it comes down to the final choice, you, your art director, your P.M., and your

D.P. must go along, and you must say whether or not it will work. I'm told that Milos Forman, when looking for that house in *Ragtime*, sent scouts out all over the place, but when they had found three or four "perfect" houses, he went out there with a group of his important team members and they talked through all the problems and all the possibilities in each place until they were certain it would do. You can't be expected to know all the technical problems that may arise in a particular location, but you *can* know what it is you want to accomplish and how you want to shoot. Ask, probe, listen, then make up your own mind based on all the alternatives.

COSTUMES

You and your producer will hire a costume designer. Make sure it's someone you meet and talk with. Is she or he familiar with the period? Is she or he experienced enough in getting the kind of detail you want or, conversely, too detail-oriented? (I've gone crazy waiting for the "right" bow tie when all I was going to see was a profile of that particular extra!) What was the last film the designer did? Call the director and have a chat. This goes for hiring everyone you have a say about, of course, but it's particularly important for those people with whom you will work closely as the days of the shoot get nearer. Some directors don't pay much attention to costumes, letting the designer work pretty much alone and approving only those outfits that seem crucial. My own preference is to participate in a lot of the costume work because (1) it's fun, and (2) I feel more secure not having surprises when the character arrives on set all dressed in something I haven't seen.

What kinds of things do you look for? I already mentioned the picky-details kind of designer. You can reassure such a person that you're not going to see the feet, so shoes don't matter, but be very sure that you *don't* see the feet during the shoot, otherwise you're going to have an irate designer on your hands, and rightfully so. Look for those details that will make a difference in the kind of character you're trying to portray. Is it a hat or is it a waistcoat? Is it the checked pants or is it the "punk" sweatshirt? What gives you the right feeling about that person? If you are knowledgeable about lighting, you'll know that a bright white shirt will distract an audience from someone's face. Most costume designers know this, too, but they may forget it in the act of buying something wonderful. They will certainly not always know what *you* think is too bright or too distracting. Speak up if you're worried. They should listen and buy an alternative that you can have handy. Watch for those clothes that won't stand up during a scene or that will be too bulky in a love scene, or that will look out of place in the set your art director is building. Remember that only you know all the details of your production plans, and that others may do things that would work independently but not within the context of the entire affair. Are there wigs? What's the makeup like? What colors do you want? Get the D.P., the art director, the makeup people, and the costume designer together at least once for a meeting to discuss these things. On small-budget films this is seldom done, but what a relief when it is!

If you're going to have a lot of extras on the set, help your costume designer out by telling him or her how they're going to be used. This may take a little more time on your part, but it could save the production a lot of time or money (if you're going to see them in silhouette, for instance), or a lot of embarrassment (if you're planning to have them appear in two or three scenes and only one costume was rented for each).

You should feel perfectly free to go to costume fittings if you have the time and it doesn't hamper the work of the designer, but don't feel you have to be there all the time. Ask to have crucial items brought to you for approval so that you can make comments before they're bought or rented (this is standard practice, and the stores or rental houses understand). Costumes, like the sets and the actors you've cast, are crucial elements in a scene. If they're wrong, they'll stick out; if they're just right, then you'll have a subtle, but important contribution to your film.

MAKEUP AND HAIR DESIGN

Like costumes, these elements are often left to the producer or the P.M. They shouldn't be. After all, your understanding of the characters and of the atmosphere they are to create is affected by the totality of the image, not just by words and scenery. When I was acting in college, I remember being surprised that I was to wear a beard for my role as the chaplain in *The Lady's Not for Burning* by Christopher Fry, because

I didn't think of that character as having facial hair. The director wanted to have me look different from the others in the cast, but I convinced her that my character was too meek a man to be asserting himself by being the only one with a beard. She acquiesced. Whether I should have had a beard or not is unimportant. What is important is that we both had conceptions of the character, and that we came to an agreement long before dress rehearsal. You and your makeup and hair design people should discuss all aspects of the characters and plan to test out any special effects you want well before the shoot. This is obviously very important when doing "period" films or tapes, but also when doing contemporary material. By the way, don't forget to consult actors and actresses if you're planning radical changes for their looks. They may *like* the way they come across on the screen and not be eager to change.

Do some research before all these consultations begin. You may be surprised to discover, for instance, that long hair was *not* the fashion in the early part of this century. Is your leading man going to let you cut his locks? Will your leading lady let you give her a red wig? If your research is carefully done, you and your designers will have an easier time persuading the actors to let you alter their appearance.

REHEARSALS

This is the time to discuss seriously with your producer when and how you will rehearse. It's no secret that in much of the world of film television, actors are expected to come to the set "prepared," which is a nice way of saying *set* in their roles so they won't have to rehearse. This may be fine for the producer—saving him money—but what does it mean for you? If this is Hollywood, with television episodes being shot one right after the other, you may have to put up with the notion. A movie-of-the week will have rehearsals. So will many a public television film or videotape, an educational documentary or reenactment, or a feature film. It's very difficult to make an impact on the acting in a film without them, and all the work you've gone through with your other team members concerning the set, costumes, makeup, and hair will be merely fluff on top of performances that have been self-generated. In chapter 7 we deal with how to cope with the *absence* of rehearsals, but here we should talk about how to handle rehearsals when you actually get the opportunity.

You will want to set a date for rehearsal as far in advance of shooting as your producer will allow. (If there are script problems, you want to have time to make changes, and the more time you have the better.) But it costs a lot of money to have a rehearsal two or three weeks early. The unions for actors—American Federation of Television and Radio Artists (AFTRA) and Screen Actors Guild (SAG)—protect their members by requiring producers to pay for every day between the time they're called in for rehearsals and the first shooting day. This means that a producer is not likely to let you have rehearsals very many days before the shoot starts. In non-unionized situations, though, or in special circumstances, you may, indeed, be able to do so. And it will be well worth the effort. Let's say you actually get rehearsals,[11] what are you going to do?

As I suggested in chapter 3, directing actors is quite different from teaching actors, and directing actors for film is different from directing actors for the stage. And finally, directing actors and rehearsing actors are two different things. Rehearsing is a way of facilitating, guiding, leading, and permitting things to happen so that you can make other things happen.

Actors have both an idea about the script and an idea about how to accomplish the goals they see in the script. They want their characters to be consistent, and they want to understand both their characters and the goals the characters have set for themselves (or the script has set for them). They also want to understand relationships. That's all very intellectual. On the other side of it is craft: how to convey those ideas to an audience. This their training has taught them, but each script, each play, each film requires amending some of those avenues of approach. In rehearsal, if you have the time, you must be able to see what it is they want to do and be able to help them change, if you can. If you can't, *leave them alone*. Of course, when you are actually making the film, you can't leave them alone; but rehearsal is a time for finding answers and asking questions, and if you're not going to be any help, then don't get in the way. This may seem ridiculous since you *are* the director, but many directors don't have the knowledge required to help

---

[11]If not a rehearsal, you may at least get a reading—a quasi-rehearsal kind of thing in which the producer, the associate producer, the continuity person, and you sit around and give the actors a chance to run through the lines of the whole script. Your continuity person "puts a watch to it" to get times; you listen for pace and rhythm; and you all try to make the most of it.

actors, so they shouldn't try. (Nothing prevents you from *learning* to act, or from learning how to work with actors; all I'm saying here is wait until you can help before you interfere.) This warning aside, just what is it you can do during rehearsal?

You listen. Just like you did at the casting readings. The first time through the script, you *just* listen. You may answer a few questions if your actors ask—What accent do you want? Is this in Vermont or South Dakota?—but you don't tell them how to play the roles. The reason for this silence is that you want to see what *they* bring to the parts, what nuances or ideas that may have escaped you. Only after they have read through do you start talking, giving them changes that you feel are crucial. It's amazing how much you will learn from that one reading; how much they have read into the script, or learned from it. To be sure, there may be one or two who are off base, but in the absence of any sure-fire instructions from you or anyone else, the actors have gone ahead and made the script theirs. (Wouldn't it be nice if you had been able to do what stage actors do—start slowly, with a reading, rehearse slowly, move up to a full production? But you can't. Unless you're very, very lucky, you will get this one rehearsal before you have to work with a full crew and a "running meter." Here, at least, you have four hours or so, with the continuity person timing scenes so you have something to judge against when you're shooting.)

You now go back and start again, scene by scene, but this time stopping each time you hear something amiss. Gently, but firmly, you suggest a characterization a shade less vigorous, or a line reading less cynical. You may hear a line mangled and ask if it's a problem. You may do some quick rewriting, or cut an ambiguous or redundant line. Questions will begin to come from the actors as they realize you are actually willing to help them, that they don't have to do it all themselves, that this time, "director" means just that. Is this reading too strong? What does this line mean? Do they have this right? You may be asked to tell them information about their character that isn't in the script: When was he born? Where did she go to college? What are her political beliefs? If you don't have an answer to these questions, don't put the actors off by saying, "It doesn't matter." If they need to know, you should find out—which might mean making it up—but that's good for a director, too. Knowing details about characters will mean that they have a life off of the page; it increases their three-dimensionality.

How do you go about asking actors to change readings? I think, as in everything else in this business, using straightforward language probably will help. If you don't understand something they're doing, ask why they're doing it. If you want a character to be less like a caricature and more like a real person, discuss the style of the film you're doing and how this character fits in. If the actor doesn't get what you're saying, be specific: "I think you're playing it more like a comic commentary on the character. As far as I'm concerned, this person could exist in the real world." The actor may still not get it, or, worse yet, may be unable to play it differently, but more likely the actor will realize that he or she is playing it too comic and not straight enough. One thing you won't do is to tell the actors, "faster, slower, louder," because that's just giving them end results that don't help them with character or with understanding the "why" of things. (Of course, there are always exceptions. If someone is speaking too softly on the set, you can ask him to speak louder because the microphone isn't picking up what he's saying. He probably won't ask you for "motivation" for that instruction.)

Some of the hardest things to deal with are the smallest. An actor may understand exactly what the character is all about and be giving you a fine interpretation, but the reading of one or two lines may be wrong. The emphasis might be on the "*should*" in the sentence, for instance, "What should I be doing?" when you want it on the "I." From time immemorial we've been told not to give actors "line" readings. This is a good rule, because line readings are a mechanical tool, one that can easily be forgotten later on. In trying to change the above reading, then, you may want to suggest that the actor think of the line as asking what he can do to help, as opposed to what *others* can do. At this point, the reading may change or it may not. You can then give up your insistence on your version. Or, perhaps the actor will say, "For God's sake, what's wrong with the way I'm reading it?" and you will give him a line reading and he will say, "Oh, that's what you wanted. Why didn't you say so?"

Silly? I don't think so. It's worth trying to work actors or actresses around to your way of thinking through understanding first, and only resort to giving them a reading at the final moment. If you have time, that is.

Speaking of time, is there time for another read through? If so, do it, listening to see if your suggestions have made a difference, if they've been incorporated into the actors' thoughts. (Unlike the theater, where changes can be worked on over a few days' time, film and television actors have to incorporate them at once.) You talk to the continuity person. How long did the scenes run? You check this against your own guesses. Is a scene too long? Too short? How about the pace? Establish some guidelines with him or her, to be checked on later (during the shoot). If you're unhappy or unsure about something, stop and rectify it now. Is a scene wrong? Is some of dialogue wrong? You may want to cancel tomorrow's shooting of a scene or the next day's until you've rewritten or checked with the prop person or the producer. Don't get off on the wrong foot by shooting something that will then have to be corrected in the editing room, if a simple rewrite or new prop or costume will correct it. And don't be afraid to make changes at the last moment. If you're sure things could be better, take the time now to make them better. Give notes for tomorrow and the next day. Remind the actors that they won't be able to use one scene to prepare for the next, because everything will be shot out of sequence, so if they have any questions about pace or motivation, they're to ask you at any time.

After the rehearsal, it sometimes pays to get one or two actors aside and give them separate notes if you have something important to say. Often one or more actors may be out of kilter with the others or, conversely, have done something especially wonderful that you want them to keep. Singling them out for this kind of note is a reinforcement that will pay off when the time comes to shoot the scene.

Rehearsals, then, are a time for ironing out all the questions actors have, but they're also a time for getting a handle on the things that don't work in a script and pulling them out. It's fun to rewrite once you've heard actors do the script. It's fun, because it means that you're molding the script to the characters, creating a bond that's less and less artificial. Some lines shouldn't be changed, but many should. It would be wonderful to have the writer at the first rehearsal so that these changes can be in the writer's language, not yours, but that's not always possible. And, sometimes, it's not desirable. If you have a writer who is likely to say, "What's wrong with you? I think that's an easy line to say," then the whole value of having the writer there is lost.

Rehearsals are most valuable for giving the actors a chance to play together and find rhythms and paths to working together. This is not a mystical but a very practical matter. Two actors, or three, or four, have to play a scene together. They will play the scene in a "master shot," but also in close-ups with the camera and crew hanging over their shoulders. They will want to feel that the actors they're playing with are real characters, with whom they have real relationships. Their craft will help them do this, but having the opportunity to work with the actors over and over again *before* being on the set is a bonus, the value of which cannot be overlooked. It is rather like the rehearsals that go on in the theater that give us the feeling, when we leave, that these people have lived together. So, you will want to use rehearsals not just for line readings, not just for an understanding among all of you as to what is *meant* by the script, but also to create an "ensemble." That means that the real relationships between characters must be established, and you and they must feel comfortable with the pace and readings of everyone. This can mean working on everything from the simplest kind of disagreement over dialect, to the complex concept of whether or not two characters really love each other and how they can convey that without using words. Sometimes this is so crucial that you will want to work on this in small groups, away from the rest of the cast.

In addition to matters of dialogue, you will, of course, want to get the actors "on their feet." You will show them the movements you have planned for them and the movements you have planned for the camera. This is a good time for you to check those camera moves, by the way. (Don't be afraid to do the stereotypic thing of holding your fingers as if they were a movie frame and viewing through them. Let people laugh!) You will find that certain moves bother some of the actors. They won't seem real to them. Listen carefully. If the moves *do* bother them, there may be a good psychological reason. It may be that to move two lovers away from each other works for your camera, but is stupid for them. Don't get caught by your ego or your weeks of preparation. That's what rehearsals are for. On the other hand, if you think the move is important—that it shows the tension between the two lovers—then keep it and explain why to your actors. Rehearsals are also good times to establish your relationship with them. Later on, during shooting, you may have to use shorthand and forget some of the niceties; whatever personal relationships were established during rehearsals will come in handy.

None of this will be possible if you're just having a reading, and you'll miss a lot of important things. The sad fact is, in film and television, that rehearsing is a "bonus," which must seem strange to theater people, because rehearsals are *crucial* to them—so crucial that it's inconceivable how we can get along without them. (Looking at all the things you can accomplish with rehearsals, it's often inconceivable to me, too.) And, of course, you *shouldn't* have to get along without them. But very often you aren't given the time to have them, no matter how hard you fight.

TIME OUT

What is it *about*, if not the script and the actors? The producer's answer may be that actors in Hollywood have long ago gotten used to working on scripts, coming on to the set, and "just doing it." You answer that this accounts for a lot of the junk coming out of the film industry. He says, "Sure, but what about the good stuff?" And you think to yourself, "Yes, what about the good stuff? How does *anyone* manage to get a good film without rehearsal?" And the answer probably is good scripts, directors who pay attention to detail, and actors who have gotten used to the system, who work on scripts by themselves, knowing they'll have to come to the set and "do it." In fact, film acting is different from stage acting, and good actors know that there are many things to adapt to: the fact that they will have to repeat a line or a scene endlessly within the space of a few hours; that they don't "project" their voices to the thirteenth row center, but only as far as the microphone hanging over their head; that gestures and movement have to be held down; and that rehearsals are a bonus, not a given. Strangely, many actors have, indeed, learned how to "deliver" under these circumstances. Not that they're not grateful for a bona fide rehearsal, but they can still act without them.

For you, of course, it's another matter. You're a director of actors, not just shots, and you want and need your rehearsal so that you can make the film the way you want it to be. Period. Nothing makes up for real rehearsals.

SPECIAL EFFECTS AND PROPS

Some years ago, I needed a couple of dead ducks. They were to be carried at the waist of a hunter and figured in a close-up in which they would be swinging madly as the hunter ran. The prop man came to me a week before the shoot and told me that only domestic ducks were available without sending to England, so I suggested that he look for a bird that was available here and could be made to look like a duck. The day of the shoot, he asked me out to the garage of the house where we were on location and showed me the three "ducks" he had prepared. They were painted with makeup and feathers and looked like ducks to me. I didn't even want to know what they had been in their previous incarnations—or where he had gotten them!

This prop man was wonderful. Nothing called for in the script escaped his attention. Were the plants going to be the right height? Don't count on it. He'd have some "lifts" just in case. Did the rifle for the hunter have the right bore? Did I want him to shoot on camera? Then he'd have to get special shells that wouldn't be too loud for the microphone but that would give enough kick so the actor playing the hunter would look right. And so on. And this wasn't a difficult film, "prop-wise."

Property men and women used to be responsible for such "simple" special effects as bullets hitting into a doorframe around a gunfighter's head, or water draining out of a glass just sitting on a table. Today, with films such as *The Matrix*, or the almost commonplace *morphing* of body parts, major special effects are handled off the set, in postproduction, using computers. What can we say about such things here? Be prepared. Think ahead. If getting the right location is inherently important to your film, then realizing that a special effect or prop has to be invented or rigged up is doubly so. You wouldn't have included it in your script if it wasn't. From making a dog look like a wolf to blowing up the Taj Mahal to having a cigarette lighter that looks like a gun, prop and special effects people are crucial. But *your preparedness and your care in alerting them are equally so.* We all like to think of directing as having to do with shots and actors. Fine, that's the glamour end of it. It also has to do with all the things we've talked about in this chapter, which add up to lots of hard work, diligence, talking to craftspeople, and looking ahead, and nowhere is that more important than having the thoughtfulness to look for prop pitfalls and alerting the right people. In the budget in chapter 2, the property person was brought on early (look at the number of days). That's no accident. Being prepared for even the simplest shoot requires lots and lots of technical preparation.

What you have done up to now is extremely useful. You have conceived a film, from script through look. You have met with your team, and you have rehearsed with actors—we hope. But your many tasks, which have proceeded simultaneously, have only begun. What about the shots—the building blocks on which your film is actually *filmed*? In the next chapter, we take a close look at them.

6

Getting Ready (III): Shots and Setups

We come now to what many directors think of as the primary role of the craft—the shots. When I quoted Bruce Beresford earlier in this book, there was little doubt that he considered how the shots were planned to be a crucial part of the directorial art. I have spent a lot of time on other matters because I believe *them* to be equally important; but, certainly, what shots you are using, and how you will cut them together, is a huge part of directing.

In chapter 4, we discussed shots as part of an overall look, but now we need to get down to the nitty-gritty of how to plan them. You will be planning shots at the same time that you are addressing other issues. Because books are linear things, we must take each aspect as if it were performed in chronological order. The planning of shots and setups occurs at all stages of the production. "Setup" is the industry term for every time you move your camera and "set it up" somewhere else. It's a very important concept in filmmaking; its importance lies in a number of areas: (1) How many setups you need to make your film, that is, how many times you need to move your camera in order to get the number of shots you've planned; (2) How you plan your setups so as to spend the maximum amount of time *shooting* and the minimum moving your camera; and (3) How many setups a good crew can get in a day. The last is a kind of question a production manager will ask, but you can see how important it is to your work.

THE SHOTS

How many shots do you need? What are they? This is not the same question we asked in chapter 4, where our goal was to visualize the film. This is a much more mundane, much more technical matter, and yet it is important, because it impinges on the look of your film in a very direct way.

To some extent, this business takes us back to very elementary matters: the grammar of film. How are we to get from shot A to shot B? How many shots are needed to cut together a sequence?

The basic sequence of shots that everyone learns is: wide shot, medium shot, close shot. In general, any sequence can be cut together if there are as many shots as there are people. In other words, a scene with two people requires two shots. (This doesn't quite work when you get down to a single person, because you can't "cut together" a single shot, but otherwise it makes sense.) As you get up to a larger number of actors, say, five, you can actually cut together a scene with as few as three shots—a wide shot of all five, then a two-shot and a three-shot. Having said that, we really have said very little. What's possible is not necessarily attractive or creative. Are your shots matched? That is, do they bear some resemblance to each other? Look at this sequence: a close shot of one actor; next, a medium or wide shot of an actress; then back to the close shot of the first actor. This gives a certain impression that you may not intend to convey, namely, that the first character is more important than the second. So, if you're going to shoot a close shot and a medium one, you will want to shoot medium shots and close shots of both actors, giving a minimum of four shots for two people. And if you add ECUs, then that's six shots. And, if you think it's necessary, how about an "establishing" shot of some sort—seven. Or, possibly, two over-the-shoulder shots—now we're up to eight. There could be more, and often are! How many do you need?

This question refers us back to chapter 4 and what it is you're trying to convey, and how complex you need to be to do it. But you must think through not only the final shots you want to have in your film, but also the shots you need to shoot in order to be able to make choices about editing when the whole thing comes down to the editing room. In other words, a beginning director will think that he or she wants to have a tracking shot of two lovers, ending in a close shot on the man, and, so, will shoot such a shot. In the editing room, however, the editor wants to "intercut" a shot of the woman. And the editor may also want a shot of the two of them, without the move. If the

"Matched" pair of over-the-shoulder shots.

"Matched" close-ups

director has been so sure of what he or she wants that the other shots haven't been made, then the option isn't there. (This is called, "cutting in the camera.") Few directors are that certain of themselves, but many still don't take these shots—they forget, they don't think about it, they . . . ? So, you won't let that happen. You will write down all the shots, and you will keep in mind the basic "grammar" lessons and give yourself options in the editing room. But not too many options. Which brings us back to the basic question, How many shots do you need? Let's try another approach.

You have a limited amount of time on the set. You can't spend all day shooting the same scene over and over again. To take eight or ten different shots of a short scene, with all the fluffs and problems with camera moves, would probably tire your actors beyond repair and weary your producer's patience. What you actually do shoot will be a compromise between giving yourself all the options you might want in the cutting room, and skimping. The number of shots is not the only problem; variety is another, and also height, angle, and size.

Let's go back to our two lovers. They are seated on a couch, not quite certain whether or not to go to the bedroom in the background. In order to accentuate the bedroom, we need to see it, but if we shoot from a low angle at the lovers, the couch back will cut off the door to the bedroom—the enticement will be lost to the audience. So this wide shot, which includes the couch, the two lovers, and the door to the bedroom in the background must be from a fairly high angle. Then, if you wish, and you have a dolly or crane to help you, the camera can lower as it pushes in on the two-shot of the two lovers. This so-called combination shot gives you, in one "setup," two needed shots: a wide or "cover" shot and a medium two-shot. The two-shot, from a lower angle, is a little more romantic than if you shot down on the lovers; however, were they lying on the bed, a *high* two-shot, looking down at them, might be quite effective.

Next, you will probably want some kind of individual shots of the two, to be able to cut back and forth between them as they talk of their feelings and prepare for the move to the bedroom. Will these be two single shots or two over-the-shoulder shots? What considerations come up? You can't get extremely "tight" (that is, close) using over-the-shoulder shots because you have to keep a piece of the shoulder of the person in the foreground in the shot. If you want to have a passionate tight shot, you will probably want to make it two tight singles. On the other hand, if you are more interested in the continuing relationship between these two people, two over-the-shoulders might do. If the scene is very short, you could even "play" it in the medium two-shot you came to from the high "cover" shot that opened the scene, but that would mean you would have no way of cutting into the scene if there's a line flub and no way of changing the pace or timing of the scene in the editing room (because there are no other shots to

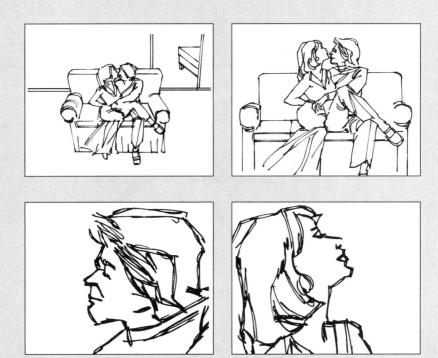

go to). So, in this case, your compromise could easily be the high shot, moving into a medium two-shot, followed by two over-the-shoulder shots or two singles. *Three* shots in all.

What about when the lovers do get up and go into the bedroom? How do you cover that? Again, there are many choices. You could move the camera around until it shoots from the doorway of the bedroom itself, seeing them on the couch in the background (this is often called a "reverse" shot) and then, when they arise and come toward the bedroom, they will be coming to camera, getting bigger and bigger until they pass under (over? by?) the camera and the shot ends (to be continued in the bedroom). You could shoot from the same high shot you started with, allowing them to go into the background, keeping them in sight all the way into the bedroom and to the bed, but keeping them small in the shot so as to be a little more "discreet." You could also track the camera with them as they get up and move into the bedroom, paying strict attention to the passionate looks and murmurs you couldn't (realistically) hear from either of the other two shots. Or, finally, you could hold onto the couch in the medium shot, letting them go out of the frame entirely, and wait for the bedroom door to "click" closed offscreen. Whichever of these choices you make, it is obvious that you must *have in mind* the eventual effect of the different shots, the effect you want to create, the time it will take to make each shot, how many options you want to give yourself in the cutting room and, yes, how many options the editor and producer will want in the cutting room.

But it is not just any old option you want in the final edit. Some shots just won't cut together. When we talk of different size shots, different angles, and different heights, we are talking about "grammar" again. Just as is true of the English language, film language has rules of its own. Some of those rules are made to be broken by innovators, but some are certainly made to be kept by beginners. For instance, I have made reference to "cover" shots, and I have suggested that these are wide shots. They are more than that; they are shots used to "cover" yourself, shots that allow something to go wrong and everything to come out all right in the end. What is it that goes wrong? Very often, it is the inability to get two shots to cut together the way you want them to. This can be for a wide variety of reasons, but let's take just two of them.

GRAMMAR

Generally, you cannot cut together two shots of the *same person* if the shots are the *same size*. Two single shots or two medium shots of the same person from the same height and angle don't go together in the cutting room without getting what we call a "jump cut,"[12] whereas a medium shot cuts very nicely to a close shot. This grammatical problem is solved by using two or three different shots, usually a wide one, a medium one, and a close one, and cutting them together. In beginning film classes, I tell students that the best way to make sure that shots cut together is to change not only the size of the shot, but the angle as well. In the early days of film, directors took their wide shot,

---

[12] In news interviews you sometimes see the shot jump a little as a portion of the interview, filmed in one continuous shot, is eliminated.

their medium shot, and their close shot (when they took the latter at all) from the same height and angle—usually straight on. Not in today's' films, where the wide shot may be from a high or low angle, the medium shots from raked angles, and the close shots from more varied angles. This new approach solves not only the problem of grammar (eliminating jump cuts and providing a smooth, varied series of shots), but helps eliminate problems of mismatching as well.

MISMATCHING

When the same scene or series of lines is played over and over again in different size shots, actors, directors, continuity people, and camera people can make mistakes, which often take the form of mismatches. A hat that was taken off on one line in the medium shot is taken off on a different line in the close-up. A person walks or moves an arm earlier in the wide shot than in the medium shot. The angle of the head is up here, down there. You don't notice this in most films, precisely because the changing size *and* angle of the various shots throw your attention *off* the mismatch and *onto* the action. So, one of the reasons for the variety of angle, height, and size of shots is to eliminate the mismatches that may have occurred when you came to them in the cutting room.

Another solution to mismatches is the "cover" shot: a wide shot that is wide enough to allow almost *any* action to go on, and to which you can cut when there aren't enough varied closer shots to cut to or when a mismatch on those closer shots can't be solved any other way.

Another way to help your editor handle mismatches is to "overlap" action. You will be shooting various angles of each scene (close-ups, medium shots, low shots, two-shots, and so forth). Each time you do so, make sure you repeat some of the action of the previous shot, especially at the beginning and end of the new one. For instance, a boy enters a room and moves to a couch, sitting on it and opening a newspaper he finds there. You may shoot such a scene, first, in a wide shot, showing everything, then in a medium shot as he reaches the couch, and finally in a close shot as he is seen reading. If each new shot repeats *none* of the action of the previous one, you may have a difficult time *matching* action, but if the medium shot repeats some of the previous action and the close-up repeats all of the previous action (that is, as much as can be seen from a close-up) your editor will have some options.

By the way, let your actors not only overlap action, but enter shots *cleanly*. Start with an empty frame, and end with an empty frame when they exit. Even though you obviously can't use an entrance to the couch in both a medium and a close shot, having clean entrances and overlapped action gives your editor an option. All "coverage"[13] of a scene should be similarly handled. I don't mean shooting every bit of action in a scene in every shot—an obvious waste of money and time. For example, the entire ten-minute dialogue should not be shot in wide, medium, close-up, and ECUs—that's overdoing it! But I do mean that *some* action should be overlapped in *every* shot. Then, when your editor is worried about mismatches of speed, movement, or behavior, the repeated action allows him or her to edit at a point that *minimizes* the mismatch. If you shoot without overlapping action, there are no options!

Of course, all this technical talk should not obscure the fact that shots are to be chosen *primarily* for the *effect* they give, not just to solve grammatical problems. The fact that you will want to shoot a variety of cover shots—especially for quick, low-budget films, where planning isn't as feasible as on more carefully organized films—gives you a wonderful chance to pick an angle and view for that shot that *also* serves you aesthetically.

The lovers go off into the bedroom; we shoot from a high angle. The door closes. We imagine them going to the bed. Our camera pans left, and we discover a window. Out the window is a brook. By the brook, two kittens are playing. The comment being made is that our two lovers are nothing more than playmates, ingenuous children. On the other hand, tilt up with your camera and discover the ornate chandelier above our heads and then cut from that chandelier to the candles on the table of the poor family who lives across the tracks, and another kind of comment is made.

And so it goes. Long shots can be beautiful, ornate, symbolic, delicate, panoramic, or simply "covering yourself." Technique serving the cause of the story, the story serving the cause of technique.

In chapter 4, we talked about an argument between a man and a

---

[13] This "coverage" is different from the cover shots just described. It means all the shots you take to get a scene from a variety of angles and in a variety of sizes. It's a crucial filmic concept: that you must cover every scene sufficiently to make editing possible later on.

woman. In this chapter, we talked about a love affair being consummated offscreen. We also talked, earlier, about storyboards and how useful it can be to sketch out the ideas you have for shots. There are two basic ways to do this: the storyboard and the "schematic" (a kind of line drawing that allows you to see where the camera is going to be in relationship to actors, how it moves, and so on). Let's take a look at a few schematic drawings and the same moves in storyboard form. This will give you an idea how to vary the basic shots we've been discussing, and two ways to visualize them, not only for the sake of variety but in order to accomplish your many artistic goals.

Using the same two people, let's look at Drawing 1. Here they are in a two-shot as the argument begins. We are going to let the woman, swinging her arms, move about the man, who is fairly stationary. As she moves, the camera has a number of choices. It can pan with her, eliminating the man entirely (Drawing 2); it can let her leave the scene, staying with the man (Drawing 3). Choice 2 gives us the "single" shot we would probably want to take of him anyway; the first one gives us the "single" on her. Another choice is to let the camera dolly to the *left* as it pans to the right, thus keeping her in the screen—facing us—and keeping him in the screen—with his back to us—and creating an over-the-shoulder shot (Drawing 4). Now as she walks back the other way, the camera can track to the *right* as she moves to the left, giving us a different over-the-shoulder onto her (Drawing 5). If the woman holds still for a while, and the man's dialogue is important, you will want to shoot an additional over-the-shoulder shot "onto" him (Drawing 6).

Or, if the desire is mainly to keep the shot open, with the woman's moves being predominant, you may let the camera dollies handle most of the scene, and "punch up" the medium moving shot with two "singles," when the woman settles down.

As you can see, it's hard to get in close on either person when one or the other is moving, forcing the other to turn (away from camera). But when they are static, it's wonderful to get in close, cutting back to the wider, moving shot for energy. Two over-the-shoulder shots are also useful, allowing us to have some movement in them (because they are wider than close shots), but giving us more detail of faces than the wider shot, which shows the woman circling the man. Complicated? Only a little. A lot of directors would prefer to keep the man and woman static the whole time, thus making it much easier to shoot—no camera movement, no tricky timing of lines and moves—but how boring!

Let's have an ending to that scene—in storyboard form. (Note the schematics next to the storyboard.) After a short period in which they argue with each other, he decides to walk out. This can be very dramatic, since he has seemed to be the passive one in this scene. Look at Drawing 7. We have this choice: he simply walks out to the right, leaving her looking after him (the look is *left* to right) in a medium shot.

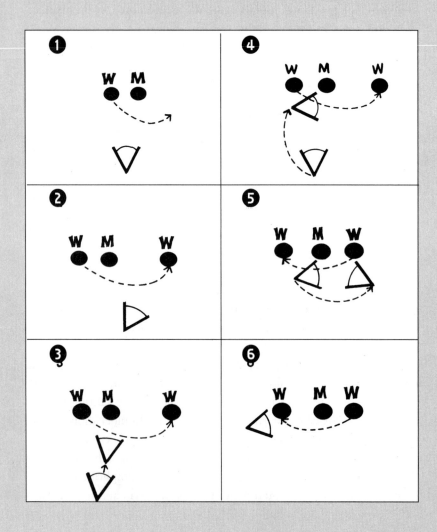

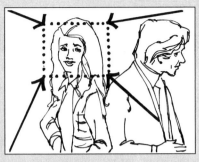

7. He leaves the shot and we "push" in on her.

8.

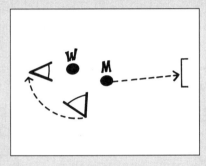

8A.

9. Or—see schematic—camera tracks left and shows him leaving in background. Then, as she turns to us we have a big close-up of her unhappy face. Some people would think this is a more elegant way to shoot the scene. It's your choice.

After he leaves, the camera moves in on her to a close shot. For variation, after he leaves, the camera moves quickly to the *left,* that is, behind her, showing him going (Drawings 8 and 8A). Now, she turns to us, indicating that she is rejecting him (Drawing 9). Or, she could do the turn first, so that as he leaves, we track left, showing him leaving in the background and her in a close shot in the foreground, with tears in her eyes (that's why she turned away).

The simple move that ends or begins a scene is not mise-en-scène directing per se, but it does give you some indication of why directors

10. The camera is shooting up from low angle.

11.

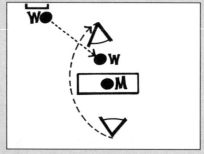

11A. Now—it sweeps around to the left as woman walks toward man (careful, don't hit her!) and gets an over-the-shoulder shot as he turns on the couch.

12. Or—he sits waiting in a wide shot.

13. . . . as she enters and he rises, we cut to a closer shot.8A.

like the fluid camera move. Let's look at another scene. Our two lovers—having reconciled their differences—are going to meet. He is seated, waiting for her. As she enters in the background, he rises to meet her (Drawing 10). We have a number of choices here. The camera must, at any rate, rise on the dolly to "carry" both of them in the shot. (The need to "carry," that is, to keep both people equally or aesthetically framed, is a constant worry when people sit or stand, or when a camera, on a low or high angle, moves closer to people.) Now, suppose the camera were to move to the left and—as he turns to greet her—move into an over-the-shoulder shot "onto" him (Drawings 11 and 11A). This movement creates a sense of excitement that a simple "cut" (to her or to him) could not and would not do. Whether it's too swift and complicated a move is something you can decide only by trying.

A simpler, also effective move, one traditionally done, would be to "tighten" (that is, dolly in) on the two of them as she comes down to the couch and he rises. An old-fashioned way to do this is to take a wide shot of him sitting there (Drawing 12), then film a separate shot of the two of them when she comes in, but tighter (Drawing 13). Not only does this take more time (two shots instead of one), but it's just not as attractive a way of making films. The earlier move emphasizes their union and is more fluid. An even more contemporary way of shooting this scene would be to use a very low angle as he sits waiting, waiting, waiting (Drawing 14). Then, in the background of his shot, we see her blurred image appear—blurred because we're using a "long" lens, with low depth-of-field (Drawing 15). He rises, and we show her coming around the end of the couch, holding the two of them in a very tight over-the-shoulder shot (Drawings 16 and 16A).

VARIATIONS. CHOICES. THAT'S WHAT IT'S ALL ABOUT

Here's still one more look at this business of combining a move with a series of static shots. Again, we're looking at the end of a sequence. Our two lovers are having dinner, alone. He is at one end of the table, she at the other. During the dinner, we have resorted to a fairly standard set of shots. Wide shot of the table, with each one seated at the extremes of the frame (Drawing 17), and close shots of each as they look off camera at the other (Drawings 18 and 19). But as the scene ends, she rises (Drawing 20), and we pull back from her close shot, pan

14. Or—he sits waiting in a close shot...

15...and she appears (slightly out of focus because of the "long" lens) behind him. [End caption]

16.

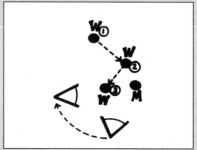

16A. In a tricky camera move—he rises and turns partway toward her as she comes down around the end of the couch. More choices!

with her as she walks to his end of the table, and push in on a tight two-shot as she hugs him from behind (Drawing 20A). We could, of course, have waited, let her exit her close-shot, and simply picked her up as she walked into his close shot, but that's not as fluid, or as meaningful, as following her on the move to him. There are, of course, dozens of variations on these themes. Your D.P. will have some ideas, but you should think of which moves make sense, and when you want to use them, how they keep the sequence of shots from becoming boring, and how they add meaning to your sequence.

Now that you have all these shots down, prepare a shot list. Your script is marked up, but that's a fifty-page document. Make a list—to carry with you at all times—of those shots that you *must* have. This

17.

18.

19.

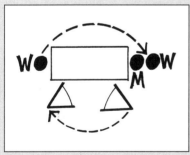

20. Here, the camera "echoes" the woman's movement, swinging left as she goes right. Because we are watching the woman, the wide swing in movement of the camera is barely noticeable. We end up with the shot above and then move in (not shown on the schematic) for a tighter two-shot.

20A.

means special shots for special effects; it means those long "cover" shots we discussed above; but it also means the everyday, mundane, bread-and-butter shots you intend to get. Make notes as to which ones you *must* have and which you can eliminate. This shot list is a very valuable tool. You may have the best memory in the world, but when it comes to the pressure of time and your script is all marked up with other notations (how the actor sloughed off that line and how you want it read, for instance), you need this list of essential shots in front of you.

SETUPS

There will be limited time in which to get your essential shots, so how can you be efficient? Answer: by limiting the number of setups you use.

Let's take a crazy example to illustrate what *not* to do. Here we are at the dinner table, with our two lovers. The camera is framed on the man as he asks the woman whether she wants to go out afterward or whether they're going to stay in. We frame them in a two-shot (Setup 1). We know that we want his next line to be in a close shot—or maybe a medium. So we move the camera (Setup 2) to his end of the table, moving all the lights at the same time. He says his line. We now know that—in editing—we'd use *her* medium or close shot, so we move the camera and lights to her end of the table (Setup 3). Obviously, this is ridiculous. We aren't going to change setups on every line. We know that we'll be shooting three major shots, so we have three major setups: the two-shot and the two close shots (or two medium shots). Fair enough. But do we always have the same number of setups as shots? Not necessarily. Here's an example.

We finish the scene with our two lovers. A few scenes later, they are again in the dining room. This time, in a bitter argument. Why not get the wide shot of that *next* scene while our camera and lights are set for *this* scene's wide shot? Why not, indeed? That would be a saved setup. (It's easier and faster to change costumes than it is to change camera and lights.) And, while we're at it, why not do the close shots from the *next scene* while we're doing the close-ups from *this* scene? There are good reasons why not: here are two actors, trying their best to surmount the problems of doing close shots, with a camera staring at them from a few feet away, and delivering the lines and the emotions of a complex scene; and you're going to ask them to do the lines from *another* scene before they've completed this one? This is an example of where saving a setup is *not* worth it.

But how do you decide when it's worth it and when it's not? When a setup can "grab" some shots that don't require actors to do double somersaults, but where lighting and grip time can be substantially saved, then it's worth doing two in one. When, on the other hand, a setup saved is a scene harmed, *don't*. In general, moving lights and camera all the way to the other side of the set (reversing directions) is a long undertaking. To get a shot or two from this side of the set while lights are here can save precious time that you need for rehearsing or for that seventeenth "take" later on. If in doubt, ask your D.P. "How long would it take to move lights?" Tell him or her your dilemma: you want to get the close-ups while the actors are "in" the scene (emotionally tuned), but don't want to waste a lot of time later on by moving lights back again for another wide or medium shot, which *could* be gotten now. The D.P. will assess the situation and tell you which will cause more trouble: moving twice or getting the shot in this setup and risking disturbing the actors.

Your production manager and your A.D. will *not* make these decisions for you. You will be expected to come to the set with your mind made up about precisely which shots you will do, and when. This is a technical responsibility that you have to shoulder, and I can assure you it's one for which many directors have gotten good (or bad) marks from producers and the crew. Look at it from their point of view. If they have to move lights and camera back and forth unnecessarily, they are going to think of you not only as disorganized, but as thoughtless. On the other hand, you don't want to waste time with more setups than are needed, so planning just which shots get made first and which second, and how many can be shot from this setup (maybe with a few minor adjustments) makes sense.

It's not always an easy decision, I'll grant that. After all, your primary objective is to get scenes that are well acted and well shot. Judging whether you should use a setup for two or more shots and risk confusing the actors isn't easy. Conversely, there are times—especially outdoors with long shots, where moving camera and crew can be arduous—when you know immediately how to "knock off" two, three, or maybe four shots from the same basic setup. And if you've got this all planned beforehand, labeled in your script, *and on your shot list,* then you're gaining not only shooting time, but *thinking* time on the set as well.

Where does all this leave "spontaneity"? This is a question asked by students who think that all this planning puts them in a bind of being committed to too much. On the contrary. Having things well-organized and planned allows a director to leave the path, stray far and wide (given time and money and a cooperative crew), and return to the same path. Sure, you can be spontaneous "all over the place" if you wish to, but without some skeleton to your film, spontaneity is a risky, if not stupid business. John Cassavetes loved improvisation, but he began his films with carefully thought-out story lines. His improvs were woven in and around strong plans. For beginning directors, spontaneity often seems to me to be a way of escaping the careful planning that, in fact, gives *freer* reign to creative ideas.

Give a little, get a little. Some of the previous discussion will appear absurd to low-budget filmmakers. They don't have the option of using a dolly every time they want to make a shot more exciting. Similarly, directors with even a modicum of experience in creating moving shots will rightly note that they take a tremendous amount of time to set up, to light, and to rehearse. One answer to that criticism is that a complicated dolly shot may in fact *save* time—by combining two or three shots in one smooth move. But that doesn't eliminate the fact that time and money will, once again, be a very important determinant of when—and if—you get to use the kind of mise-en-scène or simple dolly shots you want.

This is it. Your preparation time is over. You've selected a script, rewritten it, cast it, met with the proper teammates, chosen your look, mood, style, emotional content, and shots. You've had a rehearsal, and you're ready to shoot. Well, not quite. In the next chapter, we take a look at the possibility that all this preparation is still not enough. You need to take into consideration that—well-prepared as you may be, or *think* you may be—all may not go quite as planned.

But, first, it's time for intermission while we change reels.

AN INTERMISSION

Some Thoughts about Time

"HURRY UP PLEASE ITS TIME," says the barkeep in T. S. Eliot's *The Waste Land,* but it could be a line from the daily life of any and all directors. From the moment you arise in the morning (early, on shoot days) to the moment you fall into bed, *time is crucial.*

Overtime: After eight hours (or ten, depending on the contract) the crew gets paid time and a half for every hour it works. This adds up.

Double time: After another eight hours without interruption, the crew gets *double* its original pay scale for every hour. This really adds up.

Golden time: There are two kinds. The first is what happens to the pay scale after sixteen hours of straight work, when the pay is *three* hours for every hour worked. That adds up unbelievably fast! The second kind refers to the beautiful time of day when the sun is about to set, and everything is cast with a hue of the most splendid golden light; it's a wonderful time to shoot. The problem with the second kind of golden time is that keeping a crew around just to film it can be very expensive, leading to the first kind of golden time.

Lunch time: That's after five hours of work, usually, and everyone welcomes it.

Time to get to location: This is the time that production managers and producers worry about. How long will it take to get to the location site from the motel? Is the P.M. paying for too much travel time and too little work time?

Rehearsal time: is something you probably won't get without fighting hard for it.

Time for "one more take": Before lunch, before a coffee break, before the end of the day, before overtime, before golden time, there *may* be time for one more take.

How much time will it take to build the sets? To get the costumes? To set up for lunch? To strike the sets? To take the costumes back? It's all money.

Ninety feet per minute, twenty-four frames per second—or, for 16mm film, thirty-six feet per minute, twenty-four frames per second. That's time, too. The length of your film.

Time pressure: The producer's on your back to get more setups in each shooting day. Or to finish before the bad weather comes. Or before it costs too much money. Or before the actress has to go back to the Coast. Or—something else!

Time before the rough cut will be ready: Time it takes to get the print out of the lab. Time the editors have been working already!

"You've got five minutes before we have to break. Can you do it?" "You've got ten days for this film. Can you make it?"

No time: For a makeup check before we do this take. For going to the bathroom. To take the actors aside and give them a pep talk. For fooling around!

Wasted time: You sit and watch the grips walk in and look around, not sure where the first setup is because the D.P. or the A.D. or the P.M. didn't tell them. You watch it take two hours for the first shot, when the last shot of the day is accomplished in twenty minutes. You listen as the A.D. tells a joke and wastes your precious time.

HURRY UP PLEASE ITS TIME

7

Getting Ready (IV):
When It All Goes Wrong

It's always good to be prepared for the worst. Here's a selection of horrors.

Your lead actor gets sick. The HMIs don't arrive and are needed for your first shot. It rains. The producers say you're overbudget and can't allow you your extra day's shoot. The carefully planned shot you spent so much time on doesn't work, and the crew is waiting for your orders. An actor turns out to be half as capable as you thought he was, and twice as ornery. You can't remember what you wanted to shoot in this far corner of the cottage you've all hiked to. The video monitor goes out and no one can fix it. Everything's going very slowly today and you're not going to get to rehearse anything. The dolly was supposed to hold the video camera you rented, but it doesn't, and you're already halfway to location.

All of these examples make it clear that Murphy's Law operates with a vengeance in film and television. During the weeks and months prior to a shoot, everyone begins to believe that things will go as planned. When they don't, some directors go crazy. This chapter is about some of the disasters that could happen, and also about preparing yourself to deal with them and others like them. Knowing about disasters that may occur tomorrow allows you to prepare for them today, when you're not under so much pressure. But this chapter is also a potpourri of suggestions for ways to organize, to be ready for any kind of shoot, whether it goes smoothly or over a rocky road.

Let's take things one at a time and see if we can find a way around some of these problems.

Your lead actor gets sick. The solution depends on when it happens. If it's before the shoot, you may have time to recast. Did you keep your notes on your casting readings? Can you remember who your second choice was? If you don't want to recast, ask the producer to postpone the shoot. He should have insurance that will cover the costs. If this happens during the shoot and you've shot scenes with the lead actor already, you'll *have* to postpone the shoot or "shoot around the character," a phrase denoting filming scenes that the A.D. has planned to be shot without actors or without that *particular* actor. This is one of the reasons it pays to have that shot list we talked about in chapter 6.

The HMIs don't arrive. Here you are in the big crowd scene—the one that takes place with dozens of extras in bright sunlight. Without those lamps, you can't shoot. Period. This is your producer's problem, or your P.M.'s, but it can also affect you because your shooting schedule is limited by the money your producer has to spend. Again, if you have thought through your shooting plan for the day, you may be able to do a lot of close-ups, using alternate lighting instruments, without needing the "firepower" of the HMIs. Ask your D.P. Between him and the gaffer, you may be able to concoct a half day's shoot of just close-ups. If possible, use your extras[14] *some* part of the day, so they won't get bored from standing around. Inform your P.M. of your plans as soon as you can, so he or she can get things rolling. Don't wait for your production manager to tell you what to shoot; keep the creative initiative in your camp. And, above all, don't panic. They're only a couple of big lights.

Rain. If it starts raining in the middle of the night, your P.M. or your first A.D. will take care of things, letting everyone know which "cover set" (meaning what has already been planned for use in case of bad weather) is to be used. If it rains while you are on location, a lot will depend on the sound problems and the lights you have available. If all the shots were to be outdoors in the sun, sit down and use the time to work on tomorrow's script. But you just might think of what would happen if that particular scene were shot in the rain. Does it have to match any other scene (you know, a character walks out of the rain and into a scene that's already been shot when she was bone dry),

---

[14] There's more about handling extras in chapter 8.

or can it stand alone? You might have a very interesting scene if it were shot in the rain, and you could never repeat it again if you tried. In Hollywood, it costs a lot of money to order rain!

The producers say you're out of dough and can't allow you your extra day's shoot. First of all, this rarely happens like that. You usually get more notice. Secondly, there are few producers who are so ruthless they just tell you that's it, without giving you their suggestion as to what you can cut. But—assuming the worst—there are a number of things you can do to prepare for this kind of eventuality: (1) Make sure important scenes aren't held to the last few days of a shoot. (2) Think in advance of what you would cut (that is, not shoot at all) if you *had* to. This isn't easy, but it's a marvelous exercise back at the script rewrite stage. It helps sharpen your idea of what's crucial to the script, and it is also important in an eventuality such as this. What will happen to you, if you're skillful and lucky, is that you will find some shots or even a scene that can be eliminated; you will bargain with the producer, ask for another half a day, and come in looking like a hero or heroine. If you're unlucky, and have left things to too late, then you may have to "save it in the cutting room" or wait until the producer solves the problem for you. At any rate, as you will see in chapter 10, there are all sorts of problems that you *didn't* know about that get solved in post-production. At least this one you know about now, as terrible as it is.

That carefully planned shot doesn't work and the crew is waiting not so patiently for your orders. Of all the complaints leveled against directors, none strikes home so much as the one that goes, "He wasn't organized. We had to sit around all day waiting for him." Organization is important, but so is creativity, and, in the end, *that* may override the simple ability to organize. What organization *does* give you is the ability to plan your scenes and your shots, and the knowledge of *how* things fit together: close shots, wide shots, dolly shots, process shots, and so on. It also allows you to know, in advance, everything you're going to do; and it gives you that nice long list (that you tuck into your script and your briefcase and your spare pants) with dozens of shots that can be picked up when time allows. But what organization does *not* give you is the certainty that a shot will work.

Let's say you're on location and you've planned a tracking shot up a hillside, with your two main actors meeting the dolly halfway, then moving out to a barn in the distance, and the dolly moves with them.

This is an important shot because it gives the audience the emotional attachment to the couple they need to care passionately about if, say, one dies in the end. Now, for some aesthetic or technical reason, it just doesn't work. No matter how organized you are, it's your ability to think on your feet that will stand you in good stead here. It's your understanding of the meaning of the scene, what is needed for conveying that meaning, and the alternative shots that can be used. But here you are on location, where everything looks different. Silly things like the height of your actors, the color of the sky, and your memory of the scene can interfere with doing the shot the way you wanted; it doesn't just have to be problems with the dolly. Walk away from everyone. Take your time. What may seem like hours to the crew may only be minutes. It's your film, your shot. Recompose things and forget about what people say. If you are truly organized and truly creative then it doesn't matter how impatient your crew gets. What is crucial is that you not lose an important scene because something didn't go right. Of course, the more you've planned alternative shots in advance, and the more you've thought about potential disasters, the better off you are.

That actor isn't half as capable as you thought, but he is twice as ornery. This is not as rare a circumstance as you might imagine. It's also one of the cases where an immediate discussion with your teammates can pay off. You've been to the dailies, and you and your producer have seen the scenes that don't work. Ask the producer what he or she thinks. Any suggestions as to what you should do? If it's the acting ability that's at stake here and not your directorial capability, then you and the producer share equal blame (you cast it together) and should share responsibility for solving the problem.

Solutions? You might cut some of the lines and some of the scenes for that actor, shifting them to others. As for the orneriness, have the producer talk to the actor's agent. That often straightens things out. If it's a low-budget production and you're in charge of everything, take the actor aside and ask him if something is getting in the way of your relationship. This may not work if the actor is aware that his performance is terrible and he's being difficult *because* of that awareness, but it just might. Of course, if the actor is an important character, you do have some scenes that can't be cut. Think about the script. Is it possible to "play" more of the scenes off the leading lady, or off a subsidiary character, to use more reaction shots when you edit? Finally, stop thinking of the actor as a trained performer, and think of him as either an amateur or a student. Treat him that way, with the kind of helpful hints and techniques used for students. (Remember, I suggested that training as an actor yourself was useful?) It may all come to naught, but at least you weren't sitting on your hands. It's interesting, though, that almost any other problem can be solved *except* bad acting, which is why casting is generally thought to be such an important part of doing a film.

The video monitor blows. This situation is symptomatic of any one of the more than two hundred electronic or mechanical problems that can arise on a shoot. Some of them simply require that everyone sit down very patiently and wait until a magician-technician solves it. But even that time can be used fruitfully. In chapter 5 I said that you might end up not having any rehearsal time because so many productions are short on the money that rehearsals require. Well, now is a wonderful time to rehearse. The actors are here, the crew is here, everyone's being paid while some monstrous electronic failure occurs. Use the time for rehearsal.

In actual fact, the particular electronic gremlin I chose to use in this paragraph is *not so* monstrous. You can do without the monitor. Why? Because in the old days they didn't have "video assist" (the video monitor that is tied in to the film camera so a director can see exactly what the camera sees *during* the take and in *replay*). A director had to trust that the cameraman and DP were right that the take was okay technically, and a director had to trust his or her own instinct that the acting was good. No replay. Only retakes. And in video, many of the early news and documentary shoots were carried on without monitors because they were too cumbersome to bring. Directors watched the playback in the eyepiece of the camera, and while I think every video director should watch the scene on a monitor, when the monitor goes out, it's not a disaster. Trust your crew, trust your instincts, and watch the replay in the eyepiece. Inconvenient? Sure, but it's not a disaster.

Everything is going slowly, making it impossible for you to get to rehearse anything. Well, you didn't expect rehearsals anyhow, did you? Just a reading *and* a quiet run-through prior to the camera crew. Now here come the producer and the P.M., telling you that there just isn't enough time because someone else screwed up. All right, joking aside, what's happened is that because of some technical matters or because makeup took too long, you're going to have to take this scene without rehearsal. What do you do?

If you can't rehearse . . .

First, you alert your actors.

Second, use your camera rehearsal—that time normally reserved for the technical team to get things right—to run your actors through their lines. Normally, actors "walk through" camera rehearsals, because they're stop-and-go sorts of things. Have the cast on their toes for this one.

Third, be alert for lighting changes. Almost every scene has to have its lighting corrected once the camera has "run" it. Use this time for a bona fide rehearsal off the set. And, once you're back on set, don't let makeup and hair, gaffers and grips get in the way. Run the scene once again.

Finally, be aware that the first time through a scene is normally a "rehearsal" anyhow. No one really expects you to do a take that can be used the first time you "run" a scene with everything in place. So, there you are: "no rehearsals," but you slipped three or four in, didn't you?

The pacing seems wrong and you can't verify this with your editor. Why should the pacing be wrong, and why can't you tell? This involves something we only touched on before: the fact that all your shooting will be "out of sequence." This means, in the simplest terms, that for logistical reasons, scenes are shot when they best suit your camera, your lighting, your A.D., your P.M., and your producer, but not you or your actors. Of course, some of this makes basic sense; you shoot all the shots inside Set One before moving on to Set Two; you shoot shots pointing in one direction before moving all the lights and shooting in another direction—within reason. But the result of this is that you will shoot Scene 6a and then not shoot Scene 6b until three days later. The actors can't remember what they were doing in 6a and neither can you. How fast were they walking when they left Scene 6a for the outdoor scene in 6b? Were their hats in their left hands? How fast were they talking? To whom?

Pace is an all-important item. You will have thought about it often during your plotting of the shoot. The first time was when you were working on the length of scenes and the appropriateness of dialogue in your script. You will have thought out how your cast would read the scenes. Were they fast, slow, with a change of pace in the middle? Why that pace and not another? Once you set the pace within a scene, then you will want to establish pace *between* scenes. If all scenes are the same length and the same speed of playing, your audience will become quickly bored. Scenes that abut each other demand a *different* pace. Comedy demands one kind of pace, mystery another. But when did you establish with the actors this mystical "pace"? During rehearsal, of course. It is important that the pace within scenes be maintained. You can imagine how strange it would be for a close shot to be played at three-fourths the speed of the master. This reduces your options for editing and can make the scenes seem jerky. For the most part, like a good conductor, your internal rhythmic sense or memory, and that of your actors, will hold you in good stead. If not, talk to others on the set.

Talk it over with your continuity person. He or she will have not only made a notation as to how fast a scene ran but will have a very good idea whether your pace is being maintained, because of all people on the set, the continuity person will have been *listening* very carefully. Second, talk it over with the mixer, who also has been listening and will have an idea how the pace of this close-up matches the pace of yesterday's medium shot. Third, ask your D.P. Because of watching each scene carefully, he or she may have a notion of the pace. Finally, and only as a last resort, ask your actors. The reason you don't want to discuss pace with them, is that this brings the scene down to a rather technical matter. You want them to act on many levels. To be conscious of speed alone is to reduce the scene to a level that may harm the way it plays.

But, above all, keep in mind that pace is one of the ways that a movie progresses from scene to scene. Be prepared.

The point of this chapter is that all crises should be expected, no matter how bizarre. After all, Murphy's Law states that "If something can go wrong, it will." How much better to be prepared and have everything go right, than to be unprepared and have something go wrong. There is no god of film who guarantees you a smooth shoot. Your preparedness is your own responsibility.

The Shoot

You wake up early and know that today is quite different from all the other days you've awakened early. Yesterday, you spent four hours reading through the script with the actors. They sounded okay. Today, you start shooting. What's it going to be like? What will the succeeding days be like? In this chapter, I try to describe the character of that first shooting day, and also some of the things to look out for as the production progresses. If I miss some of them, it's because each project is different from the last; each script, each team brings its own joys, and its own problems.

You feel butterflies in your stomach. You've arrived on the set early—6:00 A.M.—because you think something may be going on that needs your attention, but when you get there the donuts and coffee are just being set out and the Teamsters (drivers) are clustered around the table. Nothing else seems to be happening. The producer smiles at you and you smile back, but he or she has other things to do and disappears through a side door. The D.P. arrives. You've already agreed on the first shot, and the D.P. goes about directing lights and telling the grip where to put the dolly track.

TIME OUT

What did you tell the A.D. about your first shot? What did you pick? In general, the first shot on any shoot should be a simple one. Since, almost without exception, it takes twice as long to get a shot at the beginning of the day as it does at the end of the day, you should pick a shot on the first day that is even easier than most first shots. But the shot shouldn't be an unimportant one. You want, in other words, to convince the cast and crew that you can accomplish something important right off the bat, but you also want to make sure that it's accomplished easily and speedily. This is a show of bravura on your part, a clever move to illustrate your capability; it also allows the actors and crew a chance to start slowly. You already know that you won't be shooting anything in sequence, because most scenes are shot in the order that makes sense for the logistics of the production, so don't pick a scene to begin with that requires a great deal of emotional preparation from the previous scene; your actors won't have anything to base their performance upon. Choose the first shot in a scene, something with a medium tone to it—not high comedy, not intense drama. You notice that I assume you will be able to pick the scene. Technically, your P.M. or A.D. will have chosen shots for every day of the shoot, but you will get a chance to go over the board with them, making suggestions in those areas that bother you.

TIME IN

On this first day of the shoot, be aware that all your actors are experiencing some of the same butterflies as you; even your crew may have some problems. I like to think that every time I start a new production I'm going to remember this, and I'm going to make a nice little speech to my crew before we begin. In practice, this never seems to happen, mainly because each member is off doing what he or she is supposed to be doing. But, oh, the first setup drags on and on. Lights have to be pulled over or off the truck; the dolly has a leak in its hydraulic system; a costume is too bright and has to be changed. (Of course, much of this could have been foreseen and forestalled, but often isn't.) The result of these delays is not only that you're behind schedule before you start, but that you and your actors are tense. Finally, the "first team" (the actors, as opposed to stand-ins) is called. Lights are adjusted for the fifth time, and a camera rehearsal is begun. Not surprisingly, it doesn't look or sound right, which is why the simplest possible shot should be selected for first—the simpler the shot, the fewer the changes necessary to get it right. An actor's voice has taken on a hard edge from waiting around; you can't see the clock you placed behind the actors, even though you *need* it to be visible. Things like that.

Even though I didn't make a big deal about losing your TV monitor a few pages back, that doesn't mean it isn't crucial to check shots through the camera. Even with video assist on a film shoot, things look differently when you peek through the lens itself. It's very important not to let your D.P. intimidate you. He or she may be the lighting/camera expert, but the shot has to match your vision—now and later. Check the shot through the eyepiece, lens, or video monitor. How else did you know that that clock wasn't visible?

So, you have this little problem before you can get the first shot "in the can," but because it's a simple shot, an easy scene, you make the changes, and you shoot. By God, it's happened. You like it, and you make one or more takes to make sure and then go on to the next scene or shot. If you can let it go at one take, do so. It makes you look like a genius.

But there *is* the serious question of how many takes a person needs.

There is, for instance, the wonderful, though possibly apocryphal, story about John Ford when he was directing one of those great Welsh classics—*How Green Was My Valley*—with a huge cast on location in Wales. Down the hill from the coal mine comes the cast of thousands, with Walter Pidgeon in the lead, singing with their great Welsh voices. They are on strike, and the scene is a great moment in the story.

After Take 1, Ford talks to the camera people (who were using two cameras to catch the whole panorama) and both acknowledge they have caught the scene. On to the next shot, says the director. Pidgeon is dumbfounded. "Aren't you going to take another?" he asks. "Was anything wrong?" queries the director, feigning horror. When the actor says he thought one always took another shot for "safety's" sake, Ford simply stalks off. Whether or not this story is true, the point is, making another take should be done for a purpose, whether that purpose is "safety"—whatever that means—or because you have something specific in mind that needs to be changed or improved. Just shooting take after take because you hope something will happen is not only fruitless, it's a waste of precious time when you could be doing something important.

After *each* day's first shot, there is a tendency to slow down again, especially if it has taken a while to shoot. Since the pressure will be put on you when things are rushed at the end of the day, or when you run out of shooting time because of a rainstorm, it's in your interest to have made a deal with the A.D. before shooting starts. Say that you are perfectly willing to give the crew breathing time after lunch, but that you want pressure put on them in the early morning shots. You know that that's when things are slow, and you want to pick up time before lunch. The A.D., who has his or her own pressure from the producer, will be delighted to find a director who understands the financial pressures of the business. What you don't tell the A.D. is that it's not financial pressure but aesthetic perfection you're looking for, and keeping things moving in the first two hours is one way to have breathing space to achieve that kind of perfection later on.

The day goes on. As it proceeds, the actors who have been called for that day's shoot begin to find their voices and their pace. The crew begins to find theirs. And, believe it or not, you begin to find yours. There should, in point of fact, be a great relief, a great surge of pleasure—assuming it's a good first day—at getting out from under that preproduction period. Things that go right on the first day have a feeling about them of perfection. Your afternoon won't be interrupted with anyone from the producer's office having seen the dailies, so you won't have that anxiety. You will consult with the P.M. at some point about tomorrow's scenes; a "call sheet" will come around about 4:30, with everything that's going to happen. And you will begin to feel that it all can be handled. By the end of the first day, you will have had enough shots in enough scenes so that a pace for those scenes has been established. So, too, a "tone." So, too, your look. You won't have seen it on film—only through the camera and in your mind's eye—but it's there nonetheless.

If you're shooting video, you will be able to reinforce your good feelings with something tangible after each take and, with film, as the days go by, you will have a chance to see the material in a screening room, and have an opportunity to match it against your vision. Don't lose that opportunity. Even if you have video assist on a film shoot (and most of us can't afford it), you will want to avail yourself of the dailies. Looking at the film on a big screen a day or more after you've shot it can be revelatory.

If you're on location, they will fly the film from the laboratory to a makeshift screening room so you, the D.P., and others can look at it. It may come a couple of days after you've shot it, so meanwhile confer on the phone with the editor or the producer. Ask if a special scene had the kind of light you wanted. Answer the producer's questions if he or she is unhappy. (Sometimes the producer is on location, sometimes not; it depends on the nature of your relationship, the kind of show, how many days you're going to be on location, and so forth. Often, the P.M. stands in for the producer. Sometimes an associate producer does.) When the scenes come on the screen, don't be surprised if the laboratory hasn't gotten the "timing" or the color right. A moody scene may have been "printed up" so that you could see everything sharply. A bright comedy scene may have been "printed down" because they misunderstood the instructions. Don't worry. Everything (or nearly everything) can be corrected later. Listen carefully for sound problems. Watch the size of close-ups. All these things can be corrected in future days' shooting.

If you don't get a chance to see dailies, as you may not if you're on the studio set and they screen during the day, ask if you can have a projectionist stay overtime the first night they're available. If not, spend some time with the producer; get his or her true feelings. Don't be defensive. Learn from what they think is wrong, and what they think is right. Of course, the first couple of days' shoot may be indecisive; crucial scenes may come later. But keep all your senses alert to things; keep pushing toward the vision you have.

EXTRAS

We've said nothing about all those people who hover at the edges and in the background of scenes. They're your responsibility, too, those "extras." The first A.D. is given the assignment of handling "background business," which is fine as long as all you're interested in is "business," the coming and going of people without any special quality to it. ("Keep busy, extras," I've heard an A.D. say.) What is the quality you want? What kind of character do your extras have? If they're just background, that is, literally nondescript figures moving to and fro, then let your skilled A.D. handle their movements. ("You two come in from here; you from here; you from there. Wait for him, then you, then you, and finally get that car in here. Don't hurry. Make it a slow pace.") But if their actions and reactions are crucial to how the scene plays (imagine a film about Hitler at Nuremberg, for example), you've got to be prepared to stand up there and tell them what the film is about and what you want them to do. You see, they won't have read the script! They may not even know what the film is about on the most *general* level. They've been hired for the day (or for days one, two, and four) and given a costume and some makeup (maybe) and told to stand "there" until called. Give them a break. Clue them in.

SOUND

We have dealt very little with audio and sound problems in this book thus far, and that is indicative of the approach of most filmmakers—to worry over picture, script, and cast. On the other hand, if you have done your best to make sure that the actors are cast for character in their voices as well as their faces, if you have rehearsed them and listened to nuances in their reading, then you will want the sound quality to be good, right? Then you have to know more than a little about some of the technical matters that can make for good—or bad—sound.

Let's start with the film versus video problem. If your production is double-system film (that is, the image is on film and the sound is on quarter-inch magnetic tape recorded on a Nagra), then you will have a good deal of control over it when you are in postproduction: editing, mixing, dubbing, and so forth. Each piece of tape is cuttable at the same place as the picture—or separately; and several sound tracks can be created to give you control over nuance, level, and variety of sounds. You can have a voice on one track, sound effects on another, music on a third, and so on. You can have your picture cut and then remove a few frames of it, simultaneously cutting out a few frames of sound in all three tracks or on only one track. Similarly, if you choose to leave the picture the way it is, but replace the cough that is in track one with a piece of sound track of a door closing, that is a fairly simple matter—a literal cutting of the tape with a "guillotine" splicer.

Not so with video. Even though the introduction of digital recording, and editing tools such as AVID and Media 100 have made the job of editing both picture and sound a hundred times more facile (see chapter 9 and chapter 10), and even though audio labs can do miracles with video sound, the expense and time required to solve audio problems on video is far beyond most low-budget operations. So if you're shooting video, make trebly sure you're aware of audio problems before they're recorded.

What are the effects of these things that a director needs to know about? First of all, there is background noise. If, during a take, a cough occurs between two words, in film it is a fairly simple matter to eliminate the cough and replace the empty space on *another track,* with "room tone" (the noise that is heard in an empty room or outdoors—crickets, traffic, the buzz of a light bulb, and so on—when "nothing" is happening). When this occurs in videotape, it requires a fairly complicated kind of editing; one cannot ever totally, accurately, fill in the space left by the eliminated cough. This means that a director has to be very responsive if an audio person cries "Halt!" If it turns out there's a real sound problem, you had better do another take, because postproduction manipulation may be very difficult. This is especially true on low-budget productions, where sound rerecording and elimination of "glitches" is almost impossible. In film, even the most elementary editor can cut out a sound problem and keep the tape in synch with the picture. In video, it takes both expertise and high-tech equipment to do so. So, when recording sound on videotape, you must take some simple preventive measures, such as doing *retakes* when any problematical sound arises.

Second, there is the question of postproduction. The individual film sound track can be "equalized" in a "mix." That is, an excessively bass or treble voice, or one with too much background hum can be individually tuned during the final mix of sound tracks, and new sounds can be added (a door closing, a telephone ringing, and so on). So can music. Add another track, put it in synch, "sweeten" the sound track, and there you have it. On the other hand, videotape-editing consoles are organized around video problems, not around audio ones. Editing rooms have computers and consoles to take care of the picture (changing colors, enhancing video, and so forth) but only rudimentary ones to handle audio. Differences between media aside, what will *you* listen for, now that you've established yourself as someone concerned with sound?

Perspective. This is a common problem. You've taken a wide shot of a duel in a glen, outdoors. The sound, because the microphone couldn't get in the picture, is nice and airy, giving the sense of distance. On the other hand, you're getting a lot of birds and airplanes because the microphone is so far away from the actors. The sound man is perfectly ready and willing to put RF (radio frequency) microphones on the actors to get their voices close up. Do you want to do that? Shouldn't the actors have a sense of distance from the camera? Sure, but what happens in editing when you cut back and forth between wide and close shots? Do you want the sound to change? Get softer and louder? Get "airier," with more perspective in it? Probably. But you *don't* want it to have more *airplanes and birds* in it. All this not only requires that you be sensitive to sound perspective, but have some idea how you want to handle the problem in concert with your audio person, of course.

The solution to the problem above? You're probably better off getting a "close" perspective with an RF and then planning to "cut over" (that is, use two different tracks) when editing and mixing, with wide shot sound on one track, close shots on another. Then, you can equalize them for distance without adding birds and airplanes at the same time.

Different Takes. It often happens that you've changed the action or the lights between Take 3 and Take 17. Or, with a microphone shadow in Take 3, you decided to have the mike held higher, so by Take 17 there is a different kind of sound from your actors from what there was in the earlier takes. This is a common problem. As long as you're sensitive to it, it can probably be handled very nicely during the mix. On the other hand, if you have a very soft-spoken actor or actress and you've asked him or her to speak louder for the latter take, you may have trouble cutting between one line on Take 3 and another line on Take 17, without it sounding as if a deaf person had just entered the room. Be aware of it.

Noise. We all were shocked the first time we listened to a recording of something we'd also heard firsthand, because we realized that the microphone was picking up all sorts of "background noise," also called "ambient sound." Airplanes, flies, birds, radiators, elevators, bed springs, you name it—it's there and it's distracting. A good mixer on the set will call your attention to these nasty noises, and you'd better decide then and there how you intend to handle them. Waiting until later, unless you're unbearably pressed for time, is not a good idea. Can you get the microphone closer? Can you send an A.D. over to the man cutting wood next door (Where was he when you scouted the location?) and ask him to hold it for a few hours? Should you go ahead with a plan to dub in the voices later (expensive)? Or what? Discuss it with your team. They've been here before. But the decision and the responsibility is yours. Just remember to be sensitive and alert to noises of all kinds.

One solution is the "wild line." This is the term used for the practice of recording an actor's line (or lines) with the microphone close to the actor and no film rolling. Why? So that the editor will have the *option* of "laying in" the wild line in place of the noisy line recorded during the filming of the shot. This also requires, by the way, that you record "wild sound" of the background to lay in on another track so that the gaps cut out of the original track won't be as noticeable. Tricky? Sure, but the wild line is a time-honored practice and a reasonable solution to the problem of microphone placement and noisy locations. (I used to work with a child actor who got softer and softer during a scene. Rather than do the scene over again, we had him read wild lines one at a time after the scene, which could be cut in during wide or medium shots— "synched up" is the industry expression—and the practice saved us lots of time.) Wild sounds of birds, automobiles, and so forth can also be a great help when the sound effects editing is going on.

Nuance. The most important sound problem is also the most important opportunity. When a microphone gets hold of an actor or actress, it transforms the sound that you've heard during rehearsal into something else. These are not gross changes, but they are important ones. Take the time to listen to your actors on the headset during the first takes of a shoot. Your A.D. will wait. Is that what you wanted? If not, ask the mixer what to do. Be alert for changes. Generally, a sound person won't want to exchange microphones during a shoot precisely because that will cause a different timbre in the sound, which will have to be corrected between takes or shots in the mix. But maybe something is wanted for one scene that a microphone change *can* accomplish. Or maybe a different microphone has to be used because of logistical problems (a shotgun, an RF, another kind?). Be aware of the differences that change will make, and then go ahead *if* you have to. But you'll know what you're listening for and what will happen when it gets transferred back to 16mm magnetic track in the editing room.

LIGHTING

Let's talk about picture again. As the shoot progresses, you will find that all sorts of things are happening. For one thing, your D.P. will have put lights up and created effects that cause quite different results from what you anticipated. You will see images that are quite wonderful. And—most importantly—you will see opportunities that you hadn't dreamed possible, ones you can convey to your D.P. Don't shrink from doing so. *If* it costs too much or takes too much time, someone will tell you!

You will begin to see subtle uses of backlight and sidelight or, conversely, you will see opportunities for more creative lighting. Take these opportunities, but don't be surprised at the time or trouble it takes. I remember shooting inside a house in November, when the wind began to blow. We didn't hear the storm, because the house was well insulated, but we noticed that the light was moving back and forth, creating all sorts of moving shadows that we didn't want. Outside the window, swaying like the Empire State Building in a tornado, was a large HMI on a scaffolding. On top of the scaffolding with the light, and holding on for dear life, was a young juicer, who had just started in the business. He had been sent up to "steady the light" but was being shaken about instead. It had taken a long time to get the lamp up there and the shot was important. Rather than wait for the wind to stop, however, I decided I'd add *sound effects* of wind blowing and shoot an exterior scene of trees shaking. Since the film was a mystery, with lots of odd things going on, this would work pretty well and allow us to keep on shooting. (If the film had been a romance or a comedy, I don't know what we would have done.) You may have to be inventive to get around some of the problems caused by your lighting. And you may, sometimes, have to give up some imaginative lighting because it will take too long or be too costly.

LENSES

The shot doesn't look the way you thought it would. You'd envisioned a tight shot through a misty morning, with the background out of focus, but when the D.P. tries to give you that—with a 105mm lens—the frame doesn't take in enough of the subject matter. There is no room to move the camera back, so he or she "throws on" (don't ask me why, but lenses are *thrown on)* a wider lens, say, a 55mm, and the focus isn't what you wanted: the background is crystal clear, distracting the audience from the foreground actor. A number of questions may occur to you at this point.

You might question why the D.P. has to change lenses at all. Why can't he just zoom to a different focal length? The answer is that zoom lenses are not the best lenses to use. First of all, "prime" lenses (so called because they are limited to a single focal length, but also implying "first-rate") are generally faster (that is, they let in more light) and the glass is generally less distorting, so they give a sharper, "cleaner" picture. But there are other reasons to avoid using zoom lenses, even in documentary work, and it's worth taking a few lines to discuss the issue.

When a camera is moved toward or away from an object, the amount the viewer sees, of both the object and the background, changes: if it gets very close we can't see the full width of either of them. But the amount cut off the object and its background differs depending on how far away each is from camera. For instance if I move toward a man standing twenty feet from a building with ornate columns but only three feet from the camera (see drawings on the following page), I will get to the man and have a close shot of him without cutting off much of what's behind him. If, on the other hand, he stands only three feet from the columns and I move toward him, I will still get a close-up of him but cut off a great deal of what's to either side of and behind him. This change in "perspective" occurs simultaneously with the change in the size of shot. With a zoom lens, however, change in size of shot occasions *no* changes in perspective, since the camera itself isn't varying its distance from either man or background. (It is the change in *relative* distance from different objects that causes variation in perspective.) This means that the way we (humans, not cameras) normally see the world—with changes in perspective as we approach two or three objects at different distances from each other and from us—is mirrored by a camera that moves and is *not* mirrored by a zoom lens.

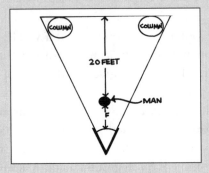

A man stands between two columns.
Let's look at two camera positions.

In the first, with the camera at twelve feet from the man, we can get a fairly wide shot like this with a normal (50mm) lens.

If we move the camera closer, say, to four feet, using the same lens we get a medium shot of the man without the columns. (They "move aside!").

If, on the other hand, we stay at twelve feet and use a zoom to get closer to the man, we also get a magnified view of the columns. The point is that sense of perspective (what happens when we physically move toward or away from objects) is lost with a zoom and retained with a physical camera move. With the zoom, the images simply get bigger, as if we were using a magni-

fying glass or an enlarger. When the camera actually moves, each change in perspective (from far to near) happens much as when we walk; with a zoom, things change the way they do if we simply moved closer to a photograph.

The result of all this? In my estimation, it is that a zoom lens provides a strange, abstract, nonaesthetic move, while a camera on a dolly (or handheld) provides a "natural" move. The zoom lens is a godsend when you are shooting news or when you can't avoid being in a tight spot and need to get a close shot of something fast. But it's a pretty crude mechanism to use when you want to get closer to an actor or actress and make the background seem "right" in relationship to the character. Do it the right way: put your camera on a dolly, lay down tracks, and move camera, lens, and dolly toward or away from the actor. An exception to this "rule" is that a good camera person, using handheld movement and a zoom lens, can provide a partial change in perspective by zooming at the same time he or she is providing lateral—that is, sidewise—movement. Since the sidewise movement is making a change in perspective, the "flat" nature of the zoom is not quite as noticeable. It is a cheap, sometimes effective way of getting around financial difficulties involved with dollies, track, and man power.

Using a zoom lens can also get you into other sloppy habits. For instance, since the zoom provides only in-and-out movement, a director or D.P. may end up forgoing the wonderful world of sideway movement because the zoom doesn't give it. Only a dolly can provide graceful, smooth, sidewise, forward, and backward movement. Use it.

A second question that could arise in the changing of lenses just described is, "Who cares?" Does the choice of lens make enough difference to bother with? Why not simply move the camera backward or forward to accommodate? One answer is that this is not always possible, but that begs the main question, to which a resounding yes must be given. The depth-of-field notion has to do with how much of a particular shot is in focus in front of, and behind, the object upon which your primary focus is fixed. The longer the lens, the less depth-of-field; the wider the lens, the more depth-of-field. Most people study depth-of-field in order to be sure to have things in focus, and you learn how to "stop down" (that is, use a higher f-stop, requiring more light) in order to achieve that greater focus.

But to have everything in focus all the time is very boring, and most directors and D.P.s purposely use long lenses, with less depth-of-field, to create "soft" backgrounds or foregrounds, with only a *selected* object in focus. In fact, control over focus is only one thing a variety of lenses can bring to a film, and you will probably have done

147

a good deal of the preparation for this concept when you started thinking about how your film or videotape was going to *look*.

Now, however, back to our shot. The D.P. has changed from 105mm to 55mm lens, and it's no longer a matter of *thinking* about the picture—you can *see* it. What difference is there in the two lenses? The 105mm not only makes the background a little less in focus, it brings the background *closer* to the camera; it sharpens the features of the actors, making them thinner, with their noses less broad and shorter. If the camera is very close to them, their eyes are in better focus than their ears, creating a sense of isolation of that crucial part of the human face. The 55mm, on the other hand, flattens out the picture a little more. Shift to a wider lens—say, 28mm—and features that were sharp are broader; you not only include more in the picture (hence, "wide" lenses), but what is included is fatter and/or wider. Everything begins to be in focus, making it harder to fasten attention on any one item.

But we've only begun. What happens to light and color when lenses of varying length are used? If the background is out of focus, the color and light on the background "spreads" to create a pattern that is quite different in effect from the same background in sharp focus. A red lantern hung on a wall behind a sea captain "smears" into a soft red smudge when he is shot with a long lens. Bright patches of light, often distracting or ugly when in focus, become attractive crystals when out of focus. And what about movement? Take this shot: a running woman, dashing through the undergrowth in pursuit of a rabbit, is followed through a long lens (with careful attention to "follow focus," as it's called). The background and the foreground are out of focus, so she is seen by the camera as if she were the only creature on earth, and almost as if we were eavesdropping from a great distance. If you use a wider lens and get closer to her, the camera is forced to move along with her. Things are in focus, and the chase seems nowhere near so "panicked." We all know the effect of filming a running horse with a long lens, as it comes right at the camera. It seems to come on and on, never getting any closer. With a wide lens, the same animal comes on much faster, going from a dot in the screen to a close-up animal in a few seconds. So, if you are trying to achieve a sense of quick movement, a wide-angle lens and a head-on shot will do it.

A discussion of the varieties of effects caused by changes of lenses could go on forever. The purpose here is not to outline all the possibilities, but to make it clear that experimentation with a variety of lenses is part and parcel of the creative baggage you bring to a shoot. When your D.P. changes lenses, you should anticipate the effect it will have; you should verify it by looking through the camera; and you should put the lesson into your lexicon for future use. Above all, you should think of shots not as fixed images, but as flexible ones, with each variation dependent upon the particular lens you choose to use.

DECORUM

You want people to behave in a certain way in order to accomplish certain goals. How do you create this situation? Well, in part, that depends on you: how you talk on the set, how you ask for people to do things, how you expect people to talk to you.

There are two sides to this. One is the question of personality— that is, who you are as a person. The second, equally important, is what has to be done in order to get a good scene.

If you're an irritable kind of person, greedy, pushy, hard to get along with at home, it's not likely you'll change on the set. If you're a nice, soft-spoken, polite person, with plenty of ego strength, you can behave well on the set and still get a good movie made. I know that goes against the image of the tough, demanding, jodhpurs-wearing director, screaming at his cohorts and exhorting them to do their utmost, despite the rains and the snakes. But in fact, the opposite works. One of the sweetest men I know is a director of one of the most expensive, time-consuming PBS shows, using seven cameras and a crew of thirty. I've never heard him raise his voice; I have always heard him say "please." And the show is impeccably directed. Just because you shout and work people ten hours overtime every night doesn't mean that the film will be "creative." Okay, but what if you're the kind of person who feels good shouting at people and who never says "please" and can't operate any other way? I guess you'll have to keep on doing that, but it certainly is unpleasant and I think you'll find that it wears thin after a while. Your teammates may respect your craft, your art, but I don't know if they'll respect you.

What do you have to do to achieve the kind of scene you want? Do you have to be hushed on a set where you're shooting a tragedy? Should you laugh and joke on a set that's doing a comedy? What kind of clothes are required? I'm afraid there's no single answer to this.

Some actors need quiet sets and peaceful surroundings to be able to concentrate on even the funniest lines. Others, even in a serious film, can make jokes just before they go into the set, so good is their concentration. So be it. Learn what your actors need—and what you need—and ask for it. Nicely.

THE LONG SHOOT

It rained yesterday, and you had to use the alternate (rain date) scenes. It rained the day before and you had to use *those* alternate scenes. It's supposed to rain tomorrow. You're depressed, and no one can blame you. But three successive days of rain is not the only depressant in a long film shoot (or a short one, for that matter). You've moved from the long buildup of the preproduction days into the fast, hectic pace of the first days of a shoot. The adrenaline is going, the actors are delivering, you're finding your feet. And then, without warning, you wake up one morning and decide you don't want to be out there shooting. Too many little things have gone wrong. Maybe the producer doesn't understand what you're doing, hasn't heaped enough praise on you. Maybe your own internal critical mechanism is at work. Whatever it is, rain or lack of praise, you're depressed. How do you cope? Part of what's happening is that your system is coping, it's adjusting to the time span. You can't keep the adrenaline going sixteen days in a row. There has to be some letdown so your body can handle it. Part of what's also happening is that the film shoot is becoming a "job." You never thought that could happen, did you? Filmmaking is so exciting, so creative, so full of wonderful events that it couldn't just degenerate into a routine. Sure it could. And does. Don't let it all disappoint you. There are a lot of good directors who shoot forty weeks a year, and for them life would be an impossible nightmare if they treated each and every shoot as if it were a creative orgy. Some of what you're doing is pure art and some is the work of a craftsperson.

Routinizing some of your work will actually help you be more creative in other parts of the work. As for the lack of praise—well, there's nothing to do but wait. If the film is as good as you think it is, then praise will come eventually, and from some very strange and wonderful places. If not, then there's always another film.

9

The Digital Realm

I made a promise earlier in this book not to get too technical. There are already wonderful books on the market that compare the physical nature of videotape with film, or talk about the way various film and video cameras work, or show how to set up different kinds of equipment and how to edit on diverse kinds of devices. Where I have ventured into technical matters, it was to demonstrate the relationship between technology and the creative direction you may wish to employ. In other words, the freedom to be a creative director often depends on a modicum of technical knowledge. This brief foray into the digital realm is another exception to my general rule to stay away from nuts and bolts, because digital directly affects many young directors and writers—and some older ones as well. I will tell you, for instance, that the ease of using digital cameras has turned me from a producer-director-writer into a director-cameraman at a late stage in my life.

Two particular advances in digital video are making an enormous difference in the way films and television are being made and will be made in the future. Any director worth his or her salt will want to understand the pros and cons of these new phenomena: the mini-DV camera and the software that lets you edit on your home computer. These technological advances are stunning because they allow low-budget productions while maintaining a remarkable degree of high-end visual quality. Let's start with the cameras.

THE CAMERAS

It has been the practice for film schools at major universities to train students in all the disciplines—writing, editing, directing, lighting, camera. I've always thought this to be a mistake. Some people are not made to handle a camera. Some can't learn to direct. Others seem born to those crafts. While it probably makes sense in undergraduate courses to let everyone take a crack at handling a camera, at least once, when they get to graduate work, where they're going to prepare for a professional career,[15] it probably makes sense to specialize. Let those who have a technical expertise and flair do that work; let those who are good at writing, and have a sense for story, learn to direct.

Now that I've said that, I'm going to flip-flop. Because the new Mini-DV cameras (DV for digital video, "mini" for, you guessed it, very small) are just perfect for becoming a hyphenate: the director-cameraman.

These cameras look very much like the home camcorders that have been on the market for a long time. They're light (often less than 3 pounds) and easy to use; they take long loads of tape (from 1 to 2 hours), and if you drop them on a moderately soft surface you've got a reasonably good chance of being able to go on shooting. The problem with the home camcorder for professional or semiprofessional use is that the tape on which those cameras record is not made for editing. Rather, if you do edit with it, it degrades in quality (in look) almost immediately. (Those tapes are the same format as your home VCR. If you've ever tried to record from one VHS tape to another, you know that the original quality goes downhill fast.)

Enter the digital era. It started in music. Engineers found a way of using the binary language of computers (0s and 1s) to code musical sounds during recording. When they translated those codes back into sound, they found that they could rerecord, dub over, and make changes as often as they wanted without losing quality. They weren't dubbing down from original tapes. They were re-coding and re-encoding the little 0s and 1s that—when strung together—made up

---

[15] You'd better read my later remarks about film schools in general in chapter 13. I'm not a big fan. And this is from someone who spent six years teaching film and television at City College of New York!

pitch, timbre, and tone. CDs are as good as they are because they use laser beams to read digitally mastered disks.

Eventually, this technique had to become translatable to video and, after a number of years and a lot of money, the techno-wizards found a way to do it. Enter, first, the digital editing systems—AVID being the most well-known—that allow editors to store an enormous amount of images in digital form on RAM disks and to randomly access the material. Then, a few years later, the industry miniaturized the electronics sufficiently to put them into digi-Beta cameras: portable "Electronic Newsgathering" (ENG) equipment that was the same size as the models invented in the late 1960s and are now put out by all the big manufacturers. This digital tape continues in the sequence of better and better quality that started with 2" recording tape in the 1950s and went through two styles of 1" tape, on up to Beta recording systems in the 1980s. Only this is far superior because you can make endless variations of your tape and not lose any picture quality—all because of those little 0s and 1s.

The next step? To keep miniaturizing and put that digital technology into smaller and smaller cameras. If this could be accomplished it would do two things: it would reduce the cost of cameras and it would make it easier to move around and make documentaries (much the way that the umbilical cord between lightweight 16mm cameras and Nagra recording devices enabled the *cinéma vérité* of the 1950s and 1960s). At first, broadcast engineers doubted it could be done. The size and amount of electronics required for high-end video cameras, even portable ones, required a bulky casing.

That something like this could be done became evident when the Hi-8 video camera and tape were invented. For a short time, back in the early 1990s, the Hi-8 industry looked like it was the answer to the consumer demand for better quality in camcorders, and for the "prosumer" market—those budding videographers who wanted cheap but good equipment. Hi-8 cameras were very much like the camcorders that first came out, but they were able to record on a new kind of videotape, one that gave a better image. In the process of working on those cameras, engineers were able to use three color chips instead of the usual one, making purer color possible. A few inventive television producers even used Hi-8 to make some or all of their on-the-streets shows.

But it wasn't long afterwards that the impossible happened: engineers found a way to use digital recording techniques developed for larger ENG equipment (costing upwards of $50,000) in small camcorders with three color chips. The price ($4,000) was a good deal higher than the home camcorder but way below the ENG gear. As usual, the old-time producers, executives, and broadcast engineers denigrated everything about the little cameras. The images weren't clean looking enough, the color wasn't pure, they didn't have interchangeable lenses, and so on. And the manufacturers, who in most cases also produced the high-end broadcast cameras, didn't disagree. These weren't intended for broadcast, they said. These were "prosumer" cameras, for use by the amateur and the budding professional. They were beautiful for what they were, but no one was pretending that they were high-end.

In my view, the industry made a mistake with that attitude. I own two of these little marvels, and I've been shooting with them, editing on digital equipment, and using the result both on television and for large-screen projection at conventions, and no one has yet to criticize the images. In short, I think the prosumer camera—and its offshoots (mid-range professional versions) are here to stay and are very valuable tools for many of the filmic uses that used to require big gear. At first, I could find almost no one who agreed with me, but more and more people are doing so. In fact, some like the slightly "degraded" look of the Mini-DV camera because it can take on the appearance of film, which still has a cachet in the world of Hollywood. The slight "grain" of DV mimics some of the aspects of that older—and more prestigious—medium.

A caveat, and a big one: The industry is changing over to high-definition digital television (HDTV). Pretty soon, according to FCC regulations, all television broadcasts will have to put out both analog and digital signals. Though the industry is having difficulty meeting the government's schedule, home TV sets will take on a different shape and clarity. It will be a setback for these little mid-grade cameras, but I have no doubt that the camera manufacturers will eventually find a way to upgrade the Mini-DV camera and make it shine a little brighter. And because they're already digital they will already be compatible with the new signals.

As one might suspect, most Hollywood and network broadcasters are not using the Mini-DV equipment. It's still considered below broadcast standards. And, for documentary makers and news organizations, especially at the networks, the small cameras look so much like home camcorders that a certain amount of status is lost. I have one colleague who won't hire me to shoot video for him because I insist on using my Mini-DV camera. "They won't think we're serious," he says, meaning the clients will think we're amateurs. And then there are the executives who don't know much about technology to begin with. For years, they've been spending $50,000 on big, heavy Beta-SP cameras (or more for the new digi-Beta cameras), and they've been persuaded that only those cameras are "broadcast capable." (To make them see things my way, I've once or twice taken to the following scheme: I transfer some of my DV material to Beta and I take it to an editor at another edit house—preferably one that is used by the prospective client. I ask the editor what stock or camera he thinks I used. Sometimes, the editor guesses BetaSP, sometimes 1", sometimes even film. Almost never do the editors guess that the camera I'm using is less than a tenth of the cost of the cameras the "big boys" use.)

The future of the industry may not be in the Mini-DV field, but a number of very inventive professionals have begun using the equipment. Most of the very popular movie Buena Vista Social Club, directed by Wim Wenders, was shot on low-end video equipment. The experimental and highly successful Time Code (conceived of and directed by Mike Figgis) was shot in one continuous take on four Mini-DV cameras shooting simultaneously. I can't guarantee that

this was the same $4,000 camera I own. They may have
used a $7,500 version that Canon makes (the XL-1) rather
than my GL-1, but it was low-end digital video nonetheless,
because there is no field camera that the big boys make
that will record more than a half hour of tape. Films shot on
Mini-DV are also showing up at festivals and on the
Internet, as I will discuss further in a moment.

So now that I've taken you on this technological trip, what does it
mean for you, the director/cameraperson?

- **Cost** The Mini-DV cameras range from $3,000 to $4,000, tens of
  thousands of dollars less than the industrial or professional models.
  The slightly larger XL-1 that Canon makes is about $7,500. It has
  interchangeable lenses and lots more gadgetry, but it's also heavier.
- **Portability** These cameras, even with microphone, cables, and
  batteries, will fit in a briefcase—albeit a large sized one. Or in a
  shopping bag. They weigh a few pounds, so handholding them is
  a cinch. The tripod required for them is lightweight and, while it's
  not the fluid-head tripod that big cameras use, with their ultra-
  smooth movements, the manufacturers are getting better daily at
  mimicking true fluid-head tripods for the small cameras.
- **Minimal size of operation** Because the camera is light, and
  because you can plug an external microphone into the camera or
  use the very good stereo microphone built in (if you're close
  enough to the subject, or want just ambient sound), you can go
  into a room with one other person (for lights) and make yourself
  almost invisible. This is especially useful for sensitive taping situations in documentaries—hospitals, for instance—but it can also be
  useful when shooting a drama in cramped spaces.
- **Experimentation** Because these cameras are lightweight, and
  because they're easy to use, tilting them, holding them high above
  your head, using different shutter speeds, fooling with color, and
  other such moves are all very easy. My first camera in this arena—
  a Sony DXC 1000—allows you to set your shutter speed at anything between 1/4 second a frame all the way up to a frame every
  1/2000 of a second. This is the kind of thing you can do with still

cameras, and allows for a wide variety of lighting conditions, without pushing gain. The 1/4 second per frame also gives the most wonderful smearing of color and slow-motion effect and works well for music scenes. Try it, you'll like it. (For some reason, Canon does not permit anything below a frame every 1/60 of a second, which is too bad.)

The downside of these cameras must also be talked about.

They may be too light. Holding a very small, very light camera and walking with it is almost impossible to do without jiggling. Even with a built-in electronic lens steadier, you will notice that the camera is wobbling. You probably can't use a Steadicam with these. So, if you're strong enough, you might want to invest in the larger Mini-DV cameras, such as the Canon XL-1, which has other virtues, as well.

The smallest of these cameras are made for idiots to use, which means the viewfinder is filled with too much information, and the options are kept to a minimum. As I said above, for instance, you can't use the Canon GL-1 below a 1/60 of a second. You can't change lenses on any of these small cameras. They have zooms, but no ability to put a really fine prime lens on them, or a super-long lens. I've put wide-angle adapters on top of my lens, but it's highly unsatisfactory. The lens is plastic, not glass, which means there is some distortion that you wouldn't get with glass. Also, the controls are tiny, which means you can easily press the wrong button or be unable to read the labels.

These cameras come with a built-in microphone that is okay. They also come with a place to plug in a microphone with a mini jack. This is not okay. These jacks pull out very easily. They aren't grounded, so that if you're taking an audio feed from someone, and using AC current from a house system, you may end up with a loud hum on your audio track. The answer: purchase a gadget that goes between the camera and the tripod that costs about $300 and takes two XLR (i.e., three-prong, grounded) audio inputs. These are the standard microphone cables, and this solves your problem, as far as hum goes.

There is no consistent time code on these cameras. (Time code is a continuous marker that tells an editing machine exactly where it is in terms of minutes, seconds, and frames.) That means that you cannot screen your tapes and take notes using real time code. You'll have tape time, but it's not going to help you in making an edit list. What I have been doing is transferring my Mini-DV tape to BetaSP at an edit house. I make a "burn-in" time-coded VHS at the same time (sometimes called "viz" code; see chapter 10) and an audiotape. That way I have everything I need for screening and eventual editing on an AVID, and I can turn the audiotape over to a transcribing house. As the next section will tell you, there is another way around the time-code problem, if you choose to edit at home.

EDITING EQUIPMENT

Here, I'm going to be very brief, because the next chapter is all about editing.

The good news is that with the software programs called, *Final Cuts* and *Final Cuts Pro*, the ability to edit digitally on your own home computer is finally at hand. Not any computer, mind you. The systems were designed for Macintosh, and they work best on those computers. Not only that, the top-end Mac. The reason is that you need a tremendous amount of memory to hold the shots in readiness for editing, and to store different versions of your film/tape. While some PCs and Macs now come with "home video editing" software, this is truly for Uncle Ted. If you want to play around, you can use that stuff. If you want to get serious about editing, you need one of the high-end programs. Cost: As of this writing, my editing guru, a top-notch editor at a Manhattan editing house, tells me that $6,000 is about what it'll cost to get a very good computer system with enough memory and speed.

Another piece of good news is that these systems are patterned after the big, expensive systems like AVID and Media 100 that I discuss in the next chapter. If you've watched an editor work on those pieces of $100,000 equipment, you'll be amazed how much you can accomplish on the home setup.

The way these digital editing systems interface with the Mini-DV cameras is another bonus. Due to an invention called "Firewire," a single cable will take the digital signals from the Mini-DV cameras directly into a slot on the back of your computer. You can then log your shots, store them in "bins" on your computer, and have them ready to edit at a moment's notice. When your rough cut is finished you can kick it back out via Firewire to a fresh tape in your camera and take it to be screened by potential buyers. Or you can finish your version (with some graphic titles if you have the software for them) on your Mac, and kick out a complete product to be transferred to Beta (or even, through laser transfer, to film) so that it can be screened.

The bad news is that it's not easy to learn how to be a good editor. This is not something for which everyone has a talent, and just because someone is a good writer or director, or even a good cameraman, doesn't mean that same person can become adept at editing. I know my own limitations in this arena, and I've held off buying a home-editing system precisely because I'd rather hire someone who is very experienced, even if it costs me a lot more.

But that's your own judgment to make. And the fact that many "filmmakers" opt to write, direct, and edit their own digital "films" is a sign that it's doable.

ONE FINAL WORD

It's well known by now that the Internet has sprouted sites where films can be shown. Directors who want to get their work seen, but can't get into festivals or onto the home screen, have started to "exhibit" their wares in cyberspace. The word is that potential buyers or distributors will watch the film or videotape on the Web site and make a judgment from that screening. And there's the added benefit of knowing that a "lot of people" are out there seeing your film, even if you're not getting paid for it.

Whatever the future potential of this realm for the exhibition, sale, and distribution of films and television programs, my own experience with viewing video on the Internet is dismal. Whether it's the baud rate of my computer (56K as of this writing) or the state of the art at this time, I don't care—the pictures I get are viewable only in a small square in a small portion of my screen; the contrast and color levels are all over the place; and most of the time I get to see them at something like 15 frames a second, rather than the standard 30. The picture holds, then jumps ahead, then holds, then jumps. All of this happens in a blurred image. How anyone can make judgments about anything except the sound (which is very good if you have even a modest system on your computer) I don't know.

Now, that's all you—as a director—need to know about digital.

10
Postproduction

You should be overjoyed. You have finished your shoot. It is "wrapped." No more sunburned shoulders, no more producer on your back, no more having to listen to that actor you misjudged misread his lines. No more 5:00 a.m. rising, with the voice of the A.D. in your ear, "Sorry, fella, time to get up. Oh, by the way, we're a little late, this morning. Better hurry."

Wrong. Your pain isn't over, just shifted to the right about 30 degrees. In fact, you're going to have to listen to that bad actor a little longer, and while you won't be getting up at 5:00 in the morning, you may have altogether sleepless nights. As for the producer, he'll be on your back just as much—maybe a little more—because, brother, you have the postproduction blues!

Here's the scenario. You have had a rather lovely time at the final party, drinking until late. But the next morning, aware that the production has to be finished within three months, you arrive at the editing room bright and early. The editor has been synching up the material during the shoot and has promised you a few scenes already "assembled." You can't wait. The last days of the shoot have given you no satisfaction. Pick-up shots, retakes, sound problems; it's been a mess.

Now, you figure, you can sit back and reap the rewards of your hard days' labor. The scene the editor picked is not a crucial one, but it's full of nuance, and you're anxious to see if it "plays." It doesn't. You squirm through it all. Too many wide shots, not enough detail. The light isn't what you remember from the dailies. Besides, even though the editor loved some of what you shot, you are now hearing that a couple of scenes can just be thrown out. How does he or she know? Where was this editor when the screen was blank? Not that something will be immediately cut out if you don't want it cut. Not at all. There's an unspoken rule that the first edit—the assembly—of a picture will almost always be as it was written and as it was shot. After that, it may be cut to shreds!

For the purpose of this chapter, I'm going to assume that you have some control over your film or videotape; that is, that you have the right to supervise the cut of the film. I'm also going to separate video-tape and film here, because the two media require very different technical facilities and very different relationships with your editor(s).

FILM

During the first few days of shooting, the editor has come around to the set or been on the phone to location to talk about wanting some "extra coverage" on a scene, by which is meant that you didn't get all the shots he or she (or the producer) thought were necessary when you shot a particular scene—you need more close-ups, over-the-shoulder shots, a pair of two-shots, and so forth. The continuity person has been giving the editor and the assistant the updated script from time to time, so they can know what has been shot, how many takes, which ones you "printed"—so there has been communication. Now, however, it's just the two of you for a while, and you have to decide what kind of a relationship you're going to have and how you're going to operate. There are a number of possibilities. (1) Go away until the assembly is cut. Look at it, then let the editor make changes for the rough cut. If they're okay, stay away again until the fine cut. (2) Sit around biting your fingernails until the assembly is done, then sit down on a daily basis with your editor, making changes until the rough cut. Ditto for the fine cut. (3) Somewhere in between the above two. Strong directors, who have good relationships and great faith in their editors, will often follow the first, whereas insecure directors or those who have hack editors will do the second. In between, of course, range many of us.

The value of letting your editor work unfettered is that he or she may have some fairly wild ideas that need to be explored. Given the time necessary to carry them out, leaving the editing room uncluttered with directorial ego will give the editor a chance not only to explore those ideas, but to clear your mind of preconceptions. Now, this is a paradox because, earlier in the book, I suggested that preconceptions were a good thing. They are, and you couldn't shoot a film without them. But to hold on to preconceptions just because you thought them up is foolish. If they work, fine. If not, throw them out. That means your ideas, the writer's, the producer's—everyone's. A scene that worked well in a certain place during the scriptwriting stages and during shooting may belong in a different place. Or it may not be needed because the scenes on either side mesh well or because a story nuance that seemed obscure during the preproduction days seems obvious on the screen, now that the shooting's done. This happens time and time again. You, however, who have been so close to this project for weeks, may not be able to see with any objectivity that the scene isn't needed, or that a character is too strong or too weak, or a dozen other possibilities. Your editor, coming to the film relatively fresh (he or she *did* see the dailies) will be able to look at the film much more objectively. Let the editor's mind go. Listen with an open mind yourself. See what happens. After the assembly, an editor will ask permission to rearrange. At the rough cut stage, if you don't like what you see, it can all be put back. But the likelihood is, if you give it a chance, it will be very exciting. Of course, if you hang around, looking over the editor's shoulder, you will give neither yourself the time to "forget" what was there, nor the editor the freedom to create something new.

By the way, this works both ways. After having been away from the film for a while, coming back to it with refreshed eyes, you are able to see things that the editor, working on it for ten days, cannot. Now it is his or her turn to ask you to make suggestions, to see things that are wrong, out of place, overdone. Here, then, is a symbiotic relationship of wonderful dimension, one that can be quite creative. (After another period of time, of course, you both will have lost objectivity, and it's time to call in the producer. Don't gang up on him. Be fair. The producer may see things, with newfound objectivity, that have eluded the two of you.) I suppose this paints the relationship between editor and director as a more than perfect one. To be honest, there are times when it is no such thing. If, for instance, the editor thinks you've done a less than satisfactory job, he or she may not tell you but go about changing things and "saving the film" (a time-honored phrase) behind your back. Ralph Rosenblum, in his marvelous book *When the Shooting*

Stops . . . the Cutting Begins, tells of such times—when directors haven't the slightest idea of what to do with their film or when the footage that came in is in drastic need of changes and additions. Rosenblum was adept at finding "stock" footage and adding it to films to make them come to life. And since I'm being honest here, this process has worked the other way as well. I've seen editors who couldn't figure out what to do with a piece of footage, and I've had to sit there, patiently handing out ideas about how to cut the film. The tragedy of that, of course, is that sometimes you can't see the opportunities in a film you've written and shot, so the film comes out second-best.

Now that you've gotten through the rough cut, you begin to notice things that no amount of shifting will cure. An actor who couldn't act his way out of the proverbial wet paper bag has been cut to shreds, but his few remaining lines make you shudder every time the scene goes by. The close shot on the lead actress during her penultimate scene is just not close enough, and a microphone shadow flickers on her eyelid. You had to abandon the tracking shot through the dining room into the kitchen because the dolly wouldn't make it through the door (the art director goofed, or was it the carpenters?) and the resulting cuts are too static. Or maybe the thunderstorm wasn't quite over and you can hear rumbles on your sound track (or was that maybe a distant freeway?). I could go on for hours. You're lucky if you notice those problems now. A peculiar thing happens as you sit at the flatbed editing table: as the film gets more and more scratched, and the picture deteriorates from cutting and recutting, sound problems and picture problems begin to disappear; that is, become unnoticed. You make a subconscious assumption that problems will clear up when the print comes out of the lab. Some problems are not going to go away. What now?

Enter music, sound effects, the dubbing session, and the "mix"; enter dissolves, fades, wipes, "opticals," and "timing." Enter magic! What can be done to cover up the rumbling thunder? Sound effects of a car going by, music, or elimination of the entire dialogue by replacing it with a "dubbed" (rerecorded) sound track. What can be done about that scene that was too bright? When the print is made, "print it down," that is, darker. What about the bad actor? Surely, you can't "dub" him in. Actually, as Fellini did, you can replace anyone's voice, if you have the stomach and talent for long sessions on the dubbing stage. But there are equally creative sound tricks to play with a bad actor. If the lines are needed but not crucial, try playing the dialogue over someone else's face. Try playing it with music mixed in, or sound effects. (The scream of a monkey, perhaps?) As for fades, dissolves, and wipes, they can soften the hard edge between cuts, or create a sense of time passing, or dizzy the audience into believing that a love affair has just concluded. A lot of editors and directors hate opticals such as wipes because they seem old-fashioned, or because they want to achieve their ends with acting and cinematography, not gimmicks. Well, so do we all. But, when the chips are down during the final days of postproduction, take the easy out, if it works.

I don't want to give the impression that sound effects, music, opticals, and the like are used only for cosmetic or repair purposes. Some of the most creative work you will do as a director is in the postproduction period. Here, an editor will suggest a wide variety of possibilities: adding footsteps as a person leaves the room; giving a good solid "clunk" to a door that closes offscreen; a dog barking during a winter scene, giving a sense of loneliness; horses (that were never filmed) being heard clip-clopping past a house; a radio blaring in a neighboring apartment; a car going by; children's voices playing nearby. All these can give a sense of a world that exists in three dimensions, outside and inside of the space created by your film and the sound you shot to be synchronized with it.

The next time you see a feature film or a television film, listen carefully to the sound track. It's a job of wizardry. There is usually a separate sound effects editor and a separate music editor, who follow the work of the film editor seriatim. They are experts at not only adding sound, but creating it.

TIME OUT

When I was brand-new in the industry, I remember watching with amazement as a middle-aged sound effects editor in a dubbing studio, holding some leather bridles and jingling them effectively in synch with the picture on the screen, created a horse going by. It was a piece of artistry. Later, when I thought I had lost all my boyish naivete, I watched open-mouthed as Susan Morse (Woody Allen's editor) and her assistant sat in a closet of a recording booth and made it appear that matches were being struck, that there were footsteps on leaves, candles burning, and other things going on to bring to life a mystery film I was making. By their use of cellophane, a pencil, and their own voices, dozens of new sounds were created.

TIME IN

Music, too, is a compelling addition for creative purposes. When I started at MGM in the 1950s, they had a large recording studio into which a symphony orchestra could be fit, for films like the remake of *Mutiny on the Bounty* or *Jumbo*. But in a small room nearby, a veteran music editor sat and listened to recordings of old scores, which he would choose and send on to still another music editor who would cut and fit them so that they created a whole "new" score for the television films we were working on. They could do everything *but* shorten or lengthen notes—although today, believe it or not, there is digital equipment that can do even that.

I am not trying to give a course in effects editing here; I am saying that a good film editor will be able to suggest a whole range of things to be done that bring to life the two-dimensional film you have been creating. Proust talked about smells and about how they brought the past back to him. Three-dimensional vision, distance cues, a sense of the world *outside of* the immediate movie frame are missing from the movie screen. Sound and music can re-create that sense of the three-dimensional world in a way that only those who have seen it can describe or imagine.

THE MIX

Nothing is so crucial to the *sound* of your film as the way it was *originally* recorded. Next in importance is "the mix," which is exactly what it sounds like: a melding together of the various tracks that have been constructed to go with the picture. In film this will vary from a very simple single dialogue track, to the complex twelve- or fourteen-track mixes not uncommon on feature films today, involving two or three different dialogue tracks (sometimes cut in the middle of a sentence, so that part of one can be put on an "echo" filter, or changed from near to distance "perspective"), two or three different sound effects tracks, two or three music tracks (with overlapping music, to be cross-faded at crucial points), and two or three special tracks, sometimes with as few as one or two sound effects on them, or even words that need special treatment-filtering, or "EQ" (equalization—putting in highs or lows).

In the old days, you had to synch up all the tracks and the picture (marked up with all sorts of symbols that gave the mixers warnings about what was going to happen next) and rehearse, then thread up the tracks again and rehearse again; then run through once more for a take and, if you made a mistake, you had to take everything down and thread up again. It was a long process, and the adrenaline started pumping as you got down to the end of a reel. In Hollywood in those days, because it was impossible to change things as you went along, they usually had three people doing the mixing—one on dialogue, one on music, one on sound effects. (It was a boon for the unions.) Today, thanks to advances in sound-recording technology, specifically in digital editing, one person can handle the entire mix. And now the old 16mm magnetic tracks are left out of the mix. Once they've been transferred to a digital medium in synch with all the other tracks, they're put aside, and digital magic takes over. The mixer punches in and out of the sound, equalizing, backing up, jumping forward, switching from one track to the next with ease. And nothing of quality is lost in the process.

During the mix itself, a director has to keep jacking himself up from the torpor that tends to take over as the mixer goes back, time and again, to refilter an effect or add a "loop" (a continuous track that is usually available at sound studios—or which is created by your editors—to lay in a *general* background of something: wind, birds, crickets, traffic, "room tone," and so on) or to do some other technical thing that seems to be endless. Then, suddenly, the mix is on again, and your ears and eyes have to be perfectly tuned to what's happening. It's not easy to do, since the loudspeakers at the front of the room are especially large and give a distorted version of the mixed track, making birds seem louder than they should or a squeal of a tire too high-pitched. You will keep checking with the mixer (as if he or she was a genius), asking, "Is that too loud?" "Can we do that again, a little softer?" A good mixer will not treat you like an idiot but will reassure you if the sound is right and redo it if you have a particular need.

Even *with* the introduction of digital technology, the process can go on endlessly (with the concomitant expense.) In fact, many of us make video programs these days without a mix, using only the video-edit console itself to aid us. Luckily, with more and more sophistication in those consoles, this presents a cost-saving alternative. However, if you are doing a mix, on film or on video, count on it taking time: easily two days for a one-hour documentary, a day and a half for a half-hour TV film, several days for a feature film. In the middle of a reel, you may realize that a track should have been "cut over," that is, part of it laid onto a separate track for EQ purposes, or that there isn't enough room tone behind a place where a cough was cut out; or you may not like the music you picked and ask that it be left empty. Some changes are simple enough to make (the cutover, for instance), but what if you hate the music? That may occasion a two- or three-hour break; you may come back tomorrow. That can be a tedious business, too, requiring extensive retuning and re-EQing of tracks to match today's mix.

All of that aside, what is it that you are looking for in a mix? Here it is in a nutshell: you are trying to balance all the sounds that were originally created and all the sounds that have been added, to make the audio portion of your film as powerful, as subtle, as meaningful, as packed with emotion as you can. You are also trying to use sound to give a third dimension to your film. This requires an unbelievable amount of attention to detail. A door click is too loud or nonexistent. Footsteps sound like galoshes and have to be soft-pedaled. The music requires a cross-fade, and two of the pieces are just plain wrong and must be left out. (Surprisingly, this can be welcome. There's such a thing as too much sound.) The birds are annoying. The crickets are too omnipresent. The wind sounds like a machine. Her voice is harsh. His is too subtle. All of this can be changed; all it takes is lots of patience and the guts to ask. Your editor, once again, will often be ahead of you, suggesting changes, making demands, taking over when you flag. Be careful not to let the mix get away from you. It's your film and, technical problems aside, you can hear what's right and what's wrong and should make your own choices.

When the mix is finished for the day, play the film back, standing or sitting in a different relationship to the speakers. If it's a film for television, have the mixer switch the sound to the TV speakers he's got hooked up. See if the sound is right on a three-inch speaker. If the sound is for the big screen, concentrate on whether it's too mixed, that is, whether you have added so much extra sound that it sounds like a Robert Altman film—voices here, voices there, effects here *and* there—and the simplicity of your original single-track film is lost. Don't say "Finished" until you are really finished. Also, don't despair. That cuckoo you can hear returning every ten seconds on the bird loop won't be noticed by everyone when it comes across Channel 5 at 9:30 at night while the neighbors are making a fuss, the garbage trucks have shown up late, and the faucet's leaking. In other words, your perfect mix will not be noticed by 90 percent of the population, nor will your imperfect one.

On the other hand, this is your final creative act (except for viewing the answer print), and if you want to be a perfectionist about it, it's your film. Enjoy!

VIDEO POSTPRODUCTION

The advances in technology that I discussed in the last chapter started to make a big difference in both film and video editing about ten years ago. The AVID console—and similar digital, random access edit bays—allowed "film style" editing to be done with video. They even allowed producers and directors to transfer work print to electronic storage bins (hard drives) with the edge numbers intact. The edit then would progress in digital form on video monitors and, when a fine cut had been achieved, the AVID would kick out an edit list (EDL) that could be used in the negative cutting room. Some directors (Steven Spielberg being a prime example) wouldn't dream of doing things this way. In fact, as of this writing, he and his editor still use the old stand-up Moviola, long gone in favor of the flatbed editing console, for most of us, about twenty years ago.

What does this mean for material shot entirely on video? It means that you can treat your video editor much the same way you treat your film editor. You can screen footage with her or him, mentioning which takes you like the best, and then leave the marked-up script and get out of the editor's way. While this works well for the pictures in your program, the sound has to be treated a little differently. If you're doing a drama or a high-budget documentary, you will want to do a mix later. This requires that you take all your audio tracks and transfer them to a different kind of electronic file and take them to a mix house that handles such files. While the results can be wonderful, the cost is high.

There is an exception to this "dump the product on your AVID editor" solution. That is the documentary. I know no producers or directors who come out of the shoot with their script intact. Almost without exception, you have to screen all your video footage at home or in your office and make careful notes of each shot and sound bite ("Logging.") You then have to rewrite your script, making notes for your editor as to exactly where to find the material that you have chosen for your documentary. (To some extent this is also true in film documentaries, but screening with an editor is more common in film than it is in video.)

There are many systems for making notes. The most useful I've found is to go through your vis-time-coded VHS without stopping, making very quick notes (like "Okay", "no good," "terrific") on your log opposite a sound bite and noting the time code.

Next, I repeat the screening, stopping to make more select notes. I then transfer the best shots and sound bites to two lists, one titled "Select sound bites," the other, "Select B-roll and cutaways." (See chapter 12.) Finally, I write my new script, adding notes and time codes to it.

TIME	SCENE & DESCRIPTION	COMMENTS
04:05:13:22 to 08:22:19	Sally's apartment – close shot (take one)	n.g.
04:10:06:04 to 14:14:23	(same – take two)	o.k.
04:16:16:04 to 18:25:00	Sally's apartment – medium shot	!

```
                        TELEVISION FORM
************************************************************************
NOTE:  SOMETIMES, THE AUDIO AND THE VIDEO ARE FROM THE SAME PIECES OF TAPE,
SOMETIMES, THEY'RE NOT, BUT IT'S ALWAYS CLEAR WHERE THEY ARE FROM.
************************************************************************
             AUDIO                          VIDEO

FADE IN:  Voice of George          FADE IN:  WIDE SHOT OF SARAH'S HOUSE
(from 03:44:28:13)                 (from 06:17:22:00)


George's dialogue                      cut to:  George on screen
continues here                         (from 03:45:59:00)
(from 03:45:59:00)

                                       cut to:  c.u.  Sarah, as she listens
                                       to George (05:17:08:08)

                                       cut to:  George:  (03:47:00:00)

Sarah:  (09:22:22:21)                  cut to Sarah:  (09:22:22:21)
(DIALOGUE HERE)
```

TIME

How long does all this take, this video editing with its logs, its strange codes, and its computerized workings, and this complex film editing with new techniques to conquer? This is a good question, and a comparison between film and video editing might be useful.

In video, first. You will want to take a few days or a week between the end of the shoot and the logging phase, even if you're using an associate director to do it for you, because duplicate tapes (with time code) have to be made, and you have to get the life back in your legs, back, and eyes before you sit down and screen for hours each day. Then, unless you're very slow, you should be able to log a normal forty-tape production in five days (eight twenty-minute tapes a day will be reasonably all you can take, but it's feasible).

Next, re-screening and note-taking will take not much more than another week, perhaps only four days. Then, making your code markings on your script should take only a few days for the first draft, provided your logs and your notes are good. Final screening, with careful annotation, is another four or five days. So far, a total of seventeen to eighteen days, or less than three weeks, if you work weekends.

Now, events progress much as they do with drama editing, or with film editing: the editor gets your annotated script, your logs of "selects," and adds her own sensitivity and creativity to the project.

Because documentaries require special knowledge of the subject matter, you or the producer may spend a little more time in the edit room, identifying which microscope shot (for instance) to use, or who the cast of characters is, but you will also want to give the editor plenty of freedom. From end of shoot to end of edit, you can get it done, and done well, with forty days, or six to seven weeks.

In film, it is almost certain that a similar production will take half again as long, and I've seen films that took easily fourteen weeks. The rough cut or assemble stage may be achieved almost twice as quickly as video (I've seen them done within a few days), but the rest of the work takes an unbelievable amount of time if you expect the editor to work carefully and to turn out the proper sound effects and music edit—*and* you want the laboratory to do its job. In video, because "lab" work is done by the computer *while* you edit, that takes a very short time. In film, however, the end of the edit signals a sound mix—two days—and a laborious lab process that can take two weeks to get the print right (see chapter 10). But what takes the most time is the careful editing of version after version, with painful attention to details; of frame-by-frame editing, with a variety of sound effects tracks, opticals, negative matching, and so on.

Of course, we've all seen editors who worked fifteen or eighteen hours a day (or even more), cramming all their expertise into four weeks and turning out a credible film. And in TV, an episode can be edited to script in a formula fashion, within the same time period: four weeks.

Whether you're working in film or video, there are a few surprises in store for you if you've kept an open mind. The first is that the project may end up looking and sounding different from what you had planned. A character may go. A scene may go. It may not be his film; it may be hers. While you were preparing and shooting this did not become apparent, but now that you're finished, it is painfully (or pleasantly) so. Your film editor may have been responsible for getting you to shift some scenes around (though it could be your producer, too, or even you). Scenes may be cut together without some of the shots you planned. Dialogue may disappear, only to reappear in strange places. You will probably resist some of this kind of cutting, only to discover that lines you thought were

1.   2.

3.   4.

imperative aren't. (A viewer who had never seen the film before tells you that it's obvious the main character is about to leave home, and you don't need the line "I'm getting out of here.")

While the editing process is going on, you will no doubt be startled by some of the suggestions that are made. For example, you believe that you can't cut from a shot of someone looking right to left (that is, at the left side of camera) to someone *else* looking right to left and expect the two to appear as if they are talking to each other (the principle of "staying on the same side of the imaginary line"). Then, in the midst of cutting, an editor will make such a cut and, miracle of miracles, it works. The film *La Nuit de Varennes* exemplifies one such situation.

In a coach, traveling along in the middle of the dusty French countryside, are three passengers (Drawing 1). We see a two-shot of the countess, who is on the left, and the writer (Drawing 2). We now cut to a two-shot of the countess and the priest (Drawing 3). She is now on the right (because she is sitting between the two of them). This is not supposed to work, because it means that she will "jump" from the left side of the screen to the right side of the screen and it will be distracting. The right way to do the scene (says the "director's handbook") is to use a three-shot of the passengers, then individual shots of each and use the two-shots only if "bridged" by one of those other shots. Or, pan from one two-shot to another (Drawing 4).

The cut described above isn't supposed to work, but it does. Why *does* it work? Probably because the editor chose just the right *moment* to make the cut, when the eyes of the audience were on the priest and not the countess; or when the sentence that the writer was saying was so cogent that we just didn't pay attention to that so-called wrong cut. And so it goes. The rules go out the window. And thank God for that, for rules are made to be learned and then broken in the arts of film and video. "Anything goes," as long as it makes the film better, and most likely it will be during the editing process that much of the rule breaking occurs. The editor Ralph Rosenblum tells of putting stock footage into a film that was designed for original material. But using stock footage is only one of the original tricks that may improve a film; there are others. Slowing footage down (via "step printing") or speeding it up. Changing the color. Printing something in high contrast. Reversing a shot in the "optical house" or on an AVID. (He was looking right to left; make him look left to right by reversing the image.) Using subliminal shots. Eliminating scenes. Interrupting a scene with another scene, then returning once, twice, or three times to the original. Doing retakes. (This usually horrifies the producer, of course, though some producers often see the need for retakes before directors do. Retakes, in limited numbers and under limited circumstances, are the best of all worlds: you've seen the film in rough cut and can tailor the retake *precisely* to the shot you need.) Redubbing the voice to make it more mysterious, more sexy, more sinister. Adding images that weren't shot, by retouching the negative (which is expensive and difficult) or intercutting new footage or using animation or stills or superimposing light flashes or . . . on and on. The opportunities in editing are numerous—but more so in film, I'm afraid, than in video (though the line between them in postproduction is becoming more and more blurred, as digital magic takes over). And it's all terribly expensive!

The *technical* mastery and tricks, however, that an editor can bring are not nearly as important as the *intellectual* ones. For whether you are using film or video, the basic notion of the edit remains: to create from the footage you have shot a version that satisfies your original vision or, if that vision has changed, the new one. In order to accomplish this goal, you must use your editor's mind. It is not surprising that the original word, "cutter," was dropped, since the work a film editor does is much more complex than cutting, work that is often similar to the work an editor in the publishing industry can do for a written work. Ideas, images, feelings, and symbols are what films and video are about, and a smart, emotionally keen editor can contribute immeasurably to what you have begun.

Now it is time for you to know your laboratory and what *it* can do.

11

The Print and the
Film Laboratory

This is a brief chapter, but one well worth reading even if you aren't—at present—responsible for seeing film into and out of the lab. Too many times a director thinks that the film is finished when the "mix" has taken place and the editing has been completed, when in fact there are a number of things to do yet that can very well determine how good the film is going to look. Let's start at the point when the film was first sent to the lab for dailies.

What kind of film was it? "Fine-grain" (that is, without noticeable grain) because you were willing to sacrifice film "speed" for smooth, creamy texture? Or did you want the picture "fast" (that is, sensitive to light) without caring about texture. (Think *Traffic*, for the difference between the two. The scenes in Mexico are shot with very grainy film, a lot of hand-held action, to make them seem like they're documentary or news footage. The other scenes are much creamier, shot on a fine-grain film and using a tripod or dolly.) Film stock is changing every day with new, sensitive, not too grainy films, but the general rule is "fast film, lots of grain; low speed, grainless." You must also choose between "indoor" and "daylight" film. The former assumes you will use lights (tungsten or quartz) with a color temperature of about 3,200° Kelvin, a reddish light; the latter assumes lamps of 5,600° Kelvin, a blue light. If you use indoor film outside, you have to continually filter it with red filters; if you use outdoor film indoors, your filters are blue. Don't switch films once you start, but do make a careful estimate of whether you'll be spending more time shooting outdoors or indoors. To complicate matters (this is a technical chapter, after all), you can, of course, shoot outdoor film indoors with HMI lamps, because they are made to put out a light about the same color temperature as the sun: 5,600° Kelvin.

Let's assume you want to use a fairly low-grain, "slow" film, for the beauty of the color and for lots of differential between shades of gray. This is something you and your D.P. discussed before shooting. It will increase, by the way, the number of lighting instruments you need, and a variety of other technical variables, but it will also mean you can go for subtle colors and lighting effects and expect to *see* them on the film when you're through.

The film goes out for its first processing. Because it is negative, it will be run through the lab and developed first, then a print will be made. The print will be what is called a "one-light" or "untimed" print. This means that the variety of colored lights or filters that are controlled by a computer and that change the way the print is exposed, scene by scene, will be limited to a small, set number (an estimate of the *average* exposure needed to print the film and not changed scene by scene. Thus, your dailies will come back looking as good as the "timer" (a person, not a machine) at the lab can make them with a one-light instruction. The practical effect of this will be that you may find a favorite scene that was supposed to be subdued looking reddish and too light, but you will know that can all be changed when the film is eventually timed the way it's supposed to be-for a final print. (By the way, if you have a low-budget production, there's no reason you *have* to get a color work print of every scene or every roll of film. It's *generally* done, but it's much less expensive to get a black-and-white print made. If you're nervous about the color quality, because you used secondhand film or for some other reason, print one roll in color to assuage your fears.)

The work print is yours to use, to cut up, to mar, to turn upside down, because you know, barring any terrible event, that the negative is safely ensconced in the lab's vault (a small charge is made yearly for storage unless you use the lab for prints or other work, but it's well worth keeping it there, not in your house). If, for any reason, you need a reprint of a scene or a shot, you can have it done from that negative, overnight.

You will have sent the film and the synched-up sound out for "edge numbers," little figures printed on both sound and picture at set intervals so that the film and sound track can be resynched if it is ever cut up and the editor can't get it back. This is a mandatory precaution.

The next step, in terms of the laboratory, doesn't come until you have finished editing. At that time, in order to make the completed print, a "negative editor" will have to be hired. Not strictly a lab's job (though the editor can often be hired through a lab), negative editing requires a skilled eye, a firm hand, and pristine circumstances (similar to a surgeon's table). Matching the original numbers from the negative to those on the print (not the same edge numbers you put on; these are manufactured with the film) the negative editor splices together the negative that has been in the vault, taking care to avoid scratching it or embedding hairs or dust in it.

After splicing, with leader, into A & B rolls[16] (for 16mm) or with opticals cut in (for 35mm), the film is "timed." Using a video reader that takes the negative and reverses it into a "positive" image, the lab technician decides *exactly* how many "lights" a scene needs to match skin tones or other visual touchstones. These numbers are put into a computer which makes a punch tape that accompanies the film as it goes through the lab processes. The film, with its punch tape, is then sent to the optical printer, which literally makes a copy of each frame onto "color positive" stock, thus yielding a "print." You then view the print, after waiting a number of days and being very nervous.

TIME OUT

There is a split in the industry these days. Many television productions (and small-budget films, too) will opt to have their scenes printed extremely well the first time around, and transferred to digital (e.g., AVID) format. They will then be edited entirely on a random-access piece of equipment and then, through the use of computers, an edit list (EDL, in filmland jargon) will be printed out and (using a complex

---

[16] A & B rolls are the two separate strands of film that are run in parallel through the optical printer, with the first shot on one roll, the second on the next, and so on. This is done so that the splice mark between one shot and the next won't show. How does the use of A & B rolls eliminate the splice? You might want to visit a film editor and ask him. It's easy to see and very hard to explain on paper.

computer program) matched to the negative for laboratory processing. For films that will be shown on the big screen in a movie theatre, the usual lab process then ensues. But for television it is becoming common not to end up with a film print, but to do a "digital cut" (more jargon) from the AVID onto videotape, making it unnecessary to do anything (save for the mix) outside of the edit room. This doesn't work for large-size film formats (such as 70mm) or where extremely complicated frame-by-frame corrective work is required, but much of the special effects work these days is digital, and that fits very well with the AVID or similar edit machine.

Another digitally-inspired innovation is making headway: Motion picture distributors and theaters have been experimenting with the transfer of the huge, heavy rolls of 35 and 70mm film to digital disks which can be projected via digital projection onto a movie screen. Some think that this means, eventually, all movies will be shown electronically. Some videotape projection is now being used in theaters, but those who want widespread distribution of video programming (or "films" shot on DV video) are more likely to have their video transferred digitally to film, which can be projected onto movie screens anywhere in the world, while the new disk method is in very few theatres. The benefit to the latter: audio is digital, making for fine sound quality. Mind you, most colleges, schools, community centers and even festivals won't have the money for this for some time to come, but it is most likely the wave of the future.

TIME IN

Just for the sake of technological expertise, let's ignore the box above and assume that you're going the old-fashioned (film lab) route: The "answer print" is the first timed print made from a spliced negative. It may make you very upset or it may be a delightful surprise. This depends not only upon the skill of the lab's timer, but upon luck, enterprise, and the complexity of the lighting and the scenes you shot. What will you be looking for?

One *Any negative editing that went wrong.* If this happens, you'll notice it in a few flash frames (frames of another shot in between the shots you had planned to adjoin each other) or, God forbid, something out of synch. If that has happened, unless the picture is going to be shown on television (where you can do miracles, editing it on video-tape), you'll have to go back to the negative editor and get him or her to correct it *and* go through another whole answer print.

Two *Color changes that you don't like.* This can range from a whole scene that is just not the color you chose, to a scene in which shots don't match *(he has ruddy complexion, she is green).* The timer, sitting with you, will be making quick notes ("up 2, more amber, down 1.5"), but don't hesitate to make sure that you agree on which direction to change things.

Three *Differences in light.* It was shot with a wonderful "low-key" look and the lab has printed it as if it were summer, and midday. You patiently explain to the timer what you had in mind, and you hope the next time you see the scene it will be quite right.

I remember one scene that was especially important at the end of a film. It was indoors, with the big HMI lamps shining in through the window. It took place during the day, but what we wanted was a cool, almost blue light (the kind often used to indicate moonlight in films), with lots of shadows that hid people's faces. The timer had given us warm sunlight (How could he tell what we had in mind?) but that did-n't work for our scene, which was about the greed that had been hiding behind closed doors in this town and was about to be revealed. It took *five* answer prints to get the scene right, and by that time there was a scratch in the film and a strange wobbling line along the left side of the print that seemed to everyone to be something that happened in drying, although it wasn't; which brings us to the next category of things to look for in answer prints.

Four *Defects.* When you are editing a work print, with all its grease pencil markings and its splices, its dirt and its smudges, you may not realize that a hair or a scratch or a tear is actually in the negative and not just in the print. When the answer print comes down the line, any such defects will show up. Strangely enough, scratches seldom happen—at least in my experience—but dirt (like black or white "snow") does, and when it does it can be a very depressing event. What are you going to do? A scene or a shot has a hair or a scratch or dirt. Did it come from the negative editing, or was it from the lab? Is it in the print or in the negative itself? Is it, in other words, correctable, or is it permanent? In order to determine this, look for the *color* of the scratch or the dirt. If you are working with negative (not reversal), the defect will be *white* if the print has been underexposed there, which means it's dirt (dirt on the negative keeps light from going through). That's correctable. If the defect is black or colored, then it's probably a scratch, because it removed emulsion, allowing too much light to pass through. It's permanent, probably. Now what? You'll have to decide whether (a) to let it go, (b) to reedit the negative and get a new print, or (c) to try one of those "miracle" processes labs sometimes recommend that can, under the right circumstances, fill in scratches (though they often leave the image a little "soft").

After you have had your second or third answer print, you'll probably be 95 percent happy, and that's the most you can expect. If you've got a perfectly splendid timer who really listened when conferring with you and the editor, then your first answer print may do. Next to consider: a "release" print. This is nothing more than the timing on your answer print as it is applied to a standard final print. In other words, it's the answer print plus one. You put it under your arm and off you go. Well, not quite.

Suppose you want a lot of prints for release purposes. If you're using 16mm, the negative won't hold up for a lot of prints (normally beyond ten). You have to make a Color Reversal Internegative (CRI). This item is a new negative made on reversal film from the spliced old negative, but on stronger stock. From it, you can make as many prints as you want without risking damage to the original negative. Of course, as in other areas of filmmaking, nothing is that simple. Take a look at the color and the focus in the prints made from the CRI. They aren't quite as crisp or as accurate as the print "struck" from the original negative. That's because they're a "third generation" away from the original. (The negative is *first* generation; a print is *second* generation; so is a CRI, which makes the print from the CRI *third* generation.) As with all such generations, there's a deterioration of quality. Sorry, but that's one of the trade-offs you get. If you're not prepared for it, it can be quite a shock. A lot of directors and producers insist on getting their own personal copy and any festival prints struck off from the original A & B roll negative, not from a CRI. By the way, this is one area in which videotape is much better than film. If you use digital videotape, you can go down four, five, six, or even seven generations (copies of copies) without seeing a difference.

The difference between 16mm and 35mm films is as big in the laboratory as it is in the work print. You'll notice it. On television, because of the size of the screen, it may not make much difference in terms of quality, but in the movie theater a 16mm film, especially if it's "blown up" optically to 35mm, will look much more grainy, much less crisp, and the colors will be less defined and pure than something shot on 35mm. But a lot of very good filmmakers are using 16mm, even Super-16 (a wide-screen variety of 16mm film used a great deal by the British) for television and even for the theater, because the reduction in cost (at all levels, not just the lab) is extraordinary. If your particular laboratory does work on both 16mm and 35mm, you should find out what they're favoring these days in terms of schedule. One of New York City's finer labs for 16mm became well known for speed and care in its work, and then took on so much feature film work in 35mm that it sometimes neglected its old 16mm customers. It's not a frivolous matter when you're sitting around waiting for your answer print and something green, faded, out of synch, and late comes on the screen. I've seen grown men cry!

12

The Documentary:
A Special Case

In several of the chapters in this book, I have brought up the special case of the documentary. I have pointed out, for instance, that scripting a documentary calls for a special kind of approach, a different way of reading and rewriting; that editing a documentary is significantly different from editing a narrative film or videotape. Some people don't think that documentaries call for "directors" per se, that producers or producer-directors (hyphenates) are required. There is much to be said for that approach, since documentaries require a kind of single-mindedness of purpose that often defies the cooperation of two leaders. But the DGA often requires television stations to hire a director for documentaries, and a producer who has never directed often comes up with a documentary film or videotape that has good content but no visual appeal. For these reasons, alone, it seems to me worth discussing this special case.

The term "documentary" is used by me to cover many kinds of nonfiction films, not only the NBC "white paper" variety, but educational, industrial, instructional, and cultural films or videotapes as well. A word or two about such productions is in order before we discuss technical and aesthetic matters.

Before television came into existence, documentaries were usually made by strong-minded, independent souls who had a powerful political, cultural, or social point to make, who raised the money themselves and supervised the entire project. Men like Joris Ivens, Robert Flaherty, and Pare Lorentz fit into that category. But when television came around, the idea of a film with a point of view caused some problems, and the documentary took on a different gloss. It was now a film or videotape that examined an important subject, but usually from various points of view. It was "objective." It was, also, a team effort.

The distinction between, and debate over, objective and nonobjective (or nonpartisan) documentary has been the subject of many books and many lectures. For the purpose of this chapter, however, the controversy is noteworthy because the two types of documentaries, to the extent that one can distinguish between them, require different kinds of preparation. One cannot imagine, for instance, the late Robert Flaherty letting someone else write a script for him, do his research for him, or supervise his editing. He also had to raise his own money and had an awfully hard time doing it. On the other hand, when Fred W. Friendly and Edward R. Murrow made their documentaries for CBS in the 1950s, a team of cohorts provided much of the work surrounding the projects and CBS, of course, provided the money.

Independent documentarians these days often work with other people—coexecutive producers, coproducers, and so on—sharing the labor and sharing the credit. Generally, where the subject matter is political, a strong producer-writer must do much of the research, the writing, the filming, while keeping a firm hand on the filmic helm. But where a cultural documentary is being made, a producer may turn over much of the filming to a director, who is called upon not so much to supply the content as the images, to interpret a script already written rather than to invent a film or videotape from scratch. Of course, there are exceptions. My own choice, for the sake of saving money as well as for the pleasure of it all, is to be a producer-director-writer-narrator, but the hubris (a valuable word for directors) of that approach and the sheer labor of it, has often made me long for the less difficult role of the coproducer or, even, just director. That has its drawbacks (it's not your film), but it has compensations as well (less work).

SCRIPT

One of the major differences in making a documentary as compared to a drama is the timing of scriptwriting. This is an ancient argument. Some people insist a documentary must be written before it is shot;

others say it cannot be written until afterward. For me, documentaries are written twice: once before the shooting, and once during the editing. Certainly, it is difficult to shoot anything unless one has done a certain amount of research and planning and that, in its barest form, is what scripts are about. But certainly, too, after a documentary is shot, its script must be altered, even to the point where it doesn't resemble the first version. The problem with rules is that there are so many different kinds of documentaries that forming a hard-and-fast rule is impossible. Even with one subject, a variety of kinds of documentaries present themselves. Here is an example.

If the Pope is coming to Washington, D.C., and you want to make a "news" documentary about his visit, it is likely that you will go out and film him, film those who arranged his visit, get comments from common citizens and from clergy, and only then, after transcribing your material and viewing it, will you know what you have. Suppose, however, that you are opposed to the visit and want to demonstrate, via film, that it is a drain on the Treasury and contrary to the First Amendment? You may very well want to do some research, write a script, and shoot to that script. At the least, you will want a shot list. Now, suppose that the purpose of your film is to educate Americans to the notion of the First Amendment, and the Pope's visit is only one small part of the film. You will probably have to write your film ahead of time (inserting "wish list" kinds of shots where the footage isn't already available or where news-type photography will be required), get it financed from some corporation or foundation, and not go out to shoot until you have done so. Finally, there could be a film about the Pope's visit that is intended to have poetry set to it and is to give a scenic view of Washington at the same time. You would be foolish to go out and shoot until you had researched your poetry, set your shots to it, planned it all the way around. That's a script in anyone's language.

But what if it doesn't photograph the way you planned? By now, you will know that the answer to that is the same as it is with any film. No film comes out just the way you planned. So, in the editing room, you will change it. A documentary is the same; it, too, changes in the editing room. You may go back and rewrite the script, adding or subtracting narration, getting stock shots or new photography, shortening, lengthening, rearranging. On one level, that's no different from what you would do with any film, no matter what its format, no matter what its content, but with documentaries you often do a lot more.

Just how does a director look at a documentary script, and what

SASQWATAMI RIVER SEQUENCE

Fade in:

1. WIDE SHOT, the River.
    Boats are going to and fro. It is obviously the middle of a busy day.

                    NARRATOR (V.O.)
            There is nothing that immediately strikes the eye.
            All activity seems normal.

2. MEDIUM SHOT, Boat activity.

                    NARRATOR (Cont.)
            If you've never been on a river like the
            SASQWATAMI, it's worth taking a closer look.
            Be curious. Go down to the docks, see what's
            happening.

(Music up)
3. MONTAGE: River Action.
    Concentrate on stevedores, but don't give the audience any suggestion
    that there's any drug activity until later. Should look a little like
    Lorentz' film, The River, in its angles and action. (1:30)

(Music under)

                    NARRATOR (V.O.)
            Don't be fooled. It's not all that it seems to
            be. Down there, on the docks, one of America's
            greatest drug transactions is going on. Which
            isn't strange, if you think about it; wherever
            there's water, there's quiet transportation.
            Wherever there's easy and quiet transportation
            there are drugs.

4. CLOSE SHOT: Stevedore handing over package to man in business
    suit. (Get a variety of shots like this, using hidden cameras
    and ultraviolet night lighting.)

Dissolve to:

5. MEDIUM SHOT, Interior D.A.'s office -- the D.A.

    During the interview that follows, get a variety of shots, and
    get the following material, in essence.

                    D.A.
            (Talks about how easy it is to transport the drugs;
            how he has two undercover men on the job, when he
            needs ten. How he suspects some of his regular
            policemen are being paid off.)

difference is there between that and a narrative script? A sample script should point to some of the differences.

What is immediately obvious? There's no dialogue, at least not in the conventional sense. Instead, there is narration. The second major difference is that the shots as they are described are likely to be less specific than in a dramatic script. In the latter, because it's all to be crafted by the actors, the set designer, and the costumers, you can put anything you like into shot descriptions and stage directions. In a documentary, you must describe things well enough so that people know what to shoot, but you cannot describe things too explicitly without looking foolish, because everyone knows that the real world cannot be manipulated the way actors and set dressings can be. So, in the accompanying script, we see that the river is to be shot "wide" the first time, with a follow-up shot ("medium") with attention paid to the activity of small boats. This leaves the director a good deal of leeway.

SHOOTING

Leeway? Don't all directors have leeway? Isn't that what being a director is all about? Yes, but in a documentary, the leeway requires that the director (or director-producer) be *very* flexible, to the point of shooting something entirely differently if it presents itself and will "serve" the script. This requires knowing a great deal about the subject matter. What kind of small boat activity is required? Why? Is it drug smuggling we're after? Or labor union recruiting? Is it sunset or daybreak? These distinctions cannot be arbitrarily decided. In advance, discussing the script with the producer, you must add details to the shots that have been listed. You must also read the narration very carefully and see if there is additional material that should be shot to cover it. And—this is the most important matter—you must shoot a wide variety of additional shots for you-don't-know-what purposes. These "cutaways" are the lifeblood of documentary shooting, providing ways of cutting around dull interviews, inadequate material, cloudy days, jiggling cameras, and the like. I don't mean the very unattractive cutaways used in news film, where the cameraman takes shots of the hands of the reporter or a wide shot of the President to cut into the speech. I mean the imaginative use of "useless" material *as well as* full "coverage" of a scene.

I have fallen into a customary verbal trap, but it's worth talking about. Like almost everyone else in the industry, I used the word "cutaway" to indicate those shots that are not of so-called principal action (such as an interview). In news, they are called "B-roll" as contrasted with the "A-roll" of interviews. The problem is, though the term is current and omnipresent, in a documentary *nothing* is a B-roll. Everything is pertinent. "Cutaway" implies something unimportant, a mere shot to get you from one place to another. But, in fact, *reaction* shots, or scenery, or a multitude of other matter, are always important. You will need these scenes to make your picture interesting, intelligent, and flowing. So:

You can never shoot too much non-interview material for a documentary!

And this is true no matter how much you've shot!

TIME IN

Here is an example of a documentary shot list for a single "scene."

You are shooting the laboratory of a research institution. Your main focus is an interview with the head of the unit, though you also want to see something in close-up of one of the experiments being performed. Your shot list would look something like the following (though your script might simply say "Interview with Dr. X: she talks about important discovery"):

1 Wide shot of Dr. X, seated at her table

2 Medium shot of Dr. X, seated at her table

3 Close shots of Dr. X, seated at her table

4 Dr. X, seen from behind, being framed through tubes and wires of experiment (Use for "fake synch.")

5 Dr. X, walking toward her office, for voiceover

6 Dr. X, talking to nurses

7 Dr. X, doing experiment; get this in variety of shots:

    (a) ECU of mouse's brain

    (b) ECU of Dr. X's eyes during operation

    (c) close-up of assistant holding gauze

    (d) medium shot of all of above

    (e) wide shot, through paraphernalia of all of above

8 Lots of extra shots of lab and people

A good list, but don't be fooled. You may have to adjust your shooting to an entirely different situation. Suppose the mouse dies. Your camera can't continue, and you can't call for the "prop person" to bring another one. Your aim in shooting is to "cover" the entire situation, with appropriate and visually interesting material, not simply to follow the list of shots existing in the script. And, what's more, you will find that the long list of shots in the script is often useless as a guide to the real situation. The producer-writer simply wasn't there when things were going on. This is a "content script," not a shooting script.

There *are* documentaries that are more similar to the narrative script and shooting that we've been discussing in other chapters: educational films, using actors; industrials; in-house promotional films. These often call for detailed scripts that are to be followed the same way that narrative scripts are followed. But, even there, you may find on location a scene or a shot that *has* to be filmed or videotaped even though its place in the script is not to be found. You would be wasting money if you did that in a normal film (it doesn't follow the strip board or the budget), but you would be neglecting your job as a documentary director if you *didn't* get those shots while shooting a documentary. In point of fact, some directors of dramas will take such "wild" shots during their films, with the gut instinct that they will "work" later. The difference in documentary work is that *dozens* of shots like that are called for, taken, and *used,* even in the most scripted of documentaries.

Which brings us back to the most hard-and-fast rule I know of in documentary shooting, one laughed about and bandied about, yet still true.

There are never enough cutaways.

This is true no matter how much material you have shot. I don't know why, but it is almost universally a fact. A ratio of *shot* to *used* footage of 12:1, 20:1, 50:1? It doesn't matter. You always come up short with the number or right kind of cutaways, because *cutaways* are the basic cutting matter of documentaries. They allow you to make transitions, to make points, to cut out vapid parts of interviews. So, shoot more than you can possibly use. Your editor will bless you for it.

EDITING

In chapter 10 we discussed the relationship between an editor and the director of a dramatic film. We hinted that in a documentary there was a large difference. This shows up in two distinct ways.

One There are large areas of a documentary where the footage that comes in may be inadequate to the task. This happens when you have been unable to shoot material to cover a scene because people have gone home, not shown up, been boring, been uncooperative, and so on. An editor, then, is required, to "find" footage to cover the sequence. Of course, it helps if a director has thought of this in advance and provided a variety of shots (from that daily "shot list" described previously). But the director may have not done that, or—and this often happens—the editor may simply feel that those shots don't cover the problem. It then becomes a creative task on the editor's part to find the shots, from elsewhere in the footage, to cover the narration. If the narration isn't crucial, the editor may suggest abandoning it. If, on the other hand, the editor and director don't like the footage that's available and the narration is truly important, another alternative may be to go to a "stock footage house" and purchase footage to cover. Editors can be very adept at doing this and can match stock film to the footage shot by the director.

Two Because the shape of a documentary often changes dramatically between the first and the last days of the shoot, what is actually required by a film editor in a documentary is a rewriting of the script. Usually this will be done by the producer, but the editor may be the first person to call attention to the shapelessness of the film, or may find the key to the new script that no one else could find. For this reason, it is as important here to leave the editor alone with that mass of film as it is in narrative filmmaking—often, more important. Let him or her find the problems and then suggest a variety of solutions. In actual fact, it is difficult for a director to participate in the editing of a documentary, since the producer must take over to see that the film or videotape suits the script needs, and since the editor is often a stand-in for the director at that point, suggesting the kinds of creative additions that the director suggested in the field during shooting.

As a producer-director, however, you will be there, and you must bring the same kind of flexibility to this edit as to all others.

There's a lot more to be said about documentaries for which there isn't room in this book. If they are your area of interest or you want to learn more about them, many good books on documentaries are available (see the Selected Bibliography).

13
Getting There

The scene: A large office in a Manhattan building. The cast: A public television executive producer and a young woman named Marsha applying for a job.

EXECUTIVE PRODUCER
　　Your resume looks fantastic, Marsha, but, frankly, I couldn't take the chance of having you direct something as big as this. You haven't directed before.

MARSHA
　　Look at the rest of my experience: I've produced two plays, been executive producer of my own film . . . and I've been an actress.

EXECUTIVE PRODUCER
　　That's an awful lot for someone as young as you.

MARSHA
　　What am I supposed to do? How can I get a job as a director without having had one already—I mean, you don't expect me to have directed five films before you hire me to direct my first one.
　　 . . . (The executive producer's eyes start to glaze over. He's heard this before.) I've got all the experience I thought

I needed. Come on! I'm good. I know what I'm doing. I'll do
it for less than scale . . .

                      EXECUTIVE PRODUCER
     I'll think about it, talk to my staff. Your resume looks
awfully good . . . .
                   SLOW FADE TO BLACK

IS THERE A CATCH-22?

To some extent, there is. You can't get a job as a director unless you've
already directed. Well, that's almost true. Many first-time directors are
people who have been given a chance to direct or who have *demanded* a chance to direct because they have had a lot of experience in the
industry (as actors, writers, producers, and so on), or because they have
written a script that someone wants produced, and they just can't be
turned down. This is especially true of feature films, but also of television series. On the other hand, if you've had no experience and have
never produced or directed even a student film, it's unlikely that someone is going to take a chance on your ideas on a project that costs
upward of a quarter of a million dollars. Yet, obviously, most people
who want to be directors are young people, and many have that glim-
mer in their eye early on, before they've spent years accumulating
experience. What do you do, how do you get an assignment directing?

   Beginnings   When I was young, at one of my early jobs, working as an associate producer on a children's television series at MGM,
I really wanted to be a director. So did a friend of mine, who was also
working on such a series. We knew that our respective bosses weren't
going to give us the chance to direct, so we set out to do something
about it.

   A secretary in our office had sent us to see some rather extraordinary puppeteers, and we decided to make a film about their work.
After numerous discussions, we saw the piece as a kind of circus into
which many of their weird creations would fit. We selected a weekend
on which all of us could do the shooting and borrowed someone's
storefront down at the beach, a location that had enough electric

power and enough space for the crab dolly we intended to rent. But the dolly, camera, and lights cost as much money as we could afford to spend on the project, so a little ingenuity had to be used for film, developing, editing, and processing.

From the film laboratory owned by MGM we acquired—free of charge—the "short ends" (remnants) of 35mm film that had been turned in, unexposed, because they were too short to use for a professional shoot. With film in hand and a promise that the studio's lab would process for us at cost, we set to work. A van was borrowed. The dolly was rented on Friday, because we knew full well that we could have it for a Saturday rental and return it on Monday morning without being charged for our Sunday shoot. Lights were rented and a basket of food packed. Friends and relatives were coerced into accompanying us to the beach.

My friend and I had been on the sets of movies for two years, but it wasn't until we reached our set that I fully realized that only *he* had ever operated the equipment we would be using. (I had been prohibited by union rules from touching most of it.) We then discovered that the camera we had rented—a 35mm Arriflex—was too light to weigh down the heavy hydraulic lift on the crab dolly. We hadn't thought about getting a dummy sound track because we knew that sound would be "laid in" later, so everything was recorded silent, something that gave us a problem later when editing (trying to remember *which* song *which* puppet sang at *which* time!). Nevertheless, the weekend was successful; by the end we had used up all the film that had been given to us, and we were excited by the circus film we had created. Next: editing.

We had learned, that winter, that all the editing rooms at the studio were left open at night. Getting on the lot was no problem (everyone knew us at the gates), so three nights a week we came back after dinner and started editing, using different moviolas and rewinds each time, so that no one editor would begin to notice his equipment had been used. I was a novice at editing, too, so I would watch my friend, begin to learn things from him, and slowly acquire some of the procedures. (I also acquired a healthy respect for the apprentices and assistant editors I had seen splicing and cutting away.) My slowness, however, gave me a chance to remain slightly objective about my partner's work, and I soon began to see that the film lacked one important element: a story. We plowed on, beginning to realize that what we had might be amusing, but by itself was only a "short," if that. (In the 1950s, movie theaters still played short subjects with feature films.)

The film needed music. We recorded off our own records onto quarter-inch tape, then rerecorded onto wider magnetic track at the studio, again gratis. The music helped, but now the film needed voices. We dubbed in our own, speeding them up to match the puppets' movement. With a burst of energy, we ended the film with little patches of material from earlier scenes, a kind of "Russian montage."

Sneaking into a mix session after one of our employer's television episodes had finished, we mixed the five tracks down to one and sent the film off to the lab for a cheap answer print. The mixers told us they loved the film, but we had begun to have sinking feelings about it. "Maybe we're too close," we told ourselves, with false optimism.

Now that it was finished, what should we do with it? We had put ourselves out on a limb by not telling our bosses about the film, correctly assuming that they might resent our spending creative energy on our own work, or that they might think that using studio equipment and manpower for free endangered their position at the studio. So we had no choice at this point but to try to sell the film at *other* studios. We got appointments, but it became clear that we wouldn't make a sell. Depression set in. Finally, we showed it to the head of MGM, asking him not to tell our employers. He promised not to and said he found the film quite amusing. The next day, our employers returned from a selling trip to New York City. They had lunch with the head of the studio, who told them about our film. I have no idea how it happened, but they seem to have gotten the wrong impression and thought we had actually tried to go behind their backs to sell the film; the next day we were both fired.

Lessons Was all that necessary? Yes, and no. It's necessary to get your feet wet. It's not necessary to be foolhardy—though it is probably a good idea to be a little reckless, a little bold, a little tougher than you think you are (or ought to be) because it's a tough, reckless, bold, often thoughtless industry you're trying to break into. And you're even trying to get one of the glamour jobs in that tough, bold, reckless industry. Are there any rules? I think there are.

One Make a film or videotape. Any film. Any videotape. The introduction of inexpensive digital cameras and home-editing gear has made that so easy now that you can do it in your spare time or while studying film. It doesn't matter: just get your creative energy out on tape and—if you're as good as you think you are—it'll show. Something is needed before a raw, untried person is going to be given a job in the industry, certainly as a director!

Two Get into an allied field. Direct plays. Produce plays. Study acting. Find your way into CBS as a typist (I did) or as a page or as an assistant to the producer. Work in cable television. Write scripts and submit them. In fact, writing is one of the most successful ways to become a director. A script is often the item that gets you into someone's office, though a thousand would-be scriptwriters are also asking the question, "How do I get someone to look at my script?"

Three Use your contacts. Everyone knows someone who knows someone who may know someone who was or is or will be in a field allied to the field you want to get into. You must use them, not callously, but adroitly and politely, to help you get interviews and jobs. If you're as brilliant and as potentially talented as you think, you'll get a job and move up in it, and you'll be noticed or make yourself noticed. But if you don't get that first job—in some area—you won't be able to persuade people to let you direct.

Are there any surefire tricks? I don't know. Everything's been tried once, and probably succeeded—at least once. Hard work and talent help, but not always. Luck, certainly. Oh, yes, there is a fourth rule: Know what you're doing!

Unions and Nonunions Marsha, in the little scenario above, had done a lot of work in the world of drama, but she probably wasn't a member of the Directors Guild of America. If the executive producer had wanted to get out of hiring her easily; he might have said, "You're not a member of the DGA." What are the rules about union membership? Does everyone have to belong? How do you get in?

It is perfectly possible to do many things in the film and television industry without ever joining a union. For instance, even in the networks, producers and associate producers aren't unionized. In much of the cable industry, in some "independent filmmaking" (feature films not made by the "majors," low-budget television production, and so forth), in educational, industrial, closed-circuit, university filmmaking, or television work, many, if not most, positions are nonunion. That includes the director, but also most of the other jobs, such as grip, D.P., electrician, art director, and so on. I know many competent and active directors who have never joined the DGA.

There are, on the other hand, many films that are totally union. That means for everyone from the secretary to the director. There are different unions. The International Alliance of Theatrical Stage Employees (IATSE) covers most of the craftspeople, such as grips, camera people, and electricians, as does a rival union, the National Association of Broadcast Engineers and Technicians (NABET). There are unions for makeup people and costumers, unions for drivers (the Teamsters), and so on. The DGA covers assistant directors, production managers, and directors in film, and directors, associate directors, and floor managers in television.

If you're going to go to work as a director for a public television station, it's unlikely, except in some of the big cities (New York, Washington, Los Angeles), that you will have to join the DGA. That's not true of many commercial stations, even small ones, but the sure way to find out is to ask. It's certainly not true of the networks, or of the major motion picture companies. There, all directors are union members.

But how do you join the DGA? It's complicated, and you really have to ask for the local rules but, in general, it goes like this.

If you are asked to direct, even if you haven't directed before, you will be permitted to join if you have the initiation fee of several thousand dollars, and you pay quarterly dues ($50 in 2001). If you want to join as an assistant director, the initiation fee is less, *but* you have to show that you are competent in certain areas, (that is, you have to take a test). In all cases, a few members of the DGA have to sign your application. (Someone has to say you're "wanted" by the profession!) So, if Marsha is wanted by the big-city PBS station, she can direct if she joins the DGA. And she can join just by paying the right fees. But if someone hasn't said they want her, then she can't get in, even if she wants to pay the fees, *unless* she has a terrific directing background—*that's* the catch-22 part.

To make matters more complicated, it's likely that the DGA will ask the E.P. *why* he wants to hire someone who isn't already a member since there are already some very competent people who can direct and *are* members.

Some E.P.s use the fact that people aren't members of the DGA as an excuse, as a way to "prove" they aren't any good as directors. The only way around *that is* to show them a film or videotape that you've produced or directed in some situation where you didn't have to be a member of the DGA.

By the way, is being a member of the DGA proof that you're a good director? Not necessarily. It's proof that you've done some professional work, and it's certainly proof that you've been well compensated for your work, for one thing the DGA does is to look after its members in terms of pay and fringe benefits. But there are members of the DGA who are not directors (they're production managers, associate or assistant directors, floor managers, and so on) and there are director members who have done a limited amount of directing, and, of course, there are hack directors who have done a lot of directing but aren't very good. And why not? It's like any other artistic field.

Will it help a budding director to join the DGA as an assistant director or production manager? Probably not. Those jobs, as I've suggested previously, are more logistical adjuncts to the producer than true assistants to the director. They don't deal with script content, "vision," editing, or any of the other things directors need to train in. It probably won't even help you to join the DGA for the prestige, if you could get in and had the initiation fee, unless you have a film to show. So, follow the rules I suggested in the first part of this chapter. Keep your eye open for jobs such as continuity person, film editor, or writer, that will get you closer to your goal, though *any* entry-level job such as intern, production assistant, or assistant producer may give you the foothold you need.

What about film schools? Will experience there help you get a job? I think this depends on how resourceful you are, and how well trained. At least once a week my telephone used to ring with some inquiry by a college student about how to "break into" the industry. And, often, the student asked about graduate school (NYU, UCLA, USC, Columbia, and others have reputable graduate schools in filmmaking). If the student has already made a film or two (by hook or by crook) and has a lot of contacts in the commercial or noncommercial film and television world, I'm not likely to suggest graduate work. If the student has no experience, but has a good liberal arts background, I more often suggest that, expensive as such places generally are, they *do* offer a good grounding in technical and creative approaches to making film and television. The same is basically true for undergraduate film and television studies, though my own eclectic background makes me much more cautious about suggesting that someone actually *major* in film as an undergraduate. What about all those other wonderful subjects that can be studied in college: English, history, psychology, mathematics, physics, archaeology? Wouldn't you rather learn those and make films later? If not, then major in film or television, but pay heed to my remarks in the beginning of this book about the *breadth* of experience.[17]

If you graduated from college or graduate school with a B.F.A. or M.F.A. in film or TV, what will it do for you in the outside world? That depends, in part, on what you did at school. If you used your time to make contacts and to make films or videotapes, then you've used your time well, but it's not a simple magic trick to get work in the industry. Francis Ford Coppola and George Lucas came out of the Los Angeles film schools; Martin Scorsese came out of NYU, but so what? Does anyone really believe that those men wouldn't have become directors if they hadn't gone to film school? They would have found other ways. And there are scores of directors of commercials and of nonunion films who never went *near* a place that educated filmmakers.

In short, as I suggested in the Introduction, there are many kinds of directors and, equally, there are many roads to becoming one. You must know your craft and find your own path. What I've given here are hints that have worked for many, but they may or may not work for you.

---

[17]Of course, astute observers will have noted that I used to teach film and video production in an undergraduate department of a major American college. How do I square this with the statement made here? Partly, by being honest with my students and telling them how I felt about undergraduate majors in film. Partly, by spending a lot of time urging my students to take wonderful courses in other departments. As I said a few pages back, the new, inexpensive digital cameras—even the camcorder-under-900-bucks types—can now be edited on your Mac or PC and deliver to the world your creative insight. So, if you've got insight, an *education,* and storytelling ability, it'll show even in a home video.

Afterword

WHAT IS A DIRECTOR?

Some of you may think I've answered this already, and some of you may think this chapter belongs at the front of the book. I *did* describe the primary work of the director ("making choices") in the Introduction. And I have given you thirteen chapters on some of the ways a director spends his or her time. On the other hand, nowhere have I spelled out the philosophical nature of what a director is; you know, the "I know what a director *does*, but what *is* a director?" kind of question.

There are usually two approaches to this kind of question. The first revolves around script and the second around image. Script, first.

Scripts tell stories—good ones, if you're skillful. They also convey meaning, which is different from story, by which I mean that a fine script, a fine story, has some deeper message to convey. It need not always be a symbolic one, or a political message, or even a serious one, but something beyond "fluff." *You Can't Take It with You*, the Kaufman and Hart comedy, is filled with firecrackers going off, women doing pirouettes, and G-men bursting in, but underneath is the *idea* that we spend most of our lives working, not enjoying life. That's not an uncommon or a startling message, but the play would come down to the final curtain a little less funny and a little less enjoyable if it weren't there. And if the director didn't understand that message, didn't know how to convey it, the play wouldn't carry its audiences nearly as well. Now, with *You Can't Take It with You*, it's not very hard to get that extra little meaning out of the play, since the playwrights have written it into the final speech of the lead character, but with many plays and with many film scripts, the underlying meaning isn't read out loud at the end by a character. It's carried somewhere—or *everywhere*—in a line here, a character delineation there, in the basic story, and so on. If a director has a good grasp of that underlying meaning, then he or she is well on the way.

But there's more to it than that. How do you get your actors to convey the meaning? Here, the pit suddenly opens wide and you have more alternatives than you can possibly imagine or want to deal with. A perfect example is *Hamlet,* where scores of directors have tried to find a way to deal with the play's theme(s). Young Hamlets, old Hamlets, female Hamlets; modern dress, Victorian dress, Elizabethan dress; swords, pistols, daggers; Freudian Hamlet, full-length Hamlet, half-pint Hamlet.

But even with a common, everyday television film, there are decisions to be made. Made correctly, the film will convey something *more* than the bare words on the script. Done incorrectly, they will give the wrong impression—or worse, *no* impression. Take two quite different series, *NYPD Blue* and *The West Wing.* Brilliant as they are, they are brilliant in different ways. The use of the handheld "jerkycam" style, lots of intercutting between actors, the cramped quarters and the streets of New York, actors with varying ethnic backgrounds and varying styles of acting—all give a *feel* of *NYPD Blue* that transcends any individual director. Yet one assumes *a* director, *some* director, designed all of this, in cooperation with the executive producer/writer; but does *anyone* doubt that it was the result of some long nights of decision-making?

Now, *The West Wing.* Here, too, a sense of reality, of actually being in the White House. But not at all like *NYPD Blue:* a very different use of camera—long, long takes with a Steadicam, actors moving in *mise-en-scène* fashion; opulent sets, eloquent speeches, always impelled by intelligence and some sense of comedic presence. Again, we don't doubt that lots of thought and planning went into this methodology, into each and every detail, down, I suspect, even to which actors should be minorities, which should be women—not with the aim of being politically correct, but of being believable: Would the Administration (*any* administration) hire this person for that job?

So, what will you do about the style of *your* movie? About casting, costumes, sets, accents, and all the things discussed above?

To even begin to answer those questions requires a good deal of training and a good deal of thought. First, a director has to understand everything about the script. All the nuances of the lines, the reason each character is *there* to begin with (and if he or she doesn't belong, should that character be thrown out), why one scene is in that place and another scene is in *that* place in the script, how the scenes sound to you in your inner ear, and how you, in the audience, will react to them. If this is your approach to scripts, then you will certainly want to insist upon having rehearsals before you put your actors in front of the camera. You will want to listen to them and then explain each and every nuance of the script, letting them know how you want scenes played. And, in the editing phase, you will think over and over again about which scenes to reorient and where to cut a shot so that the *dialogue* emphasizes the proper point in the script.

What if you start with *image?* Is it any easier, any more straightforward? And why would someone start with the picture rather than the words? After all, isn't everything in the dialogue?

Some people start with images because it's easier for them. Others, because what they feel first about the script is best translated into pictures. Still others, because they don't have a firm grasp on the meaning of every line of dialogue but can conjure up hundreds of pictures. Others, because working with actors isn't their strong suit, but looking through a camera is. Finally, there are those who assert that because a film is made up of images, if you don't start with pictures, you're left with nothing but words, which in *their* minds is boring.

And then there are some directors for whom the frame, the image, or the shot is easier to deal with than those funny people, the actors. I've heard them say, "I really don't like actors." Does this make it impossible for them to direct? Strangely enough, no. For what some people lack in their ability to work with humans, they make up in their ability to conjure up images. But this has its drawbacks; for the image alone, without a tie to the meaning of the script, cannot convey anything more than a pretty picture. Remember my discussion in chapter 4 about *The Long Riders?* One gorgeous image after another, but—for me—tied to very little meaning. You can come away from such a picture thrilled with the images and bored with the film. But, strangely enough, that doesn't mean you shouldn't direct. It simply means you have to make one art serve the other. And it means you have to have colleagues who are strong in the facilities you lack. For instance, as an imagist, you wouldn't want to rewrite the script yourself. Conversely, as a brilliant stage director, you might want to have a fantastic D.P. to create images for you.

Isn't this simply saying that a half-talented director needs to surround himself with talented people? Not quite. While it's true that many great directors have ability in every facet of the field—dialogue, image, writing, working with actors—many a good craftsman has one or two strong suits and can not only get work in the field, but can contribute some important films or videotapes to the craft. Of course, a wise director knows his or her own strengths and defects. It would be foolhardy for a director strong in images alone to take on the direction of a work of Shakespeare or Ibsen. It would be equally ridiculous for a director whose strong suit is mainly directing actors to direct a film in which there is almost no dialogue, where the story hangs on pictures.

What is a director? A man or woman who is good at creating or translating images, or dialogue, into film or videotape.

What is a director? Someone passionate about details. Not meaningless ones, but details that *shine* on the screen, or fill in the background so that one *feels* the three-dimensionality of the picture, of the people "up there."

What is a director? As you can tell from the chapters in this book that are *not* about "vision," a director is someone who can learn to be *organized* and who understands that organization is an aid, not a detriment, to vision.

What is a director? Someone with a great knack for storytelling. Someone who notices framing and where the light is coming from. Someone with an "eye" and an "ear." Someone with knowledge about a great many things, and with a thirst for knowledge about a great many more.

A director is also someone who can tie together the various strands of the art; who "sees" something that few others see and who knows how to make what he or she sees fit a pattern. The craft, as we have seen, is important, but so is the vision.

I am not suggesting a genius when I outline these characteristics. But neither am I suggesting that a director is simply anyone who wants to put a camera in front of a subject. Directing is "paying attention" and leading and seeing and hearing and caring and knowing and, well, *directing.*

Good luck.

Christopher Lukas

Glossary

NOTE: In this glossary, terms found in the book that are of special importance to the work of a director are defined. Unless special mention is made, all terms should be considered as applying both to film and to videotape productions. All of the following terms can be found in chapter 3, so no definitions for these will be given in the Glossary: Producer, Associate Producer, Executive Producer, Writer, Story Editor, Production Manager, Unit Manager, Location Scout, P.O.C. (production office coordinator), Assistant Director, Second Assistant Director, Cinematographer, Camera Operator, Assistant Camera, Mixer, Gaffer, Juicer, Boom Operator, Recordist, Grip, Continuity, Best Boy, Makeup, Hairdresser, Wardrobe, Costume Designer, Art Director (Scenic Designer, Production Designer), Property Person ("Props"), Film Editor, Assistant Editor, Lighting Director, Audio Person, Videotape Operator, Associate Director, Cable Puller, Videotape Editor, and Dialogue Coach. In addition, various technical terms are sprinkled throughout the chapters.

Auteur A French word that means "author." Used by the French director François Truffaut in an article in Cahiers du Cinéma ("film notebooks"), it set into motion the notion of directors as "authors" because it was mistranslated when the article appeared in the United States. Truffaut, apparently, did not intend readers to believe that directors eclipsed all other creative forces on a film, but American critics used the term in that way for at least a decade.

Avid This is the trade name of one of the first and still most used non-linear (digital) editing consoles. It—and others like it—have transformed the editing of video from a cumbersome process into a fascinating blend of magic and film-style editing.

Beat (1) A pause in time. Used in scripts to indicate that the actor should halt briefly before his next line. (2) More importantly, a portion of a scene that should be considered an integral part all by itself. Thus, each scene will have a number of beats, just as each script will have many scenes. Rehearsing beats helps actors feel the scene as it is broken into meaningful parts. Similarly, it helps to film or videotape beats in their entirety, retaining the integrity of the moment.

Bounce light See Lighting.

Camera Angle A term that conveys both how high or low a camera will be and the direction from which it will be shooting. Thus, a director may ask for a low-angle shot that is done shooting over-the-shoulder. "Over-the-shoulder" is as much an "angle" as is the "low" shot the director asked for.

Clapstick The flat wooden board upon which information relating to each scene (in film) is written and that is held in front of the camera before each take. Now there are electronic slates that put a flash onto the film itself while the number of the scene and take are spoken by the audio man into a microphone and transferred onto audiotape without putting a clapstick right in front of the actors' faces.

Close-up See Shots.

Coverage How many shots you've taken. More specifically, the concept that any scene should be covered from a variety of angles, so that an editor will be able to cut it together without problems.

Crane Refers to a large four-wheeled vehicle, with a large, movable "tongue" that will hold a camera and operator(s). The flexibility of the crane allows the camera to be held at ground level or high in the air.

Cut The most basic way of getting from one shot to another without overlap or fade. Sometimes called a "direct cut."

Cutaway The term used, or misused, for shots that can be employed as buffers between two other shots that don't "work" because of mismatches or "grammatical" problems. (See chapter 11, "The Print and the Film Laboratory" and chapter 12, "The Documentary.")

Dailies The film footage that was shot yesterday. Usually shown in the afternoon (it has been rushed through the laboratory, hence the alternative word "rushes"), so that producers can decide if anything needs to be reshot today.

Depth-of-field A technical term of great importance to filmmaking and video productions. Every lens has its own properties in terms of focus. When focusing on any object at a particular distance, a 50mm lens will be able to show other objects (behind and in front of the primary object) in greater focus than a 105mm lens focused at the same primary object at the same distance from the camera. How great the span is through which a lens can hold two objects in focus is called the depth-of-field. It varies with the distance from the camera and for each particular f-stop being used. A chart is necessary to determine a particular depth-of-field.

Directors Guild of America (DGA) The bargaining unit (union) for all directors, production managers, and assistant directors in film; and for directors, associate directors, and production assistants in television.

Dissolve A simultaneous fade-in/fade-out, whereby one shot disappears from view as another appears. These overlapped shots can be varied in length either in the laboratory (film) or through a special effects generator (video).

Documentary A nonfiction film or videotape in which a point of view about an issue takes the producer-director through an investigative route toward a product that presents that point of view. In television, the point of view has often been traded in for a "balanced" presentation.

Dolly A kind of small, open-bodied cart, which runs on "track" and has wheels that can turn in various directions. The camera (and, sometimes, crew members) sit on it. For use in trucking (or "tracking") shots. There are many kinds of dollies, starting with the smallest that weighs only two hundred pounds, and going up to large ones that hold mammoth cameras and three or four crew members. They have a variety of names such as "crab," "cricket," and so on.

Double system Refers to the separate recording of sound and picture onto two different media—the film and the sound track—and also to the projection of the finished product using either two separate pieces of equipment (a projector and an audio tape recorder) or a special projector. Videotape is never double system, since the sound track is always wedded to the videotape itself. Film editing cannot be accomplished with finesse unless double-system recording is used.

Dubbing (1) The replacement of original sound material by new and better sound. (2) The use of English-speaking voices to replace foreign dialogue in a film.

Edge numbers Matching numbers printed onto the edge of the film and the sound track after the film has been "synched," so that the two can always be put back in synch during editing.

Equalization Creating a new sound track that matches bass and treble for all portions of the film or videotape; bringing one sound level "up" or another "down."

Establishing Shot See Shots.

Extreme Close-Up (ECU) See Shots.

F-stop Refers to the size of the opening in the lens that corresponds to the iris in the human eye and that determines how much light is allowed into the camera to expose the film (or the tube that creates images on videotape). Another word for f-stop is "aperture." These apertures remain the same for all lenses and all cameras and are denoted by the following numbers: 1.4, 2, 2.8, 4, 5.6, 8,11,16, 22. The higher the number, the less light is allowed into the camera; each higher f-stop decreases the light allowed in by exactly one half. When we change from a low f-stop to a high one, we say we are "stopping down." Conversely, moving from a high to a low f-stop is "opening up."

Fade-in A device used in both film and video, whereby the picture starts in black and becomes gradually apparent ("fades in"). Created in the laboratory or the final editing process (video), not as one shoots.

Fill light See Lighting.

Fine cut The third and final of the three "cuts" in the creation of a film or videotape. This is the product at its final length, with all scenes and lines of dialogue intact and in the place they will eventually play. Music and sound effects may still be missing.

Frame The actual piece of celluloid (in film) that is held in front of the projector for one forty-eighth of a second and is marked by a solid black line at top and bottom. The progression of twenty-four such "frames" per second gives the illusion of "motion" in moving pictures. In video, there are thirty such frames per second, created by the sweep of an electron beam across the face of the television screen. "Frame" also refers to the way in which directors conceive of a shot.

Gaffer's tape Looks like plumber's tape (the silver tape used to wrap pipes) but is much more powerful. No production should go anywhere without it. Used for taping lamps to the ceiling, furniture to the floor, and a million other things. This is one of dozens of tools used by the grips to make life on the set easier. In fact, a new gimmick or gadget is invented almost every day: something to hang lights from office ceilings on location, without drilling into the woodwork; a new kind of koukalouris (or "cookie"—a cellulose cutout that casts just the right kind of shadow on a wall); a new way of hanging equipment on the back of a dolly.

Genre In filmmaking, refers to the kind of style or content matter; for instance, film noir (stark, contrasty black-and-white films of the 1930s), detective story, Western, or comedy.

Grammar The way in which a film or videotape should be edited. (Similar to the way in which the order and use of words in various languages should be grammatically correct.) This usually requires that a shot vary in either "angle" or size (or both) from one cut to the next; that is, that a close-up (see Shots) of a person not be edited onto a close-up of the same person from the same angle, or that two medium shots from the same height or direction not be cut together.

Gyroscopic devices Used to make moving shots (on board a helicopter, a train, a car) steady. The camera is mounted on a device that counteracts jiggles and joggles by rotating a wheel within a wheel, such as in a child's toy gyroscope. The Steadicam works on somewhat different principles to accomplish the same ends.

Halogen mercury incandescent (HMI) This low-wattage, high-output, low-heat lamp replaced the old "arc" lamps for the purpose of creating light that looks like sunlight.

Independent Any director or other film/video professional who operates without a steady salary, that is, outside of an institution such as a movie studio or television station.

Industrial Akin to a documentary but generally used for telling about a corporation rather than taking a point of view about some issue. Differs from a commercial in that it is longer and not so hard sell.

Inkie See Lighting

Jump cut Unlike other cuts this is something you don't try to achieve. It is the expression used to denote an edit of two shots that are so close together in size or angle that it appears, when they are cut together, that something has been left out. Often, this happens when dialogue has been omitted (for example, in an interview in a documentary) and no cutaways have been shot to intervene between the two grossly similar (in this case, identical) shots. But jump cuts also occur when a medium shot and a close shot are too similar in size, even though no dialogue has actually been left out. The person appears to jump in the frame because, no matter how carefully the film has been shot, he or she does not occupy the same space in both shots. By using a larger shot for the medium or a closer one for the close-up, the change in angle and size obscures the mismatch of position.

Key light See Lighting.

Lighting How scenes are lit. Classically, the chief and strongest light source is called the "key" light. Shadows are filled in by "fill" light, and a "back" light is used from the top or behind the subject to create a sense of three-dimensionality and to separate the subject from the background. "Fill-in" light is not to be confused with "fill," but is a secondary light source used to lighten the face of a person who is primarily lit from behind or the side by the sun or other extremely bright light source. Lighting instruments have very specific but esoteric names, such as "2K" for a 2000-watt lamp, or "Inkie" for a 350-watt lamp (it's diminutive of "incandescent).

Long shot See Shots.

Mag track Short for "Magnetic track." The 16mm-wide piece of plastic (Mylar) to which oxide fragments have been adhered and that has been passed across a sound head for the purpose of recording sound upon it. There is also quarter-inch magnetic track, which is usually reserved for original recording on a small tape recorder. From that original, the 16mm mag track is made.

Matching Making sure that the action that occurred in Take 1 of a shot is repeated in other takes, or that the action that occurs in a medium shot is repeated in the same sequence in the close-up. This is in order to avoid mismatches when editing.

Medium shot See Shots.

Mise-en-scène From the French mettre-en-scène (to stage or produce). Used to denote a stylistic approach to directing, wherein camera and actors are kept in motion, allowing a variety of shots to be "built" into one long, moving shot. (For a fuller discussion, see chapter 6.)

Mix What is done when all sound is mixed together in a special sound chamber (film) or on an AVID or at a "sound house" in order to equalize or blend all the effects for a product.

Monitor Functions like a television set, except that it can receive video (pictures) directly from a camera or videotape recorder, not just over the air. The same for audio (sound).

Montage (1) The use of multiple images, usually dissolved together, to show the passage of time. (2) The creation of meaning and story through the cutting together of various shots. (3) Sergei Eisenstein's semi-mystical analysis of film editing. (4) The meaning discussed in full in chapter 4: a stylistic approach to shooting, whereby timing, pace, look, and dialogue are controlled by the editing of many shots.

MOS A silent shot. From the early German directors in Hollywood who used to state, "Dis shot is mitout sound." (Honest!)

Murphy's Law If something can go wrong—it will!

One-light print See Prints.

Opticals Fades, dissolves, wipes, and any and all other visual devices added after the original material has been shot. In video, there are an almost unlimited number of such gimmicks available when completing a tape through a special effects generator board. In film, more limited effects are possible, and all have to be completed in the laboratory or sent out to an "optical house," where a camera shoots the optical from a print of the original shot, or from the negative itself. Opticals, these days, include blowing up or shrinking the original shot, moving in on a portion of the scene; and many other effects.

Outtake A shot that is not considered good enough to use in the film or videotape, or is left unprinted (film) after a day's shoot.

Pan Camera movement in which the camera head swivels right or left to take in another part of the potential environment.

Pilot A film or videotape created before any other episodes of a television series, in order to sell the series to a potential sponsor or network.

Point of view (POV) Literally, a shot that shows how a person's eyes would see something. This is different from the normal close-up or long shot of a scene, which is shot from slightly to the left or right of an individual's POV, so that the returning look of a person in that scene will not be directly into the camera.

Postproduction Anything done after the shooting stops.

Prints For film only. When the footage is first sent to the laboratory, it is generally developed and printed in a quick fashion for the dailies. This print is called the "work print" and is used by the editor to make all versions of the film. The work print is exposed in the printer at the laboratory by turning on a number of "lights" (with filters). Generally, the laboratory sends the film through the printer with a single set of lights on, to give it an average color and exposure ratio. This is called—naturally—a "one-light print." When more careful printing is required, in order to see texture and color that is more closely allied to the final product, a "timed print" is ordered. This takes more time and costs more, since each shot is individually examined (in the negative) and different light settings are punched into the computer so that flesh tones and other colors match from shot to shot.

An "answer print" is the first fully timed print made from the cut negative after the film has been sent fully edited to the laboratory. A "release print" is a print made from either the original negative or a color reversal internegative (CRI)—a duplicate negative made to protect the original from wear and tear—after one or more answer prints have been approved for color and balance.

Racking focus Changing the focus between two or more objects while operating the camera.

Release print See Prints.

Rough cut This is the second of the three cuts of a film or videotape, the first being the assembly, the third being the fine cut. The rough cut is the editor's vision of the product, with some scenes shortened, others cut out, and still others rearranged in order. The rough cut is without special sound tracks, music, or other subtleties. There may be many rough cuts before moving on to a fine cut.

Rushes See Dailies.

Script Sometimes called the "shooting script," it is the final version of what you intend to shoot as a film or videotape.

Setups Every time the camera is moved from one place to another, and lights are changed to suit the move, a setup is said to have taken place. On any one shooting day, the number of setups is used as at least one measure of the progress of the film.

Shotgun This is a microphone with a long barrel that can be used from a moderate distance to get audio in a documentary. It has a narrow field of pick-up so that, unlike an omni microphone, it collects sound only from the person at whom it's pointed.

Shots Each time the camera is turned on or off, pointed in a different direction, or moved, it creates a different shot. The grammar of film and video making requires that different kinds of shots be defined. An "establishing" shot, or "long" shot, reveals the entire panorama in front of the camera, so that geography can be established.

("Wide" is sometimes substituted for "long.") A "medium" shot is closer and usually limited to one person (though "medium two-shots" have been used), "cutting" him (that is, framing him in a certain fashion) at the top of the head and above the waist. A "close" shot usually involves only the head, whereas an "ECU" (extreme close-up) cuts a person below the hairline and above the chin. Because of variations in personal taste and artistic dictates, there are variations in how these shots are defined. There are also "medium close-ups," "medium long shots," and so on. "Cover shot" is sometimes used for a long shot but is also used to refer (in television) to a wide shot held on one camera in case anything goes wrong with other shots on closer cameras.

Terms such as "reverse shot" and "reaction shot" need some explanation. A "reverse" is a shot taken from nearly 180 degrees opposite to the initial setup for a scene. It is usually used in order to see the face of the actor whose back was toward camera in the original shot. If both actors appear in both shots, the shots are termed "over-the-shoulder shots." To see what an actor is thinking while another actor is talking is called a "reaction shot."

Single system The recording of picture and sound on the same piece of film. This is done for newsfilm shooting, seldom (anymore) for documentary, never for motion pictures. Videotape is, basically, single-system recording, though editing techniques have allowed picture and sound to be separately handled.

Soft Out of focus.

Special effects A term used for all those marvelous magical things that happen that look real but aren't: gunshots, bombs, flying nuns, and so forth.

Storyboard A cartoonlike layout in which major shots are drawn so that cinematographer, producer, art director, and other team members can see what you, the director, have in mind. On short projects, such as commercials, almost every shot is carefully drawn and colored in.

Story line The first, very brief synopsis of an idea for a film or tele-play.

Synchronized When the sound track and the picture of a person talking start and end in the same place, they are said to be synchro-nized or "in synch." When one or the other has been moved forward or backward, and a person consequently moves his lips at a time dif-ferent from when we hear his voice, the tracks are said to be "out of synch." This sometimes happens in double-system film editing because the tracks are edited separately. Edge numbers are used to put things to rights again.

Tight A term describing the framing of a shot that is close, as opposed to "wide" or "long."

Tilt Camera movement in which the camera head moves up or down to take in another part of the environment.

Time coding Digital (sound) code with matching (visual) num-bers that is put on videotape and read by a special machine to enable shots to be found and edited either manually or by computer. (See chapter 9.)

Timed print See Prints.

Tracking Shot A moving shot. Usually done on a dolly, it can be a move in, out (that is, away from), sideways, up or down, or a com-bination of all four. See Zoom.

Treatment Somewhere between a story line and a shooting script, the treatment will use normal paragraph-style writing to complete-ly lay out the substance and plot of a film or videotape. Everything is revealed in sequence, but dialogue is not given except in snatch-es needed to reveal the plot and feel of the eventual script.

Video An abbreviation for "videotape." These are a few of its definitions: (1) Something to be differentiated from film.

(2) Something to be shot with a television camera, but not necessarily broadcast. (3) A piece of music to which an action has been concocted and that is shot on videotape—originally for use on MTV.

VTR Videotape recording. Used for both the recording and the machine on which it is recorded.

Wide shot See Shots.

Work Print See Prints.

Zoom A special lens that incorporates several "focal lengths," enabling a single camera position to be used for different sized shots. Also refers to the actual use of the lens as it goes from one such focal length to another (as in zooming in or zooming out.) This is in contradistinction to a tracking shot, in which the size of the image is changed by actually moving the camera toward or away from the subject.

Selected Bibliography

What follows is a very short list of books that you may find useful in order to bone up on:

- 📹 Film production in general, and technical matters
- 📹 Editing
- 📹 The documentary

Most of these are available in paperback editions.

I. FILM PRODUCTION IN GENERAL, AND TECHNICAL MATTERS

Alton, John. *Painting With Light*. Berkeley: U. of California Press, 1995.

Beal, Steven. *The Complete Idiot's Guide to Making Home Videos*. New York: Alpha Books, 1999.

Bernstein, Steven. *Film Production*. Woburn, Mass.: Focal Press, 1994.

Bloedow, Jerry. *Filmmaking Foundations*. Woburn, Mass.: Focal Press, 1991.

Honthaner, Eve Light. *The Complete Film Production Handbook*. Woburn, Mass.: Focal Press, 1996.

Maltin, Leonard. *The Art of the Cinematographer : A Survey and Interviews With Five Masters*. Mineola, N.Y.: Dover, 1978

Musburger, Robert B. *Single-Camera Video Production*. Woburn, Mass.: Focal Press, 1999.

Videomaker Magazine. *"The Videomaker Handbook: A Comprehensive Guide to Making Video."* Woburn, Mass.: Focal Press, 1996.

II. FILM EDITING.

Reisz, Karel, and Gavin Millar. *Technique of Film Editing.* 2nd Edition. Woburn, : Focal Press, 1995.

Rosenblum, Ralph, and Robert Karen. *When the Shooting Stops, the Cutting Begins: A Film Editor's Story.* Cambridge, Mass.: Da Capo Press, 1988.

III. DOCUMENTARY

Barnouw, Erik. *Documentary: A History of the Non-Fiction Film.* 2nd Rev. Ed. New York: Oxford University Press, 1993.

Rosenthal, Alan. *Writing, Directing, and Producing Documentary Films and Videos,* Revised Edition. Carbondale, Ill.: Southern Illinois U. P., 1996.

Snyder, Robert L. *Pare Lorentz and the Documentary Film.* Reno: U. of Nevada Press, 1993.

About The Author

CHRISTOPHER LUKAS has been a television producer, director, and writer for over 40 years. In the world of public television, he has worked for its most prestigious organizations: WNET (where he was Director of Programming as well as a long-time producer), KQED, WTTW, and the Corporation for Public Broadcasting. Mr. Lukas has several Emmy Awards to his credit. He taught in and was Chairman of the Department of Communications at City College of New York (1982-1987). After returning to the world of broadcasting in 1987, he spent ten years as Vice President and senior producer for the documentary production firm, AHP, Inc., and has recently pioneered the use of small-format digital video for both on-air and institutional use.

Index

BOOKS FROM ALLWORT

Directing for Film and Television, Revised E
by Christopher Lukas (paperback, 6 x 9, 256 pag(

Producing for Hollywood: A Guide for Ind(
by Paul Mason and Don Gold (paperback, 6 x 9,

Making Independent Films: Advice from th
by Liz Stubbs and Richard Rodriguez (paperbac)
224 pages, $16.95)

Casting Director's Secrets: Inside Tips for S
by Ginger Howard Friedman (paperback, 6 x 9, ;

Get the Picture? The Movie Lover's Guide
by Jim Piper (paperback, 6 x 9, 240 pages, $18.95)

The Health & Safety Guide for Film, TV & Theater
by Monona Rossol (paperback, 6 x 9, 256 pages, $19.95)

Technical Theater for Nontechnical People
by Drew Campbell (paperback, 6 x 9, 256 pages, $18.95)

Creating Your Own Monologue by Glenn Alterman
(paperback, 6 x 9, 192 pages, $14.95)

Promoting Your Acting Career
by Glen Alterman (paperback, 6 x 9, 224 pages, $18.95)

Clues to Acting Shakespeare
by Wesley Van Tassel (paperback, 6 x 9, 208 pages, $16.95)

An Actor's Guide—Your First Year in Hollywood, Revised
Edition by Michael Saint Nicholas (paperback, 6 x 9, 272 pages, $18.95)

Booking and Tour Management for the Performing Arts,
Third Edition by Rena Shagan (paperback, 6 ? 9, 288 pages, $19.95)

Please write to request our free catalog. To order by credit card, call 1-800-491-2808
or send a check or money order to Allworth Press, 10 East 23rd Street, Suite 210,
New York, NY 10010. Include $5 for shipping and handling for the first book
ordered and $1 for each additional book. Ten dollars plus $1 for each additional
book if ordering from Canada. New York State residents must add sales tax.

To see our complete catalog on the World Wide Web, or to order online, you can
find us at *www.allworth.com*.